God the
Economist

M. Douglas Meeks

God the Economist

THE DOCTRINE OF GOD AND POLITICAL ECONOMY

Fortress Press
MINNEAPOLIS

COPYRIGHT ©1989 BY AUGSBURG FORTRESS

Library of Congress Cataloging-in-Publication Data

Meeks, M. Douglas.
   God the economist : the doctrine of God and political economy / M.
Douglas Meeks.
     p. cm.
     Bibliography: p.
     Includes index.
     ISBN 0-8006-2329-0
     1. Economics—Religious aspects—Christianity. 2. God.
3. Trinity. I. Title.
BR115.E3M38 1989
338.9—dc20   89-12013
                                             CIP

Printed in the United States of America   1-2329

93   92   91   90   2   3   4   5   6   7   8   9   10

FOR BLAIR

Contents

Preface

God does not appear in the modern market. For most economists this is as it should be. It is in no way necessary, according to modern economic theory, to consider God when thinking about economy. Indeed, the absence of God in economic matters is viewed as necessary to the great advances in modern economy. The difficulty with modern market economics, however, is that human livelihood is also left out of the theory and practice of the market economy. This is not the result of the market *per se* but of certain modern assumptions about the human being and nature that stand behind the market. Are there significant connections, though masked, between the absence of God and the disregard for human livelihood?

But is God really absent from the modern economy? One could hardly claim that God concepts are absent from the social order that surrounds and shores up the market economy. Even though modern people tend to think of and live before God in ways shaped by the demands of the accumulation of wealth ostensibly through the market logic and rules, the economy nevertheless continues to require certain narrow views of God for its justification. In another sense, then, the modern market economy could not exist, as has no economy in history, without some form of divine sanction of its assumptions. Are there widespread views of God which seem to make it tolerable that many people in our society and in other parts of the world are denied livelihood?

This is serious business for the Christian church, for it is in jeopardy of recognizing God as a principle of its society's economy rather than as the God who is constituted by the community of persons who come to expression in Jesus Christ and the Holy Spirit. Thus, however unusual it might seem, I propose to bring the church's teaching about God, the doctrine of the Trinity, to bear on the masked connections between God and economy. I will treat the Trinity as the way of understanding what the Bible calls the "economy of God."

The fact that I am a theologian and not an economist will be immediately and to some painfully obvious. The limited objective of this interdisciplinary study is to engage church people, including economists, concerned about what the church should teach publicly about economy and to grapple with some difficult foundational issues that must be worked through, it seems to me, as the church deals more faithfully and responsibly with its commission to economic justice.

Just as we will be proposing definitions of economy that will seem strange in the academy of economists, so we will be speaking of God in modes somewhat unfamiliar in theological circles. In other words, I will argue in ways that likely will be appreciated only by those who can, at least momentarily, attenuate reigning logics in both economy and theology. My own assumption is that coming history will require both economists and theologians radically to rethink what they are up to. The present study cannot claim to go very far in that direction. Its limited intention is to ask some questions and make some proposals that might lead theologians and economists to think in each others' presence.

The most pleasant part of writing a book is thanking those who helped to make it possible. To Jürgen Moltmann and Walter Brueggemann I owe gratitude for their unfailing encouragement as well as the gifts of their thought and wisdom. Parts of this book were presented in the context of two working groups in the American Academy of Religion. In this setting several colleagues gave me important formal and informal responses: Frederick Herzog, John B. Cobb, Jr., Letty M. Russell, Joseph Prabhu, Gustavo Gutiérrez, Norman Gottwald, Lee Cormie, Francis Schüssler Fiorenza, Shannon Clarkson, Anselm K. Min, David J. Lull, and Clarke Chapman.

I am grateful to the Association of Theological Schools for a grant which supported a term free for research and to the Institute for Ecumenical and Cultural Research at St. John's Abbey and University for an extremely valuable setting for interdisciplinary discussion and writing. While at the Institute I learned much about the subject matter of this book from many discussion partners, especially Robert S. Bilheimer, Daniel R. Finn, Michael Vertin, and Antony Ugolnik.

In the last few years I have been privileged to be a part of working groups in the Oxford Institute of Methodist Theological Studies and the United Church of Christ, which have striven to relate Christian faith to the economic life of our society. Among the many persons in these contexts who have made important contributions to my thinking are: James Weaver, Rebecca Blank, Max Stackhouse, Roger Shinn, Jon Gunnemann, Alfred Krass, Brian E. Beck, Theodore Runyon, José Míguez Bonino, Philip Wogaman, Bruce Birch, David Watson, and Donald Dayton. Also in the setting of the church I am thankful for the relationships I've had with members of the National Council of Churches Stewardship Commission. To President Eugene S. Wehrli and my faculty colleagues at Eden Theological Seminary I am grateful for a generative and supportive collegium. Harold Rast, formerly of Fortress Press, and Michael West have been patient and superb editors. My secretary, Kay Boyle, contributed her many stenographic skills but more importantly her indomitable spirit.

I am thankful that in their criticism of their father my sons, Douglas and John, are not timid, for they generally save me from what could be an even greater foolishness just as they often embolden me with their affection.

In the writing of this book as in all things in my life my spouse Blair has shown an uncommon economy of grace and love, which had not a little to do with the argument herein.

Introduction

North American churches seem to be able to wrestle on a relatively sustained basis with almost all public issues except those touching on economy. Pastors find it excruciatingly perplexing to preach and teach on the economic life of Christians and of the society in which they live. Church leaders, theological professors, and ecclesiastical bodies often falter when the world wants to know what they have to say about economy.

What are the reasons for this? No doubt they are complex and varied. But one key reason has to do with what Christians think about God and how they live before God. The church's teaching on economy has been so timid because it has been unwilling in its modern forms to ask about the life and work of God in relation to economy. To be responsible about its own economy and its society's economy the church should know what difference its teaching about God makes for its teaching about economy.

Recently there have been numerous studies of the relationship of Christian ethics and economics.[1] Our intention is not to give an exhaustive ethical treatment of economic questions.[2] Rather, we shall inquire about a possible reconceptualization of both God and economy that might enhance a more faithful and imaginative wrestling by the church with the massive economic questions of our time.[3] The reform of our teaching about God and of our views of economy should proceed hand in hand. Thus we shall be concerned with the relation of the Christian doctrine of God to political economy. In its most comprehensive sense, political economy involves the social relationships of power that exist in the human attempt to gain livelihood for the community and its members.

There is a deficit of theological work with regard to political economy. God concepts have been criticized in relation to racism, sexism, the technological mastery of the environment, and ordinary people's loss of the democratic control of their lives. But not enough attention has been given to how God concepts in North Atlantic church and society relate to the deepest assumptions of the market society.

A New Metaphor for God

My claim is that, according to the faith shaped by the biblical traditions, the metaphor *Economist* is a decisive and fully appropriate way of describing the character and work of God. Retrieving this metaphor should help in overcoming the church's paralysis in bringing its faith to bear on economic life in our time.

It should be clear from the beginning, however, that we do not mean *economist* in its ordinary usage over the last two hundred years. *Economist* has its special meaning according to the classical, neoclassical, and Marxist economic traditions. Above all, it has come to mean a scientist who follows exact canons of thought, measurement, and verification in relation to things economic. Whether they are in the tradition of Adam Smith, Alfred Marshall, or Karl Marx, almost all economists in our time believe they are practitioners of a "hard science" whose modes of operation and parameters of concern are uncompromisingly determined by economic "laws." They view economics as a genuinely modern science, in part because they study constructs, such as the supply-demand-price mechanism, which did not exist, at least in their present form, in the past and in part because they employ sciences and conceptions of the human being that did not appear before the Enlightenment. If the word *economist* can mean only what most modern economists mean by it, then its application to God is of course injudicious.

But the word *economy* is an ancient word. It has a long history and is filled with a rich array of meanings and functions.[4] *Economy* has rendered meanings qualitatively different from the narrow definitions of the term in modernity. Older senses of economy accord more fully with what we shall mean by *Economist* as metaphor for God. We shall employ premodern understandings of economy and thereby claim that the modern definitions of economics are not exhaustive of the economic dimension of human existence. A church that worships the God known in Israel and in Jesus Christ and that seeks to live in responsibility to its Lord in the world will require a broader meaning of economy than that propounded in the market society today. The church's tradition of teaching on economy should not be jettisoned simply because some claim that the meaning of economics is now so radically different that the tradition has nothing to contribute to economic affairs. The life of the church today needs the richness of the economic metaphors for God, which have been largely repressed.

The Greek word from which we derive *economy, oikonomia,* is a compound of *oikos,* household, and *nomos,* law or management. *Economy* means literally "the law or the management of the household." Household is connected with the production, distribution, and consumption of the necessities of life. When we use the word *household,* we shall mean not the modern notion of a family consuming unit but rather the site of economy, the site of human livelihood. In an attenuated sense, then, we shall refer to whole economies as households. Without household people will not survive, for household is the mediation of what it takes to live. How, then, does our understanding of God relate to what Daniel Bell calls the "public household"?[5]

There is, of course, no scientific economic theory in the modern sense in the Bible, even though the Bible is centrally concerned with economy. The Bible cannot solve any technical economic problems facing us today. Nor is there a *Christian* economic system that can be set over against monetarist, Keynesian, structuralist, or socialist economics, even though Christian faith relates to all aspects of economic life. A Christian does not have to be a socialist any more than a Christian has to be a capitalist. A baptized Christian only has to be a disciple of Jesus Christ and an apostle of Christ's mission in the world. As such, every Christian should be prepared to think about economics and to participate in economic life according to the criterion of God's righteousness in Jesus Christ.

To live economically according to God's righteousness, the church should give up the notion that God is noneconomic. The church sometimes thinks and lives as if God were outside the pale of economy, so the "dangerous memories" of God's indwelling the world will not intrude on the present economic reality. The Bible's renderings of God will not allow this. If we find no ready-made economic solutions to our dilemmas, we nevertheless find in the biblical traditions the shape of God's economy to which, for Christians, our economic systems should correspond as much as possible under the conditions of history. God's own economy is God's life, work, and suffering for the life of the creation. As such it is meant as ground of the human economy for life. God's "law of the household" is the economy of life against death and cannot be disregarded by our economy with impunity.

In the broadest terms, we shall argue, God's law of the household is God's Torah and God's Gospel. The Torah and the Gospel display, when they are historically appropriated in faith, certain concrete tendencies of economy. When we treat *oikonomia* theologically we are concerned with how God is redeeming the world. This is not to conflate theology and economics or to take away the relative autonomy of the science of economics. Rather, it is an attempt to show that faith in the God of the Bible has economic implications that derive from who God is and from God's own redemptive history with the world. And in the Christian mission in the world these implications should extend to the economic life of the world, even if the Bible cannot be immediately translated into economic theory and policy. Speaking of God for the sake of Jesus Christ, as Christian theology does, means that economic existence is lived in the horizon of God's economy.

Many of the biblical traditions represent God as engaged in creating, sustaining, and recreating households. *Household* can refer to the people Israel or the church of Jesus Christ, to families, to a royal court or dynasty, to a place of God's abode, or, in the most comprehensive sense, to the whole creation. God has made Godself responsible for the households of Israel and the church, the households of the nations, and the household of everything God has brought into being. The *oikonomia tou theou* (economy of God) applies to the life of the Christian community (Col. 1:25; 1 Cor. 9:17; Eph. 3:2; 1 Tim. 1:4) as well as to God's work of creating salvation for the household of the creation (Eph. 1:9–10; 3:9–10). Because of the peculiar promises made by this God, the life of God is inextricably connected with the livelihood and future of these households.

ECONOMY, POLITICS, AND POWER

We shall consider God and economy in relation to a society whose engendering cry is "liberty and justice for all" but whose tendencies are to sacrifice either liberty or justice for the sake of the other. Some say that the search for the equality of access to livelihood has to be relinquished lest we lose our liberty. Others say that liberty should be eliminated if that proves necessary to create the just conditions in which all people can have dignity. Few would disagree that the future of democracy depends on the outcome of this contest between liberty and justice.

We cannot, however, overlook the fact that this contest is taking place in a society shaped by the accumulation of wealth based on the exchange of property rights. Accumulation of wealth and exchange have replaced livelihood as the center of economy. The values of our economic organization are often held higher than human dignity. The more the few gain power and privilege through property rights at the expense of the many, the more democracy is injured and no longer counted on as the shape of our future. The same result applies when other elites condemn liberty and rights in the name of equality. In reality the only historical, objectively given way to move beyond the threats to liberty and justice, at least in our society, is democracy. It is under this assumption that we shall try to consider God and economy together.

To do this we shall inevitably encounter the ambiguity of the liberal tradition.[6] The liberal tradition has been the fertile ground from which has arisen the modern theory of the market as guarantor of liberty as well as the assumptions which make our market society a threat to both liberty and justice. To be sure, the liberal theory is a theory of liberation from despotism and poverty. And, as the dominant ideology of the age, it has gone a long way toward achieving such liberation at least for a portion of the populations of the democratic industrialized nations. But the liberal theory is flawed. It tends to denigrate politics by assuming that blocking the power of the state removes all threats to domination within a market-driven society. It masks the forms of domination to which its own assumptions contribute. Its culture makes use of notions of domination mediated by traditional God concepts.

Liberal society has produced the conditions that make new forms of democratic society both necessary and possible. The liberal tradition has also provided us with the discourse of rights, which has pervaded almost the entire world, and with a focus on personal rights. It is unimaginable to anticipate a democratic future for our society without the strengthening of personal rights and the simultaneous reshaping of property rights. This means that the discourse of rights should be critically preserved and its correlation to the theological traditions of righteousness and covenant reflected upon.

While everyone speaks the language of rights, however, it often sounds in our public life like the cacophony of Babel. The National Rifle Association claims the right to own and fire automatic weapons while citizens and police claim the right of safe passage in the streets. In this dissonance of rights, one characteristic stands out: rights defined by the privileged in the economic sphere of life are allowed to define rights in many other spheres. For example, in a society asserting that all should receive justice equally, it is nevertheless the case that justice in our courts has been reduced to a commodity available to those with purchasing power. Again, whereas most of the tradition has assumed health care as a right, health is now widely regarded as a commodity to be bought and sold. Thus many people give up on the discourse of rights. But in our time, besides rights, there is little else to which to appeal but brutal power politics or violence. Those without rights erupt aggressively or succumb to quiet despair or to the nihilism of drugs. We are discovering ever so slowly that if the democratic life of the appeal to rights is to thrive, it must presuppose a community or household of common social meanings. Our society is thus faced with the decisive problem of finding such communal shared meanings of social goods without destroying the diversity which personal democratic rights requires. Where shall we turn for a nondominative view of rights arising out of common social meanings?

The two great antidomination traditions of modernity, liberalism and Marxism, are both beset with a unitary view of power. The one says domination is lodged in the state and can be overcome only by the liberty that emerges from the rules of the market. The other says that domination comes from the privilege of capital deriving from the rules of property and can be overcome only by allowing the state to eclipse the private realm. But both are short-sighted in that their slant on reality does not allow them to see the pervasiveness of domination in many other spheres of life, especially the very spheres that they define as the nondominative solution to domination.

The liberal tradition has become blind to the fact that domination takes place not only in the state but also in the economic sphere.[7] The Marxist tradition has uncovered a peculiar kind of domination, namely exploitation through privilege deriving from property rules. But it is unable to see the domination that takes place in the state as well as in many cultural spheres of life. Neither tradition is able to give significant criticism of institutions in which women and people of color are oppressed and the ecosphere ruined. Both traditions thus fail in the end to assert the value of democracy, which we understand to be the organized struggle, through the expansion of rights, against privilege and domination in all dimensions of life.

If God and economy are inextricably connected, we shall have to go against the modern stream by holding that economy is political. Power, authority, and politics cannot be removed from the economic sphere, the arguments of neoclassical economics notwithstanding. Thus when we argue that Economist is an appropriate, much-needed metaphor for God, we are not supporting the liberal separation of politics and economy, the one public and the other private. We are rather trying to retrieve the economic metaphors of God in order to set God and political economy in a critical relationship. Politics and economy are necessary to each other just as the political and economic dimensions of God's life with the creation are necessary to each other.

Why bring God into this picture? Because some views of God are a major part of the problem. By offering a simple unitary picture of power they justify economic and political structures of domination. Against these views of God we will set a trinitarian understanding of God and our life before God. The Trinity will be viewed as a hermeneutic of God's history of righteousness with the world, which in turn provides a covenant discourse of rights that the church can appropriate as it relates its faith to the public economic reality.

THE COMPONENTS
OF POLITICAL ECONOMY

There are at least four basic components of every political economy: power/rule, property, work, and needs/consumption. How a community or society decides the character and structures of these spheres will shape its future and provide the framework in which the meanings of liberty and justice arise. These are not just external, structural questions. It is true that most human beings will feel that the relationships of power, property, work, and consumption in which they live are forced upon them, that they have no essential control over them. But the prevailing modes of these components of political economy have been produced by human values and decisions shaped by the rudimentary faith of masses of people. No particular political economy exists for long without fundamental support of its assumptions by most of the people among whom it flourishes.

It will of course be difficult to maintain that economic relationships are chosen or condoned in countries like the United States or the Soviet Union, where the public universe of discourse maintains the absolute inevitability of a particular economy. Yet in the long run, political economies are shorn up by a faith by which people agree to live with the modes of power, property, work, and consumption presently determining political economy. We cannot ask about the future of the global *oikos* unless we ask about all four of these components, about their interdependence, and about their religious grounding in various perceptions of God.

The first component of political economy is power/rule. It is an ancient question: What kind of politics serves a humane economy and what kind of economy serves a humane politics? At least out of the West's memory it should be clear that politics and economy belong together. One cannot eclipse or replace the other, though our past and our present are full of attempts to collapse one into the other. How shall we relate *oikos* and *polis* and how shall both be related to *kosmos*? What is the system of authority, power, and coercion that stands behind the economic system? What is the principle of the legitimation of an economic system? Because God concepts have always been used to depict and justify authority, power, and coercion, God concepts have always been at work in political economy, even if it was claimed that the economic system excluded God.

The second component is property. What does possession or ownership mean? Who has rights over resources and capital, and why? Who should control planning and investment policies and monetary and fiscal systems? What are the rights of nature? Does nature have property rights?

The third component is work. How does a society understand production? What is meaningful work? Does work justify human beings and generate their lives? Is meaningful, remunerative work for those who desire it a human right? Who should control the work process? Who should plan production? Should investment and planning processes be accountable to those whose work carries forward the production process?

The fourth component is consumption and human needs. Are there ways in which our understanding of needs affects ways in which we distribute resources, goods, and income? What is a human need as opposed to a human want? Does human freedom mean the right to luxury when the needs of others are not being met? Are there limits to human satisfaction? Should human satisfaction be connected with the consumption of commodities? Are there kinds of incentive and motivation that do not lead inexorably to the narcissism of our society?

Christian theology is concerned to ask what Christian faith can contribute in each of these four dimensions toward a more humane economy. When we ask about power/rule, property, work, and consumption we are asking about four principal ways in which human beings have dominated and exploited each other. Christian politico-economic theology will criticize assumptions, theories, and systems of domination in each of these dimensions. It will try to make clear at every point that economy exists for the sake of the human community and its relationship to God and the creation. The criterion of a just economic system will be whether it serves the life and future of this community.

THE TRIUNE GOD
AND THE PROBLEMS WE FACE

Several clusters of problems will appear prominently in our juxtaposition of God and economy. They involve implications of setting a critical view of the Triune God over against God concepts that are still influencing basic economic assumptions in our society. The doctrine of the Trinity is the Christian way of demythologizing God concepts that undergird utopian and ideological uses of economic assumptions. Trinitarian views of God's freedom and power will be set over against claims made about liberty and justice in the modern market society assumptions about property, work, and consumption.

Economy and Fate

No other assumption is so detrimental to the church's attempt to be faithful in the economic sphere of life as the claim that economic reality is determined by fate or unchanging laws. Both capitalist and Marxist theories claim that things are the way they are economically because economy is rooted in the inevitability of nature or history, abstractly conceived. Economic theory claims to be the most "realist" of all theories. But in point of fact much of modern economic theory has a utopian cast. It tries to make the economy conform to human and social conditions that could exist only in a nonhistorical world.

Such a view of the immutable ground of economic laws is supported by a conception of God as an unchanging, eternal substance or an unchanging, absolute self. The biblical traditions, however, render God as a community of persons dwelling (making a home) among the creation and the people who are called into being by God's power of righteousness out of the power of the *nihil* (Exod. 3, Genesis 1–2, John 1). God incarnate dwells in the history of God's creatures, for whom God has become Economist. Only with a doctrine of God's radical immanence in the Spirit will Christian theology be able to make its own peculiar contribution to public economy. The households for life that God desires to build are neither determined by a natural principle nor closed according to a universally defined human nature.

Economy is not fated. Economy is historical. In principle everything about economy can be rethought and changed. Poverty is not an eternal condition of nature nor an intention of God.[8] If economic reality is not grounded in nature or its laws nor can be derived from the unchanging character of human nature, it is unwise, for example, to try to build an economy on the claim that the greedy character of the human being cannot be changed. Modern economic theory often views human nature as immutable, as God's nature used to be conceived. But human nature is not eternally given and fixed. Sin is always present in human economy, no matter what the economy's structure. But sin cannot be made a justification of any economic system. Sin is no excuse for capitalism or socialism, nor can either claim to be a solution to sin. Systems that justify themselves on the basis of a rigid, unchangeable human nature idolatrously deny the eschatological power of God the Holy Spirit to create human beings anew and transform conditions in which they live.

That the structure of no economy is eternally fixed is demonstrated by the rise of the modern market society itself. The market economy had to show that feudalism and mercantilism were not eternally fixed. But now both "free" market and "state" market societies define the public household as if their own assumptions and structures were indeed eternal. It is assumed that everything can be changed except the "laws" that brought about modern improvements in the household. But to live in the immanence of God the Economist is to know that all economic "laws" are historical and will be judged by God's economy.

Economy, Domination, and Equality

The main problem of all economy is domination. "God" has been the epitome of power and authority in most societies. Thus "God" can be used as an agency of domination in economy as well as in politics. By removing God from modern economy, economics thought it had eliminated the last vestige of coercion, that is, the ways the state uses God concepts to dominate human beings. But economics remains unaware of the ways in which domination *within the economy* is still supported unconsciously by deformed God concepts. It is precisely for this reason that it is so urgent for Christian theology to juxtapose God and economy.

The biblical traditions show that domination is always mediated by some configuration of social goods.[9] The egalitarian thrust of God's economy (Torah and Gospel) is to free the households of Israel and the church, the household of the nations, and the household of the creation from domination. It envisions a society in which no social good can serve as a means of domination. It does this by proscribing the use of things for the purpose of domination. The Torah and Gospel intend a "shared understanding of social goods" that requires what Michael Walzer has called a "complex equality."[10]

Equality means the thrust to abolish the differences that result from wealth, racial and sexual supremacy, ecological rape, and meritocratic privilege.[11] Equality works against the experience of subordination. It works against some people having to fawn, defer, bow, and scrape because other people or groups have power over them. The equalitarian impetus of God's economy is against all forms of domination by which the powerful "grind the faces of the poor." It intends the end of the master-slave relationship.

The egalitarian thrust of God's economy is meant to serve freedom. It does not aim at eliminating differences among human beings. It does not intend a conformist and leveled society. Rather, equality in the household of God means that radically different persons embrace and yet remain radically different. We do not have to be the same or have the same amount of things. What God's household seeks to eliminate is domination over others, which prevents their access to what they need in order to keep their calling to be God's image, child, disciple, and friend.

Economy and Possessive Individualism

The theological attempt to describe God's unity in terms of monarchically defined substance or subjectivity provides a ground for what C.B. Macpherson calls the "possessive individualism" of the modern market society.[12] The "individual" is an abstraction that can fit into the thought pattern of modern economics. A critical doctrine of God, however, should show that God is not a radical individual but rather a community of diverse persons that finds unity in self-giving love rather than in substantialist or subjectivist principles of identity.[13]

The ancient Cappadocian doctrine of *perichōrēsis* or the "mutual coinherence" of the persons of the Trinity is a model of interrelationships of the members of the household that God intends. All the persons of the triune community have their own characteristics and their own tasks. Yet they are constituted as persons precisely by their relationships with the other persons of the community.

The same should be said for human economic community. There is in reality no such thing as a radically individual and isolated human being. We are what we are as a result of being constituted by our relationships with the other members of the communities in which we live. All social goods are given to us communally. Such communal coinherence should be the presupposition of distributive justice.

There cannot be a just society until there is a society. There cannot be a just community until there is a community. It is not meaningful to speak of justice until we are involved in living communities that in their relationships and conflicts are struggling for justice. The substantive life of society is prior to and intimates what justice is. Once we know the stories, the identity, the interests and loves, the passions and commitments, the hates and fears of a community, then we may begin to speak of justice.

Economy and Scarcity

As the introduction to almost every contemporary economics textbook shows, one of the most basic assumptions of modern economics is scarcity.[14] Scarcity, it is claimed, is the universal presupposition of exchange relationships. No matter how much society will be able to produce, it is claimed, there will always be scarcity. There is never enough to go around because the human being always wants more. There is no limit to human wanting.

The biblical traditions uncover God as the Economist who constructs the household with a radically different assumption: *If* the righteousness of God is present, there is always enough to go around.[15] From the manna in the desert, to Jesus' feeding of the multitudes, to the Lord's Supper, the biblical traditions depict the superabundance (*plērōma*) of God's Spirit as the starting point of God's household and its practice of hospitality. Thus should the doctrine of God follow the biblical claim of the fullness of God's being rather than the modern economic assumption of the formal emptiness of God's being, which can be filled or negated by human impulses to self-possession, autonomous individualism, and greed.

A brief map of our journey is in order. Chapter 1 considers our present economic quandaries and reasons the church has kept

God and economy separated. Chapter 2 inquires about ways in which theology and political economy might be correlated. In chapter 3 we trace some of the historical and theological implications of God's official absence from the market and the surreptitious presence of God concepts in the assumptions behind modern economistic theory. The next chapter investigates some biblical warrants for using Economist as a metaphor for God. The final three chapters examine some of our society's basic assumptions about property, work, and needs. By making a trinitarian critique of God concepts entailed in these assumptions, we seek to open up new possibilities for the church to struggle with economic questions on the assumptive level and to live both before God and in face of the massive problems that emerge in a society extolling liberty and justice in which the denial of livelihood to many people raises radical questions about liberty and justice.

Chapter 1	# God's Economy and the Church

WE LIVE IN A TIME WHEN THERE IS NO BASIC agreement on solutions to economic problems or even on what the problems are.[1] We do not know for certain whether we are facing sea changes or merely significant adjustments in the world's economic order. But there are clear signs that the old ways of thinking economy are not working, even if many North Americans seem content with the predictable oscillation between optimism and pessimism in things economic.

This is certainly not the first time in history that large numbers of people have feared economic collapse. But it is the first time in living memory that there seems to be no viable theory of economy. The great theories of demand-side and supply-side economics behind the cycles and swings of the economic systems of the developed countries seem to have played themselves out. We are living between the time of relative certainty about economy and the time of a new economy which is surely coming but whose contours are only dimly perceived.

ECONOMIC PERPLEXITY

Over the last few years, we have come to know these things about the North American economy: the rate of poverty has risen; officially "acceptable" unemployment has risen by about 1 percent after each recession of recent times; we do not really know how to keep interest rates and inflation under control; there seems to be no way to control deficits in the national budget; the United States, for the first time in its history, has become the major debtor nation; farmers are tempted to despair over the loss of their land; workers are told that industrialization in North America is coming to an end; many people are afraid of falling out of the middle class after three generations of their families have labored arduously to enter it.[2]

The Richter scale can register the seismic reverberations of an earthquake but not the resulting havoc, destruction, and despair that beset human life. The same is true for economic mechanisms that measure fiscal and monetary flows and Gross National Product. We have an ever-more-highly tuned economic apparatus that does not register the suffering of persons, families, and communities. Euphoria over a high-technology, information-based economy and the other megatrends does not even acknowledge the presence of the poor and minorities trapped outside of the market economy, much less offer a hopeful prospect for them.

A large proportion of our people do not participate in the wealth of the American household.[3] What is the obligation we owe to those who have been structurally and culturally excluded from the household? Over thirty-three million persons have fallen below what our government defines as official poverty (annual income of $10,600 for a family of four).[4] This amounts to the combined populations of Alaska, California, Hawaii, Oregon, and Washington. Forty-six million U.S. citizens are excluded from career employment, locked into menial, dead-end jobs, or into sheer joblessness. The growing prosperity of the majority is not "trickling down" to the destitute. An inadequate, misconceived welfare system visits the tragedy of parents on their children's children.[5]

In our public household poverty does not threaten us equally. Racism and sexism are entrenched. Only 12 percent of all white persons are officially poor, but 35 percent of blacks and 28 percent of Hispanics are poor. In our public household a woman who heads a household has a one-in-three chance of being poor. If she is black, the chance is one in two. In households headed by women, 71 percent of the children are poor.

In our public household many do not even have a shelter. Persons in our society who have neither a job nor a family are homeless people. The number of homeless people, already in the hundreds of thousands, is the fastest-growing poverty statistic. Many of these people have jobs and work hard, yet are not able to find homes for themselves and their families. People are being made homeless by budget slicing in housing and welfare programs, by deinstitutionalization, and by speculative development projects, which raise real estate values so high that some cities have no housing for the poor. The cycle of poverty and homelessness leads to drug and other kinds of death-serving addiction.

The storehouse and table of our economy are plentifully stocked with food. But because food is a market commodity, many do not have the means of taking a place at table. Not all the poor are hungry, but almost all the hungry are poor. Our household allocations for child nutrition and food stamps have fallen as an ever-growing number of soup kitchens valiantly try to do the impossible.

Even less does the suffering of the poor in the global household appear in the sophisticated measurements and rules of our public household.[6] We have cut off food assistance to Third World countries so that we can afford to send bullet-proof vests to the Filipino police and fighter planes to El Salvador. We are willing to sell agricultural and commercial technology, which is often not culturally suitable to peasant societies, on the condition that we can control the products.[7] The result is increased poverty and dependence for millions of people in the Third World.

The starting point for economic thinking should be the suffering caused by the present household arrangements. Why can we not see what is before our eyes? Why does the economic suffering around us not register with us?

SCARCITY, SATIATION, AND SECURITY

Our public household has become crazed by three simultaneous phenomena: scarcity, satiation, and security. Since 1973 Americans have lived with the gnawing premonition that the overflowing cornucopia will cease to be the realistic symbol of American economy. The land of unlimited possibilities might after all be finite in its resources and in its ability to solve all of its problems technologically and economically. The sense of scarcity does hateful things to the human animal. Territorial, survival, and competitive instincts appear, instincts that are not healthy for homemaking and for enlarging the table for those who do not have enough to survive the day. The sense of scarcity makes the members of the household less accepting and compassionate.

At the same time our public household is beleaguered by a pervasive sense of satiation. Many of us have too much and consume too much. It is all we can do to dream up the next purchase and simulate hunger for the next meal. We count on there being a medicant to take for every mood, every overstuffing, every success. Satiation makes the household members drowsy and inattentive to their own and other's suffering. It takes away the incentive to reconstruct the household so more persons can be included.

The double-jolting experience of scarcity and satiation in our public household has issued in a compulsion to security. Ours is an economy of security, in which people are driven to tie down advantages and privileges and to hedge all bets against the uncertainty of history. People and societies ridden by scarcity and satiation will devote an inordinate amount of energy to defending gains and possessions. No expenditure of resources will seem too much to secure the present arrangements of the household by means of the state's police forces and the national structure of the household by means of the state's armed forces. As the history of the Vietnam War makes clear, internal security and external defense bolster each other and mold each other. The expansion of nuclear arsenals to support the doctrines of assured destruction and unlimited defense leave the public household without means for the everyday welfare and security of its people. People insecure in their jobs, housing, and streets contribute to a pervasive sense of malaise, which in turn is met by increased security measures. Compulsion to security leaves no energy for imagining a different, more just world.

The conspiracy of scarcity, satiation, and security issues in a household without memory and hope. We are a society of amnesia. Our everyday modalities of life make us forgetful. It is increasingly difficult to remember not only our public history but also our personal stories. Indeed there may be some actors in the economy who benefit from the forgetfulness of others. Those who enjoy the present arrangements of the household do not like the dangerous memories of the past which envision different household arrangements.

Scarcity, satiation, and security produce not only amnesia, but also anesthesia. Drugs, alcohol, overconsumption, narcotics for overconsumption, passive absorption in television, and the compulsion to batten down the hatches all have the effect of making us insensitive to the suffering around us and too inert to remember what we have a right to hope for. To think together God's economy and our economy requires memory and hope, for only they can break the torpidity into which we have fallen and enable us to suffer with those who suffer in our public household. In life before God, memory and hope set before us the universal household for which God is working.

THE SEPARATION OF
THEOLOGY AND ECONOMICS

Whenever economics as a science or economy as a system denies Christians the opportunity to live for the sake of God's universal household, there will necessarily be a conflict of interests. Neither theology nor economics has taken this conflict seriously enough. Rather, both, living as they do with their salvational claims, have conveniently divided up the spheres in which they could properly make their claims about "saving." Economics has staked out the market and has invented frameworks, such as the price-supply-demand mechanism, which are assumed to be autonomous and self-validating systems and thus impenetrable to criticism. Theology, on the other hand, has tended to take over the internal life of the human being, with its questions of meaning, purpose, and value. Its field is also viewed as impervious to the other sciences.

This is a convenient division of labor and turf. For then neither theology nor economics can be called into question by the other. But just as clearly neither theology nor economics can call the other into question. It is a marriage of separation in which there is never any serious quarrel because there is no basic ground for argument. It is assumed that they are always talking about fundamentally different things when they talk separately about their own thing. But this unknowing mutual disregard cannot go on forever, for the struggle over the meaning of the redemption of the household belongs too focally to each.

The worship and life of churches in our society appear isolated from the economic context. Christians have often been unaware of the ways in which economic systems have distorted Christian faith and the way in which perverted religious notions have dehumanized economic relationships. The predominant economic values have sometimes been virulently anti-Christian. Yet church people have tended to assume that the economic environment of the church had nothing to do with faith. Theologians, moreover, seem assiduously trained not to see critically the connections between God and economy. When these convictions hold sway it is easy to make surreptitious use of the Christian faith as religious legitimization of assumptions behind prevailing economic systems.

When we ask how Christians should understand themselves economically, we are faced with two kinds of problems: First, we are confronted with ways in which economic realities influence our relationship to God. Are there elements of the modern market society (in both capitalist and socialist forms) antagonistic to the peculiarly Christian understanding of God? Do some economic claims and conditions in our society lead to false worship? Do some systemic elements of our economic life lead to consistent inhibition of prayer, of personal sharing of life and goods, and of personal commitment to the church's life and ministry? Do some of our economic conditions lead to a bias against promises of fidelity in family and communal relationships?

Second, we have to contend with ways in which our conceptions of and worship of God influence our economic life. Do false concepts of God generate or provide fertile ground for the dehumanization of life in various economies? Do some views of God expressed in our worship and everyday life prevent us from living in solidarity with the victims of existing economic systems throughout the world?

The first line of questioning suggests that unjust economic conditions destroy the true worship of the Triune God. The second suggests that worshiping God in distorted ways contributes to the dehumanization of economic life. Both kinds of questions imply that God and economy must be thought together, that theology and economy are correlative.

This, however, has been largely denied in the North Atlantic context. At least since the beginning of the nineteenth century the standard way of dealing with the problematic "God and economics" has been to separate God from an ever more narrowly defined sphere of economics. In matters of faith and economics our churches still follow the lead of the preeminent American "theologian," Andrew Carnegie. In an article published in 1889 Carnegie argued that it would not behoove the Christian faith to say anything about how money was made, since the process of producing wealth is determined by inexorable natural laws, such as the laws of the survival of the fittest and the competition of tooth and fang.[8] These laws determine the acquisition of wealth and fully justify the discrepancy in wealth between rich and poor. Property, extraction, production, and market operate according to fixed natural laws. The Christian religion, Carnegie maintained, becomes pertinent only after the production process has run its course and money has been made and reinvested. Only then should Christianity enter the scene to help successful producers and acquisitors know how to disperse their surplus money prudentially, that is, charitably.

Carnegie even provided the rules for distributing surplus money. It should be given only to the "deserving poor" and only to those who support the system under which the wealth was produced in the first place. In other words, Christian faith has to do with charity, and charity does not extend to the basic questions of economics. Thus we have the basic understanding of stewardship in old-line and newer churches in North America: the voluntary giving of left-over money and time. And this is often as far as the church goes in dealing with economy.

Even though worship and theology seem separated from economics in our time, the Jewish and Christian faiths have traditionally expressed deep concern for the questions of economy. And despite Carnegie's claim about charity, the Bible says much more about work, property, and consumption than it does about "charity" and "philanthropy."

FAITH AND THE
AMBIGUITY OF ECONOMICS

That these traditions demonstrate such a thoroughgoing ambiguity about the basic issues of economics, however, suggests that faith gives no easy answers to economic quandaries. The daily life of economics stimulates constant, open questions of faith. Faith, on the other hand, just as constantly calls economy into question. This is no new story.

The Christian faith's ambiguity about economy is reflected in the religious orders of the West. There are three problems of human existence which persistently appear with great ambiguity: wealth (property, work, and consumption), sexuality, and knowledge. The ambiguity is that human beings cannot live without these realities, but they can hardly live with them.

Economy, sexuality, and knowledge are the chief fields in which idolatry takes place, which is another way of saying that power is formed around these facets of reality and that politics dances incessantly around them. In these fields human power is most readily distorted and turns into human domination which destroys the lives of other human beings, perverts our relationship with nature, and alienates us from God. Economy, sexuality, and knowledge (which seem to be intrinsically related) are the dimensions in which human beings seem to be most independently creative. In these areas of life we dream that we can create our own world and even the next generation. Here we are most prone to arrogate the claim to self-sufficiency and the power to subjugate our environment, other persons, and even our own bodies. The gifts and claims of God can be most radically denied in these areas.

Denying God's right in these dimensions of life, human beings forget their creatureliness and, like Cain, construct a counter-creation, the city, which symbolizes, in some of the biblical traditions, the human urge to secure the future by dominating human beings and nature. For the sake of their mastery through wealth, sexuality, and knowledge human beings erect fortified walls, which separate them from creation (which now becomes nature, the stuff for our use), from other human beings (who now become enemies), and from God (who now is to be coerced by appeasement or escaped in dread). It is no wonder, then, that in the Christian tradition the vows of poverty, chastity, and obedience have been thought to grace a better way of serving God in history.

On the other hand, however, it has been realized that the human being cannot do without property, work, consumption, sexuality, and knowledge. They are necessary for the human being to be the image of God, which means to be human. They are gifts of God for the doing of God's will. They are part of God's economy of creation and redemption. They cannot be negated without denying the peculiarly human, since they are all needed to fulfill the divine calling that makes the human being human. The city as the human project is not to be utterly negated. Indeed God finally accepts the city, utterly transformed, as the ultimate shape of the new creation (Revelation 21).

The vows of poverty, chastity, and obedience, which ground the project of the religious orders, have not been meant for the most part to annihilate property, work, consumption, sexuality, and knowledge, but rather to bring them under the strictest discipline of God's word and liturgy of communal living. Here these facets of life are to find their liberating discipline under obedience to Jesus Christ. The vows are meant to make certain that these most necessary and most-subject-to-perversion powers of human life remain means and not ends. The vows, in their best conception, are intended to have a humanizing impact on the world, not to be world-escaping. Whenever the religious orders or the churches as a whole lose the courage to be radically different from the world in order to contribute to the transformation of the world, they lose their *raison d'être*.

The Reformation did not eliminate the concern for bringing wealth, sexuality, and knowledge under the disciplining of God's Word. Rather the Reformation claimed that such disciplining was not meant just for the religious orders but for ordinary Christians in everyday life. Reformation theology maintained much of the medieval ethic of economy.

It is widely assumed in the modern world, however, that the triumph of capitalism required overcoming this ethic. Market ways of thinking had to demystify traditional economic world views. But in so doing they eclipsed the sense that everything about economy is creaturely and that God's economy should ground human economy. And thus these new ways of thinking were subject to their own mystification. We stand today before the arduous and painful task of demythologizing our economic assumptions, assumptions we have supposed to be beyond scrutiny.

One place in which this should happen is the household of Jesus Christ, the church, for its very being is the *oikonomia tou theou* (economy of God). Despite its constant, gnawing sense of ambiguity about economy the church can persevere in the scrutiny of all economic claims because of the promised presence of God the Holy Spirit who is incessantly seeking to create a home, a household, in which God's creatures can live abundantly.

THE CHURCH'S *OIKONOMIA*

The doctrine of the church is the doctrine of the economy of God's household (Col. 1:25; 1 Cor. 9:17; Eph. 3:2). Because the church exists for the sake of God's love of the world (John 3:16), there can be no sound teaching about the church that does not include the relationship of the church to our society's economy and the world's economy.

The church is meant to be that place in history where God's interests for the world meet the interests of the world *in the presence and power of the Holy Spirit.*[9] The Holy Spirit seeks to transform a portion of the world into the church so that, as transformed world, the church may live for the future of the world. According to Paul, the presence of the Holy Spirit means that we have to die either to the world or to the Spirit of God. But if we live in the Spirit of God this means solidarity with the world—we are to die to the world so that we might live for the transformation of the world.

This is an insight with consequences. If we strive to put church, world, and the Triune God together in our time and place, we discover that theology must begin with an ideology critique of the church. Our initial question should be the ancient one: *Cui bono?* For whose good are we doing theology in the first place? Whose interests is the church serving by its existence? God's interest is transforming the world into a household in which all of God's creatures can find abundant life. God's economy in Israel and Jesus Christ is to begin with the poor and oppressed, those who are most threatened by death and evil, in order to build a new household for all of God's creatures.

God's economy is meant for this world. Therefore it entails a conflict with all those who would build households excluding the poor and oppressed, the uneducated, those less than adequate at bargaining, and those without political power. God's economy also entails a conflict with those who would exclude nature from home as if it were mere stuff to be manipulated for our ends. If the church is already captivated by the interests of the world, can it serve the transformation of the world into a home for the homeless?

This is a disconcerting matter for theology because in order to engage in such criticism of interests, theology has to name names. It will soon become clear that the church is not captivated by every imaginable interest in the world but by a few particular interests that are often specifically the interests of those of us who call ourselves disciples of Christ. The more we press the question the more we realize that the first thing theology should serve is the liberation of the household of Jesus Christ from many of our own self-interests. If the church is already beholden to our economic, political, and cultural interests, can it serve God's liberation of the poor and the dying in the world?

North American theology is continually threatened with the temptation to forget the church. Are not our churches among the most segregated, sexist, and classist institutions in our society? Has not much of the rest of the world declared a moratorium on even listening to us? Have we not lost the right to speak to the world? Whenever the North American white churches intervene in economics and politics, there is the suspicion that they are serving their own interests. By what right or whose right can we claim any authority to do anything in the world?

It is sheer confusion to think that North American churches could make a difference in our political economy or effect a transformation of our society without their own radical conversion.

Without transforming its own economy, the church cannot have much effect on its society's economy. In the next decades theology will have to be done in the midst of God's struggle to transform the economy of the *oikos tou theou* (household of God). No theology will be able to escape this exigency.

This is the reason we must also be delivered from a second confusion, namely, the delusion that Christian theologians should give up on the churches in which they find themselves. This seems to be an ever present temptation among theologians and pastors: Either to give up hope for the church completely or to work on issues that are separated from their own church situation. Sometimes we focus on the liberation of the poor and the oppressed without even being aware that their poverty and oppression are immediately connected with our sin and our death-serving systems.[10] Is it that everything looks possible except our own liberation, except the transformation of the churches of which we are a part, except the transformation of that part of the world glued together by our interests and values?

The enormous unrest in the global economy is affecting the ecumenical church. Economic justice has become the central question of the *oikoumenē*. Churches are not separated merely by questions of doctrine, authority, polity, ministry, and sacraments. Even if they will be on the ecumenical agenda for some time to come, tremendous strides have been made in overcoming these divisions. What remains as an infinitely more difficult question is how the churches can live together in a world so deeply divided by economic ideologies and interests. The ecumenical movement has passed into a new phase. The divisions that threaten and deter the unity of Christ's church are no longer simply between communions. Rather, these divisions run through every communion, dividing congregations and denominations according to the prevailing spectrum of economic ideologies and the urgent life and death questions of the world economy. Those who would serve the ecumenical church can no longer overlook this reality.

Ecumenical work, especially in the North Atlantic community, should devote itself to a new conciliar existence focused on the part the doctrines, structures, and mission of the churches play in maintaining ideological economic divisions or the possibilities they contain for overcoming these divisions. Indeed, the ideological divisions of East and West and those within the West have religious/theological roots. The ecumenical movement has the responsibility to work theologically at removing at least the religious/theological components of the deadly threat to the whole inhabited world and even the whole creation posed by these economic antagonisms.

In this crisis situation theology will not be able, as it never has been able, to offer technical economic solutions. But Christian theology is responsible to the baptized community, which is called to live God's economy within this world of threatened economic chaos. The church in North America is in an especially precarious position because it has so little wherewithal to respond to the economic situation. The so-called *avant-garde* churches of North America, from the time of abolition to the present, have given significant leadership for human emancipation in the areas of civil, political, and legal rights. But like the rest of this society they have a deficit in the theory and practice of economic rights.

To be sure, there have been important exceptions in our theological traditions.[11] One thinks of abiding insights from the Pentecostal and evangelical traditions, the millennialist and utopian experiments, the Social Gospel, the Chicago school of Christian ethicists, and from the 1930s, when Reinhold Niebuhr and others experimented with socialist thought. North American Roman Catholics are presently seeking to appropriate the rich heritage of economic thought in the social teaching of papal encyclicals in the last one hundred years.[12] And the Protestant denominations are also beginning to wrestle with economic questions.[13] Yet we still have before us the task of critically juxtaposing theology and political economy.

If theology in the North Atlantic societies cannot escape the questions we have raised, then its first task becomes the criticism of the God concepts prevalent in our churches and socioeconomic structures. God concepts have always been and still are at work in economic life.[14] God concepts are effectively interwoven with the rudimentary assumptions of political economy.

"God concepts," it should be understood, may or may not use the term God or the language of theology. To discover them we must uncover what it is that we worship, what we regard as having ultimacy. In this sense all people, including atheists and agnostics, hold God concepts. And whatever we hold to be divine or ultimate will determine our life interests, the shape of our lives, and the institutions of our society.

In the conversation about what the church should teach on economy, we shall have to examine (1) which God concepts have been projected by specific economic beliefs and systems and (2) which God concepts enhance and justify economic beliefs and systems. The task of Christian theology in dialogue with economics, however, is not simply critically to analyze existing God concepts in economics but (3) to serve the church's mission to contribute to the transformation of existing dehumanizing economic systems. Thus theology should make its contribution to the humanization of economy.

Chapter 2 | # Reconceptualizing God and Economy

OR THE NEW TESTAMENT WRITERS AND the early theologians, "economy was the knowledge of God's works, and that meant not only knowledge of [God's] two great works, creating the world and saving [human beings], but also every detail in the life of the world that might have to do with God. Matters of life and death, good and evil, order and disorder, the governing of the state and the significance of the home, all belonged to economy."[1] Thus the redemptive work of God has traditionally been referred to as God's "economy." The relationship of the Triune God to the world has been called traditionally the "economic Trinity." A doctrine of God faithful to the biblical traditions will be economic.

THE SEMANTIC FIELDS OF THEOLOGY AND ECONOMY

In our time, to be sure, it will seem strange to juxtapose God and economy. But it should not be. The semantic fields of economy and biblical renderings of God are surprisingly similar. Words heard in the religious sphere are often also heard in banks and brokerage firms, labor unions and corporate executive offices. In both fields one regularly hears such words as trust, fidelity, fiduciary, promissory, confidence, debt, redemption, saving, security, futures, bond, and so on. It is as unimaginable to enter into basic economic relationships without these words as it is to speak biblically of God without them. Biblical God language is fundamentally economic. Economic language is fundamentally kin to the language of God's promissory history. As examples of the semantic similarity between economics and biblical language we can note the clusters of faith, salvation, and debt words.

If, to begin with, we consider *fides* (faith) and its derivatives, we shall discover that biblical religion and economics share the words fidelity, fiduciary, and confidence as the foundational words of everything that concerns them. That so many savings and loan companies and other economic organizations are named with "fidelity" and "trust" is a tribute to the fact that no economy can exist without a basic faith, which its constituents express in the relationships and structures of the economy.

Economic systems always have to be justified and legitimated. Without faith in what justifies them economic systems will exist by means of nothing but sheer coercion. Hence some economists are candid enough to speak of the whole science of economics or at least the economy which that science studies as depending on some kind of faith. This leads some economists, such as Robert Heilbroner, to speak of a "deep and pervasive crisis of faith" regarding the economy. Faith in this context does not refer to belief in an ecclesial doctrine but rather to "the propelling, all-embracing visions which direct persons in everything they feel, think, and do. Insofar as an opinion or conviction becomes a matter of faith in this sense, its influence will inescapably be noticeable in the architecture of society."[2]

For many business people and economists the object of faith is not important as long as the precious "commodity" of faith can undergird the functioning of the economy. Any source of faith evidently would suffice. But in the North Atlantic market societies Christianity has often been used to support and justify the prevailing economy. Thus, J.P. Morgan, New York's leading banker, believed that economic panics must be quelled by the restoration of confidence. He began his program to control the panic of 1907 by summoning the Protestant clergy of the city and instructing them: "It is time for reaffirming faith. Beseech your congregations on Sunday to leave their money in the banks."[3] The more economics can be mystified by persuading people that economic systems are grounded in nature itself or are determined by a mystifying agent such as Adam Smith's "invisible hand," the less faith in the system itself need be stressed. But people still need faith in whatever grounds or upholds the economic system. Economics cannot be separated from the religious dimensions of life, despite the claim of modern economic theory to the contrary.[4]

Biblical religion and economics also share a cluster of salvational words. Both speak of redemption, saving, security, profit, and so on. All premodern economies have been related to the fundamental question of daily sustenance and survival. "Give us this day our daily bread." Without a functioning economy, however primitive, people do not survive the day. But the modern science of economics reaches far beyond survival. It has taken on a messianic aura because it is assumed that if the economic system, whether capitalist or communist, should crumble, so too would everything else worth saving. Claims for the value of whole civilizations have now been attached to the peculiarly economic and thus people are willing to risk the future on this or that economics.

Finally, biblical God language and economics overlap in their focus on debt. We pray, "Forgive us our debts as we forgive our debtors." This prayer has been spiritualized and privatized, as if it referred merely to our individual, familial, or small group life. But the biblical prayer language of debt is not unrelated to debts on a much larger scale, the scale of the global household.

We are faced with such a situation in the present world economy. The specter of default by Third World debtor nations necessitates a redefinition of the global household. There are currently five nations with an aggregate debt of approximately $800 billion: Brazil, Argentina, Mexico, Venezuela, and Poland. If any two of these nations were to default, some economists contend, the entire world monetary system could collapse. Much of the debt is outstanding loans from United States banks, and a large part of the money was originally the enormous oil profits of the OPEC nations, which were sent to American banks during the 1970s. The banks, not wanting to pay even a day's interest on such large sums of money, made quick and often unwise loans to speculators in developing countries.[5]

It is highly unlikely that the countries just mentioned and others will ever be able to realize the trading surpluses necessary to pay back these debts (about half of it owed to private commercial banks). Many economists, not only in the less developed countries, are saying that the debts can never be paid back. They must be "forgiven."

Meanwhile, the International Monetary Fund (IMF) and its main patrons are causing immense suffering by making loans to these countries to pay interest (not principal) depend on austerity programs intended to deprive a country's citizens of an amount of consumption equivalent to the loan or at least interest on the loan. There has been no rise in real living standards in these countries for many years, and in many cases there has been a sharp fall. Even the best administered economies among the less developed countries are suffering a loss in wealth production far greater than the surplus needed to pay interest.

The people of the developing nations are thus threatened with the loss of their "daily bread." When Brazilian peasants are forced to plant soybeans, which will bring foreign currency in Northern markets, instead of black beans, on which they have subsisted for decades, the resulting starvation and undernourishment become a cost of repayment that is more than any humane government can demand.

The poor in the global household are paying for the relative stability of the Northern economies. How much longer, realistically, can the poor follow the IMF advice to "tighten their belts"? "Will it be *politically* feasible, on a sustained basis, for the governments of the debtor countries to enforce the measures that would be required to achieve even the payment of interest? To say, as some do, that there is no need for the capital to be repaid is no comfort because that would mean repaying interest on the debt for all eternity. Can it be seriously expected that hundreds of millions of the world's poorest populations would be content for long to toil away in order to transfer resources to their rich rentier creditors?"[6]

"Forgive us our debts, as we forgive our debtors" can no longer be spiritualized and privatized. Given the military strike force of the northern hemisphere nations, who are ready to protect their interests if default threatens a collapse of the international financial system, a humane future depends on new institutionalized relationships of those within the global household. Instead of "rescheduling" or "servicing" the debts of countries who cannot repay them, responsible international discourse may require dealing seriously with the implications of forgiving these debts. In North America that would mean deciding how the necessary relinquishment by North Americans can be shared justly. The issue is exacerbated by the fact that the United States has itself now become the largest debtor nation.[7] Who within the public household will suffer and pay for this debt? Can Americans actually learn to accept a lower standard of living in just ways, ways that do not require some members of the public household to suffer while others continue to flourish? The question of peace for some decades will be essentially such household questions.

These commonalities of the semantic fields of economy and biblical God language show that it is not so strange after all to juxtapose God language and economic language.

OIKOS AS CORRELATIVE TERM

As a way of correlating God and economy I propose the term *oikos*.[8] In the broadest sense I will mean by *oikos* access to livelihood. The household living relationships of the *oikos* are the institutional relationships aimed at the survival of human beings in society. *Oikos* is the way persons dwell in the world toward viability in relation to family, state, market, nature, and God. *Oikos* is the heart of both ecclesiology and political economy. A number of reasons recommend this approach.

In the first place, the Christian faith has rather consistently rendered God in relation to *oikos*. The *oikonomia tou theou* (the economy of God), however the church critically appropriates this, is the heart of the church's being. The basic problem is that the church is alienated from both the biblical sense of the economy of God and a critical awareness of its actual situation within our society's prevailing economy. There is insufficient awareness of the way in which the assumptions behind market society have influenced the church and of the way in which the church's worship of God blindly condones prevailing economics.

The God-*oikos* relationship represents the possibility of a God-economy correlation, which, on the whole, modern theology has thought to be impossible, wrong-headed, unnecessary, or dangerous. *Oikos* is thus a conceptual and praxis matrix for the question of how God and economy were correlated in the socioeconomic situations depicted in the Scriptures and the tradition as well as a format for economic analysis of our society.

Recent research has shown the pivotal theological, liturgical, and social implications of the concept of *oikos* for the primitive Christian communities.[9] "The *oikos* or household constituted for the Christian movement as well as for its environment a chief basis, paradigm and reference point for religious and moral as well as social, political, and economic organization, interaction, and ideology."[10] It is evident that "the household had a dominant influence not only on the structure and internal conduct of the early Christian groups but also upon their theological perspectives and socioreligious symbols."[11]

The Old Testament traditions had already appropriated *oikos* (or *bayith*) from their environments and used it with decisive theological intentionality.[12] Israel's life in relation to God and its historical environment is often described in terms of having a home or being at home in opposition to being homeless or being uprooted from home. The household is at the heart of most Israelite definitions of community. *Oikos* is a principal way of speaking of God's covenantal bond with Israel (Exod. 19:4–5). God has created Israel as a household out of many tribes and is accordingly viewed as a constructor and ruler of the household. The wrath of God brings down unfaithful households and restores anew the household of faith (Jer. 31:28; 33:7; Amos 9:11).[13]

Peri oikonomia (concerning economy) is a way Paul can sum up his entire theology of the church or a way of describing the whole life of the church. The *oikonomia tou theou*—the management of the household of God—could be used to describe not only Paul's responsibility and service to the community (Col. 1:25; cf. I Cor. 9:17; Eph. 3:2; 1 Tim. 1:4). This action of domestic administration could also be employed to symbolize God's arrangements for the redemption of the world: "For he has made known to us in all wisdom and insight the mystery of his will, according to his purpose which he set forth in Christ as a plan for the fulness of time (*eis oikonomian tou plērōmatos tōn kairōn*) . . ." (Eph. 1:9–10; cf. Eph. 3:9–10). The whole of creation is seen as an *oikos* for whose redemption (ultimate livelihood) God as its Economist has become responsible through God's promises.

Second, *oikos* and the *oik*-paranymns (economy, ecology, *oikoumenē*) point to the interrelatedness of God's work of creating, reconciling, and redeeming. From the perspective of the biblical traditions *oikos* can be understood first as the household in which God wants to give people access to life; second, it is the household of the creation in which God wants God's creatures to live together in symbiosis; third, the *oikos* is the world that God wants to make into a home by establishing God's justice and peace among the peoples and nations. God's oikic work integrates economy, ecology, and *oikoumenē* and demonstrates that redemption must be found interdependently in all of these dimensions.

Within the economy of God, economy, ecology, and *oikoumenē* are concerned with peculiar questions. The question of economy is, Will everyone in the household get what it takes to live? The question of ecology is, Will nature be given its rights or must it protest by dying, thereby cutting off the existence of human beings? The question of *oikoumenē* is, Will the world become mutually habitable by the peoples of the earth? Will all people be able to live in the world as a home? Thus the traditional content of economy has been *livelihood*, of ecology *symbiosis with nature*, and of *oikoumenē mutually recognized and supportive habitat in peace*. The integrity of God's righteousness and of human justice holds these three concerns together as mutually interdependent. Economic justice includes the question of justice for the land and justice for the peoples on the land. Slavery of human beings and slavery of the land have always accompanied each other. Every economic question is also an ecological and ecumenic question and vice versa.[14]

The God-*oikos* correlation also points to the interrelatedness of the dimensions of oppression and liberation. Racism and sexism are deeply embedded in the various definitions of *oikos* in Western societies. In modern definitions of the *oikos* (in particular, the neoclassical theory), in which the *oikos* is assimilable to the market, the domination of the *kosmos* (including the ecosphere) and the *polis* are added to the other oppressive definitions of the *oikos*. That is, in an economy predominantly defined by market arrangements the domination of nature through technology and the eclipsing of participatory politics by the values and mechanisms of the market are added to the ancient oppressions of sexism and racism.

It has to be asked whether racism, sexism, ecological rape, and denigration of democracy can be effectively combated without a simultaneous radical criticism of *oikos* in our society. This is not to say that original sin lies in the dimension of economics. But it is to insist that all dimensions of oppression are interrelated with the economic sphere and that no one of these dimensions in our time can be affected in isolation from it. They are all problems of the *oikos*. They all belong to what might be called a "social or moral ecology."[15] A humane social ecology will recognize that the rigid disciplinary boundaries of modern economics have been historically constructed and have emerged from certain interests. Disciplinary definitions of economics that preclude an interchange with ecology and ecumenics reduce economics to an otherworldly science or a science bound by unexamined interests.

The same is true for the church's teaching about itself. A church that is unaware of its own place in God's economy, on the one hand, and in the presently defined *oikos* (political economy) of our society, on the other hand, will define itself abstractly while it uncritically serves the requisites of the prevailing *oikos* (which in the North Atlantic societies is *oikos* as market).

Third, *oikos* has become a research interface for a number of fields, for example, sociology of Jewish and Christian Scriptures, social anthropology, phenomenology, and history of economics. *Oikos* can thus be a key for both social analysis and hermeneutic. *Oikos* is a way of speaking of the collaborative character of the disciplines and fields that serve the church. Theological disciplines exist for the sake of the formation of the *oikos tou theou* and its life in God's *oikonomia* in the world. It may be that other disciplines, while using different language, have similar objectives.

Fourth, *oikos* also suggests itself as a soteriological/praxis key, that is, as a way of speaking about access to the source of life, God's righteousness. It encompasses the questions of inclusion in the household as well as solidarity with those who are excluded from the household, both of which are primary signs of liberation.

To receive God's justice is to receive access to home. What is home? In Robert Frost's poem "The Death of the Hired Man," home is defined as "the place where, when you have to go there, they have to take you in."[16] Poetic descriptions of "home" would suggest these characteristics. Home is where everyone knows your name. Home is where you can always count on being confronted, forgiven, loved, and cared for. Home is where there is always a place for you at the table. And, finally, home is where you can count on sharing what is on the table. However rudimentary, these traits of "home" apply to all oikic sites. According to the creation narratives not just human beings but every one of God's creatures has a right to a name and access to "table."[17]

To be a part of a home or a household is to have access to life. The heart of justice is participation in God's economy or God's household. Unless the power of God's love creates household, justice will disintegrate into meaninglessness.

Finally, *oikos* is an ecclesiological key for speaking of the church as the "household of God," existing for the sake of God's liberation of the polis and the kosmos through God's liberation of the poor, the oppressed, the sinners, and the dying. To be no longer "strangers and aliens" but "members of the household of God" (Eph. 2:19–22; cf. Heb. 10:21) means becoming a part of God's attempt to bring all of God's creatures into God's economy of life.

The transformation of the church in our time depends on its rediscovery of its own *oikos* nature. A church that does not take seriously its character as the "household of God" will form its members only partially, which means that it will actually aid them in adapting to the predominantly defined *oikos* of the society. Thus theology in our time should think concretely, praxiologically, in the midst of the church's economy. Theology will not be able to overlook the fact that the economy of the church in North America has increasingly been conformed to market modes of living. Calls for the renewal and transformation of the church that do not deal concretely with this fact will be partial and ideological in character.

GOD'S JUSTICE
AND THE MARKET LOGIC

The friction between biblical religion and any prevailing economics comes at the point of defining the household, at defining *economy*. The modern history of economics changed the meaning of economy.[18] This is what theology should question today. When Jews and Christians speak of God biblically they are compelled to speak economically. They cannot do this if they uncritically accept the standard definitions of economics in the modern world. These definitions will squeeze out the peculiarly biblical understandings of God's economy. Therefore theology today is faced with a struggle over a fundamental redefinition of economy or the household.

The crisis for the Christian church in North America is that it has become too much absorbed into the market society in whose logic God's grace and God's justice cannot appear. The more the market logic threatens to become the church's way of organizing its life, the more the economy of the church is defined by the prevailing economy of our society and the more market rules determine what we mean by justice. In this situation what the biblical traditions mean by stewardship also cannot appear.

Nothing in our society is taught more effectively than the doctrine of the market. It is taught with surpassing self-certainty and discipline, incredible imagination and not a little reinforcement. We shall not get very far in our task if we do not discern the differences between the logic of the market economy and the logic of God's economy. I am not arguing against the logic of the market *per se*. Who can argue against the market? Every developed country has markets, including the Soviet Union and its satellites. The modern market is one of the most powerful social arrangements in our memory. Its successes are immense. It has wrought astounding "miracles" in raising the standard of living for millions of people over the last 150 years. As a system of distributing commodities it is unparalleled in effect.

The problems are basically two. The first is the pretension of the market logic when it is considered a complete system for the distribution of all social goods. The market logic is pretentious when it enters many spheres of human social life and threatens to determine the whole of life. In our time the market logic is again presented as the fundamental way of organizing all of life. The second problem has to do with the way the privileges of capital bring about domination in the market despite the official claims that the market is free of domination. It is important to maintain the many valuable dimensions of the market while criticizing the pervasive misuse of the modern market through directing all of its mechanisms to the gaining of power through the accumulation of wealth. Japan, the Soviet Union, China, and the European Common Market threaten to eclipse the American economy in large part because they are learning the value of the market while keeping it free from outworn assumptions of the control of the market by capital.

When the logic of the market overreaches its proper sphere and begins to determine distribution in all social spheres we have what Karl Polanyi has called the "market society." Exchange relationships replace all other social relationships. The logic of accumulation and exchange invades every dimension of life. When this happens many persons are excluded from livelihood. "Surplus people," those who cannot be fit into the existing modes of production and consumption, are created.[19]

The market is the great instrument of distribution. According to the most zealous prophets of the market, there is nothing that is not potentially a commodity for exchange. If that is the case, they argue, we can solve our problems of water distribution, clean air, or adequate health care distribution by transfiguring water, air, and health into commodities and putting them into the market. The market can work, it is claimed, without systems of justice based on natural law or, for that matter, any sense of justice that is extraneous to the market itself. The great fascination of the market is the assumption that we have finally found a way of organizing mass human behavior without domination, authority, and coercion. The market works naturally, impersonally, automatically. There are some good aspects to the anonymous, automatic workings of the market. But it does not distribute all social goods justly. Moreover, if a giant economic organization is able to determine distribution of social goods in other spheres, such as political offices, courts and legislatures, educational institutions, security and welfare, human recognition, then we can properly speak of domination.[20]

Christian theology should call into question the logic of the market, not to overcome it (such would be preposterous), but to put it in its place, in its own proper sphere, and to free many social spheres in which, if they are forced to live by the logic of the market, human beings succumb to the powers of death. The gospel also has a logic; it is a logic which comes from the Logos, Jesus Christ. The logic of the gospel is meant for the world, which God loves with God's whole being. The church is an agency of God's gospel economy for the world. The church simply cannot be such a servant of God's passion for the world if it is determined by the market logic.

The households of God, Israel and the Church, have always known that there are certain spheres of life which cannot be submitted to the exchange relationship, the logic of the market. For example, they have always known that if sexuality is made a commodity of exchange it becomes prostitution. "Bought sex is not the same."[21] According to Hosea prostitution is the apt metaphor to describe God's people when they reduce human relationships to exchange relationships and human beings to commodities.

Israel and the church have always known, if they could remember, that healing could not be placed in the logic of the market. Hospitals were originally established by the church in order to practice hospitality to the poor and strangers of society. Once hospitals are run exhaustively according to the logic of exchange in which decisions are made not by the mercy of hospitality or the canons of medical science but by the compulsion to profit, they lose their *raison d'être*. When they organize themselves according to the market logic, even church hospitals are no longer able to accept and care for the poor, the stranger, and the dying.[22] Similarly, once church schools, colleges, and universities, founded in order to provide a peculiar kind of learning that would serve the public speaking of the gospel, are organized according to the market logic, they subtly construe learning and research as commodity relationships. They no longer support the learning for which they came into existence.

Israel and the church have always known that parent-child relationships cannot be put into the market logic. If this happens, the generation of the generations loses its most necessary elements, memory and hope. But family life in our society not only maintains the age-old patterns of patriarchy with its control through property but also succumbs to the valuing of human relationships according to exchange ratios.

Other social goods that Israel and the church have always known cannot be placed exhaustively or at all into the market include kinship, recognition, offices, food, housing, and farm fields. If the market cannot fulfill its promise of distributing all things or if it cannot do this justly, then we must conceive of household relationships without domination. A just household does this by communicating its shared meanings of the social objects it must distribute, share, divide, and exchange and then by recognizing the peculiar logics and means of distribution that correspond to those meanings.

Searching for such a household of justice with peculiar shared meanings of social goods has always been a struggle of God's people. The memory of Jews and Christians is that our life with God began in Pharaoh's household; the memory of Christians is that we were first called to mission in Caesar's household. The way Pharaoh and Caesar defined the household led to slavery and death. The Jewish and Christian ways of living in the "household of God" make them opposed to the definitions of economy given by Pharaoh and Caesar. They were definitions of economy from which God has freed God's people through the Torah and Jesus Christ. The biblical perspective on the *oikonomia tou theou* correlates the character of God with the creation of a household of freedom against a household of slavery (Pharaoh's and Caesar's economy). The creation of this new economy emphasizes access to livelihood for those who have been excluded from what it takes to live. The Torah is God's economy for Israel; the Gospel is the new economy for the New Israel. The God of Israel and of Jesus Christ seeks to create a household from whose livelihood no one will be excluded. Indeed God's economy serves God's promise that the whole creation will have eschatologically the shape of such an inclusive access to life.

Christians speak of God for the sake of Jesus Christ and live for the interests of Jesus Christ. The interest of God in Jesus Christ is that the poor, the oppressed, the sinners, and the dying may live and live abundantly. We know from the beginning that it will not be easy for us to relate the interests of Jesus Christ to economy because we know in our own lives how much we are religiously bound to our own economic self-interests. It will be a struggle first of all with ourselves. We so much live in the world through market modes of economizing that it will require great imagination and courage simply to envision alternative modes of being. Our dwelling is a market dwelling. But for us to make any contribution as Christians to a redefinition of the public household, it will be necessary consistently to speak of the interests of Jesus Christ to whom belongs all authority and sovereignty in history.

In what follows I will argue that *oikos* delimited to capitalist definitions of market: (1) reduces "God" to the motivations and mechanisms of the market, (2) excludes from the *oikos* (that is, from livelihood) those who do not have a property in the market mechanism, (3) maintains many of the exclusionary (racist and sexist) factors of the ancient definition of the *oikos*, and (4) systematically reduces nature to the "stuff" of technological production. The God–*oikos* correlation of certain biblical traditions, on the other hand, suggests a God–economy correlation in which are proposed radically alternative conditions of access to *oikos* or livelihood. This correlation can contribute to the church's praxis of economic justice beyond the narrow constraints of the modern market logic.

WAYS OF
CORRELATING GOD AND ECONOMY

Three of the various ways of correlating God and economy can be termed (1) disclosive, (2) critical, and (3) transformative.[23] The disclosive approach emphasizes the way God concepts influence economics. Divinity finds its image in human and social constructs. The way we think about God ultimately will be the way we think about ourselves and our institutions. This approach points to the disclosive potential of religious symbols in our contemporary social structures. As can be seen in the work of Max Weber, this method discloses the way God concepts play a crucial role in the shaping, explaining, and legitimizing of economic structures and practices.[24]

A second approach, the critical method, stresses the way God concepts are actually produced by the economic conditions of society. God concepts, it is claimed, emerge out of the modes of property, work, and consumption in society. God concepts simply reflect the social, economic, and political conditions. This approach recognizes that human beings project their own gods. They produce gods out of their wish desires, their aspirations, and out of a compulsion to legitimize their power advantages. This way of thinking was taken up in the modern world by Karl Marx, who asked why society is so unhealthily religious and reminded us of the rather constant biblical claim that human destructiveness through idolatry takes place largely through the economic dimensions of property, work, and consumption.[25]

Theology must make use of both the disclosive and critical ways of approaching the God-economy correlation. But these approaches do not by themselves suffice as means of helping the church toward a transformed and transforming praxis in economy.

The disclosive method seeks to detect the normative intent and actual effect of God symbols in economy. It can also detect the way the rationalization of society subjectivizes religious beliefs and weakens the power of religious symbols. But it does not engender the praxis by which doctrines and symbols are restored with power to make a difference in the present. Theology cannot be reduced to hermeneutic or the analysis of symbols. The critical method, on the other hand, unmasks God concepts as deformed ideology of a deformed society. Its concern is to liberate human beings from a distorting transcendence. But simply being able to show that certain concepts of the divine are projections of existing oppressive economic conditions or of liberation movements against these conditions or simply being able to criticize existing God concepts does not yet show how faith in God can convert persons and make a difference in the transformation of economic conditions. Theology cannot be reduced to social analysis or social criticism.

The third correlative approach may be called transformative. This approach understands praxis not only as the goal but also the foundation of theory.[26] Theory is critical to the extent that it explicates its foundation not in terms of axioms, principles, ideal types, social analyses, and so on, but in transformative praxis. The difference in this method is that it begins with the intent of conversion and is controlled by this intent. The norm of theology is given in conversion through the power of the Holy Spirit. The critical correlation is placed in conversion rather than in disclosure or criticism, though disclosure and criticism are necessary elements of conversion.

Thus this method is concerned with the transformative character of religious truth and not only the questions of relevance, meaning, the distortion of religious truth, and the adequate depiction and etiology of actual social conditions.[27] To speak of the truth of faith one must speak of how faith transforms human action. Transformation lived out in praxis is the condition for understanding to take place.

THE CONTEXT OF A
TRANSFORMATIVE CORRELATION

Where does such a transformative correlation of God and economy take place? First, it can be said that a theological correlation of the God of Jesus Christ and economy should take place in the midst of and for the sake of those who have been denied access to the household in our society and to the global household. This context and starting point is indicated by God's own economy and God's own character, not simply by social analysis. As we shall see, God's own economic work begins with those who have been excluded from the household. God suffers because of the way human beings have defined the household and have structured it so as to prevent access to some people. Theology should find its context among those whose freedom is denied by existing economic arrangements.

Theology sets out in critical solidarity with victims of the way property, work, and consumption are practiced. Victims of the way the household is presently defined by the market assumptions of the developed world are the ones who yearn for a new definition of the household. Who are these victims? They are those who have no claim on what it takes to live and thus have no access to the household. They are those who have no work or whose work distorts their lives and who thus cannot contribute to the household. The conditions and relationships of their work often destroy the possibility of home. They are those whose lives are distorted by the modes of consumption in our consumer society, which puts consumption of luxuries ahead of the needs of others and defines certain people culturally as losers. Christian theology, because of who God is, begins in solidarity with those for whom the relationships, rules, and structures of the household will have to be changed if they are to be included.

But we must speak of "victims" in an even more comprehensive sense. Damage to human beings in an economy that closes the public household takes many forms. Few people are not oppressed or repressed in one way or another by means of the prevailing structures and practice of property, work, and consumption. It is not only the unemployed and those who are permanently defined as "losers" in our society who are hurt by the economic structures of our society. Even those who seem successful according to present household rules are dehumanized by structures of a household that excludes the unsuccessful. The conditions that exclude some from the household distort the life of all those who are already in the household.

Accordingly, in the North Atlantic societies one has to be wary of doing theology *for* the poor. Those nurtured in the liberal tradition are especially tempted to translate liberation theologies into comfortably objective reflections on the plight of the oppressed. We who do theology in predominantly white, middle-class churches should not distance ourselves with theories about the liberation of the oppressed. Our sin is often the evil that the oppressed experience. Therefore our theology should serve the liberation of oppressors, that is, our own liberation from our sin, our own conversion in order to serve God's liberation of the poor and oppressed. And this includes the conversion of our own modes of property, work, and consumption.

This means that Christian transformative correlation of God and economy should also be lodged in the church. The church is God's attempt to build a household that will join God in making the world into home. Theology finds its bearings by asking what kind of household God is trying to build for the sake of God's threatened creation. God's economic work and the economic work to which God calls the disciples of Jesus Christ is different from the economies that human beings normally dream and produce. God's ways of building a household for God's economic work are Word, Sacrament, and Towel.

The strange message of the peculiar economic work of God in Jesus Christ will not be heard anywhere except from the community that lives in response to God's Word. The Word of God is both promise and commission. It promises God's dwelling with God's people and a dwelling for God's people. "The word became flesh and dwelt among us" (John 1:14). The Word, enfleshed in Jesus, announces the end of anxiety and fear, the assurance of forgiveness, and the hope for participation in God's ultimate home without sin, evil, and death.

On the basis of these promises and their partial realization God sends disciples or economists into the world. Those who hear and respond find the beginning of their redemption by entering into God's economic work for the creation. They are made just by God's grace and are thus relieved of the compulsion to produce their salvation through their own work. They are sanctified and empowered by God the Holy Spirit to enter into God's economic work of distributing the gifts of life, a work for which they would not be prepared in any other way. The glorification of God's ultimate home in which all of God's creatures will find place already radiates signs of glorification in God's household under the conditions of history.

Baptism is entrance into God's economic work through the death and resurrection of Jesus Christ. Those who are baptized receive preveniently God's gracious promise of forgiveness and of power against death. In that promise they hear God's call to participate in God's own history of distributing righteousness.

God creates a new home for those who have heard this promise and this commission by calling a meal. Like all households, God's household is structured around a table. The Eucharist is God's economic act par excellence in the household of Jesus Christ. In it is made present God's own self-giving, God's own economy by which God intends to make the world into a home.

Economics should be basically about the relationships of those within the household. The "towel" is a chief symbol of God's new creation of persons within the "household of God." In Jesus' taking up the towel, God's power for life is disclosed as servanthood. The household is constituted by *diakonia*, by the mutual self-giving of the persons of the household in service to each other. *Diakonia* is not simply church members serving each other. Rather it is the praxis by which Christian disciples learn how to engage in the economic work of God in the world.

The "household of God" exists as an agent of God's work to make the world into a household in which all of God's creatures will find access to life. The church's public acts of evangelization and mission will have increasingly to focus on God's economy in relation to the world's existing economies.

Chapter 3 | God and the Market Logic

 O OTHER CHARACTERISTIC SO CLEARLY marks the separation of the modern economy from the economies of antiquity and the medieval age as the absence of God in the former.[1] It is not only that God is not desired; God is also not needed in the modern market. It is true, of course, that God concepts are required in order to undergird the values that make human beings good candidates for participation in the market and to ground the ideologies that justify the market. But within the parameters of the market itself it is unwise, if not impossible, so agrees the vast majority of modern human beings, to allow God entrance. Presidents may refer to God in political addresses as an element of the control functions of politics. But in their peculiarly economic activity, their corporation executives, economists, and consumers at the local hardware store do not think to call on God for any conceivable purpose, however religious they perceive themselves to be.

THE ECLIPSE OF GOD IN THE MARKET

The gradual exclusion of God from the market is a complicated history.[2] The period of the rise of the notion of "natural liberty" and the consequent market view of the human being and society was also the period of the decline of the traditional concepts of God. The seventeenth and eighteenth centuries saw an increasing divorce of God and the church from public life and from philosophical thought. "There was a clear correlation between the minimalizing and neutralizing of God as a philosophical theme and the growth of some modern forms of humanist and political life which permit no disturbing presence from the idea of God."[3] If we differentiate between the period of classical political economy, beginning with the publication of Adam Smith's *Wealth of Nations* in 1776 and the period of the "science of economic analysis" beginning in roughly the 1880s, we can say that political economy had almost completely removed God as a concern of its work and that economics as a mathematical and mechanistic science, arriving rather late in the Enlightenment collegium, was from the beginning determined to exclude the "disturbing presence" of God from its bailiwick.

With his theories of the price system and the division of labor Adam Smith was the first to envision a vast economic universe that could function on its own.[4] In fact, the main point was that it should be left to function on its own. Behind his vision was Newtonian celestial mechanics with its concept of the universe as ruled by differential equations rather than by angels. In ways that many think are still the best conceptions on the subject, Smith depicted the *self-regulating character* of the economy and the theory of "natural" economic equilibrium. There resulted the science of economics, which could assume exclusive responsibility for the site of economy, now understood as working according to the laws of the market.

Modern liberal theology has for the most part acceded to this state of affairs. It has generally spoken of God as a dimension of human experience and has dutifully left the economic as well as political and natural dimensions to the sciences and technologies which can discern the laws of the accumulation of capital, of the rational control of people, and of the extraction of resources from nature. *Oikos* underwent extreme truncation: *oikos became market.* In his *Philosophy of Right* Hegel already described a society whose public life was totally determined by the "laws" of production and consumption.[5] Hegel noted a small area of life left free, namely, the private, the interior, the intimate, the familial. Much of modern liberal theology has traded on this area of life as the only dimension left to theology and the church. Theology has put itself in the position of having little to say about access to livelihood.

Contemporary conservative televangelists and religious movements want to reclaim God for the political, cultural, and natural realms, but they are only interested in a God who, on principle and by his very nature, can be excluded from the mechanisms and liberty of the market. These movements are still "liberal" in their understanding of how God is related to the market.

Until liberal theology entered the scene it was customary to reflect on God's power in relation to political power and authority. The history of the West was largely the history of the struggle over the nature of power within the controversy between state and church. In our society, however, power is denominated in the form of capital. This does not mean that state power is no longer an authoritarian threat to human dignity and the faithful worship of the Triune God known in Jesus Christ. But it does mean that theology should be more focally concerned with domination in the economic sphere in relation to other social sites of domination, such as racist and patriarchal institutions and politics.

The problem is that under the regime of capital it seems a logical mistake to juxtapose God and questions of economy. In the modern world the church-state antagonism over authority has been replaced by the configuration of state and market.[6] State authority and market exchange/production are the two basic ways in which modern society is organized. But wherever theology presupposes the rightness of the liberal theory of liberty, with its partitions of state, economy, and religion, it assumes that the rules and structures of the market mechanism of the new social formation under the regime of capital are *sui generis* and not subject to criticism. For this reason theology could for a long time join other cultural expressions in being essentially apolitical, privatistic, and individualistic. Theology, like other disciplines, has been susceptible to the partitions of human life demanded by liberal theory: private-public, individual-social, equality-hierarchy.

Why, under the regime of capital, is it unwise and unnecessary to conceive God and economy together? This perception is due essentially to the enormously powerful fascination and success of the modern market.

Devising a market so pervasive that it has produced a "market society" is the great modern revolution. The nineteenth century, consolidating trends that began as early as the sixteenth century, created a peculiar kind of economy: the supply-demand-price mechanism. As this market mechanism grew into one of the most powerful forces ever to appear in human history, there arose an officially accepted doctrine that applied to the whole of economy. Together with the pervasion of market institutions in all developed societies there appeared the idea of economic law.

The necessity of this economic law was extended first to the whole economy and then to the whole of society. First a market economy was produced and then a *market society.* Karl Polanyi describes in this way the process which took place between roughly 1815 and 1845:

> The price-making market, which previously existed only in samples in various ports of trade and stock exchanges, showed its staggering capacity for organizing human beings as if they were mere chunks of raw material and combining them, together with the surface of mother earth, which could now be freely marketed, into industrial units under the command of private persons mainly engaged in buying and selling for profit. Within an extremely brief period, the commodity fiction, as applied to labor and land, transformed the very substance of human society. Here was the identification of economy and market *in practice.* Man's ultimate dependence on nature and his fellows for the means of his survival was put under the control of that newfangled institutional creation of superlative power, the market, which developed overnight from lowly beginnings. This institutional gadget, which became the dominant force in the economy—now justly described as a *market economy*— then gave rise to yet another, even more extreme development, namely a whole society embedded in the mechanism of its own economy—a *market society.*[7]

Within three decades this revolution radically changed the developed world, shaping human energies for the greatest exploits of the modern world. So thorough is social organization through exchange that no developed country, including the Soviet Union, is without labor markets and consumer markets; state socialist countries exclude only money and investment markets.

MARKET AND LIBERTY

The liberal theory is a theory of liberation from despotism and poverty. The great promise of the modern market is that through its own control mechanisms, exchange and production, it can organize millions of human beings and coordinate massive human energies *without external authority.* For Hobbes the disorder and dissolution caused by the natural strife of human beings could be ameliorated only by each giving up his or her liberty to a sovereign. Mandeville's *Fable of the Bees,* however, showed that the market could reconcile self-interest with rational order and could at the same time overcome despotism. Of all conceivable laws, market laws can best regulate human passions. The distribution of income, the allocation of resources, and the growth of the economy can all be accomplished by the market without coercion. Thus, it is claimed, the control of human behavior in the market mechanism works without domination, coercion, and exploitation. And if such logic works without domination in the sphere of the exchange of commodities, why not expand it to the other realms of society as well? It is a human dream come true: social organization without coercion; life without politics. It is the triumph of a culture that attributes evil and misery to the political sphere. The market is extolled because it offers human relationship without rulership. Since some form of social control is inevitable, it is best to choose noncoercive means for it.[8]

What would constitute a "free" means of social control?[9] If economy can be identified essentially with the logic of *costly choice* and if costly choice can be identified essentially with the distinctively human reality of free will, we have the ground for a nondominative social relationship.

Classical liberal theory set out precisely to make such identifications; in the end, however, its assumptions promote liberty in such a way that domination is masked. It postulates a population not yet engaged in economic cooperation and asks how its members might be organized. The answer: They can be organized by being drawn into mutually advantageous, freely chosen exchanges. This does not impair their liberty, for each enters into exchange for his or her own advantage, that is, *voluntarily*.[10] The market does not coerce because it is based on "free choice." People "vote" their preferences. Individuals' decisions are made impersonally, in terms of their wants. One responds in the market system only if the proffered benefits are attractive. This is, it is claimed, different from an authority system in which one is required to obey commands regardless of benefit and to work where assigned.

The other side of the coin, however, is that the market works by a kind of fate. People are deliberate in their decisions but the results of their decisions are unintended. Market forces, then, are said to be automatic, unconscious, mechanistic, and unintended. As such, the market can take the place of state and church and even the family, insofar as they have depended on authority. Naturally, the God concepts that provided these institutions with authority systems could also be replaced. The coherence of the system is derived not from tradition or command but from the unintended outcome of self-interested, self-guided activities of individuals. Taking on the character of necessity and inevitability, economic law could seemingly fulfill all public functions that "God" had previously performed. The market, were its laws obeyed, promises a free and harmonious way of integrating and coordinating society without authority and coercion.

Thus for the first time in history human beings are said to have devised a mechanism that enhances freedom because its logic is free choice. Market relationships do not involve coercion and therefore contain no necessity of external power and authority. Because in the West "God" has been the epitome of power and authority (as well as goodness), there is then putatively no need for God in a system that works without coercion. On this assumption, "costly choice" presents itself as a logic which can govern social actions not only in the field of distributive practices, but also in the fields of appropriative, political, and cultural practices. Consequently, we have the ground on which the modern market economy has produced the modern market society through the transportation of practices from one social field to another.[11] That is, power as the structure of rules and rights of the interplay of property rights has been extended to virtually all spheres of society.

But precisely this is domination: the expansion of the logic of distributing commodities to nearly all spheres of social goods in society. The problem of despotism has not been overcome, only masked. Such dominative power destroys the access to livelihood of many persons, distorts human life as possessive individualism, and undermines democracy. The question facing North Atlantic societies is whether democratic practices can be transported into the various social spheres so that democracy becomes the principle by which human life is formed and by which the rules regulating our lives are determined and transformed. Will we be able to learn democratic means of redefining social goods and agreeing on alternative ways of distributing those goods whose character is destroyed by any kind of domination, including domination in the market?

THE PECULIARLY ECONOMIC: EXCHANGE OR LIVELIHOOD?

With the rise of ubiquitous exchange relationships economic reality now began to take on a decidedly new cast. The ancient understanding of economy as concerned basically with *livelihood* was replaced by the modern notion of *exchange* as the content of the study of economy. According to modern economic orthodoxy we have a peculiarly economic slant on human activity when there is an ends-means or an output-input relationship. The economic presupposes a transformation of goods and services from one form to another, but we are speaking of the peculiarly economic only when there has been in these activities a *gain in value*. When people choose between alternatives in a particular way, that is, by incurring a loss through choosing what is worth more, we refer to an economic reality.[12] What constitutes an economic choice is that people give up something of value in order to get what they value more.

Thus the peculiar characteristic of economic reality is *costly choice*.[13] An exchange relationship is one in which a costly choice is involved. Economics, as the logic of choice, requires that we ask two questions before making a choice: What is it worth to me? What do I have to give up to get it?[14] Any aspect of life can be looked at from an economic perspective when we ask, Who pays the costs of a costly choice? In principle anything can be exchanged, put into the market to be bought and sold.[15] Lionel Robbins's classic definition of economics, as well as any other, demonstrates the components of the modern definition: "Economics is the science which studies human behaviour as a relationship between ends and scarce means which have alternative uses."[16] This seemingly comprehensive definition of the economic is, especially from the perspective of the tradition, terribly cramping.

Karl Polanyi has insightfully detected what has been lost. He makes a distinction between "formal" and "substantive" definitions of economics.[17] While the substantive definition denotes *livelihood*, the formal definition denotes *scarcity*. The two meanings have separate roots; they have nothing in common. The formal definition of market exchange excludes *livelihood* from the shaping of the household. As we shall see, this is the most fateful development in modern economy. It accompanies the eclipse of God from the market.

The substantive definition has to do with the mode of living through the day. It points to the fact that human beings, like all other living things, cannot exist for long without a physical environment that sustains them and without fellow beings who provide institutions through which they can relate to their surroundings. The wants to be satisfied are by no means exclusively bodily needs, but so long as wants depend for their fulfillment on material objects, the reference is economy.

The formal meaning of economics, on the other hand, springs from the *logical* character of the means–end relationship. It should be clear that the means–end relationship is not restricted to any particular field of human endeavor, but modern consciousness has become increasingly convinced that this rationality belongs essentially to economics. For it is this rationality that gives us the peculiar notions of economizing, economical, maximizing, efficiency, or making the best of one's means.

Polanyi argues, however, that the modern "marketing mind" has combined these two definitions and has thereby produced what he calls the "economistic fallacy," the "central illusion of an age in terms of a logical error." The harmless kind of logical error involved was that "a broad, generic phenomenon was somehow taken to be identical with the species with which we happen to be familiar."[18] That is, human economy in general was equated with its *market* form.[19]

The peculiarity of the economistic transformation can be seen most clearly in the violent break with the conditions that preceded it. This violent break was made possible by the massively pervasive "commodity fiction" by which land and labor were treated as if they had been produced for sale; they were made into commodities. Land and labor were now thought under supply and demand ratios and insofar as they were known essentially in terms of their market price, they could be effectively reduced to rents and wages.[20] Land and labor were given their own markets. In order to gauge the true scope of this break with the past, according to Polanyi, we have to remember that land is only another name for nature and labor another name for human beings. Only then can we see the totalistic tendencies of the modern market.

Once land, labor, and money are submitted to the economic laws of the market, the institutions of the whole society are increasingly determined by its economic systems. Implicit faith in the market mechanism has created the delusion of economic determinism as the general law for all human society. The commodity fiction handed the human being and nature over to an automaton governed according to its own internal laws. The automaton would produce material welfare only if its laws were obeyed. And these laws were no longer seen as human devices but as laws of nature itself.[21]

The laws made clear that the great mechanism of the market was governed exclusively by the human (nature-based) incentives of *hunger* and *gain* (that is, the fear of going without the necessities of life and the expectation of profit). Thus the nineteenth- and twentieth-century market society has ideologically organized itself around hunger and gain as the sole effective motives for the individual's participation in economic life.

It was now assumed that the substantive ingredients of the compound definition of economics could be forgotten. The economic laws of the supply-demand-price mechanism and the human incentives of hunger and gain would decide who could have access to the *oikos*/market. The results have been clear. In market society one-fifth to one-fourth of its members have been excluded from the livelihood of the public household. The human cost in establishing and maintaining this set of modern institutions has been immense. Since England's poor laws at the time of enclosures, as Polanyi has shown, societies, classes, and groups have organized in order to protect themselves against the pretentiousness and severity of the market and to prevent its extension.[22]

THEOLOGICAL CRITIQUE
OF THE LIBERAL THEORY

Political theology and liberation theology have broken with the liberal theological acceptance of the liberal theory of liberty. Political theology recognizes that market society, far from eschewing God concepts, employs them ideologically precisely to justify conditions of domination that lie "outside" the market.[23] Whereas the market rules themselves exclude God, the actual assumptions about the human being and society presupposed by these rules require certain ideologies that have made use of authoritarian God concepts. These God concepts are expressed in the complex forms of civil religion and in the public practices that surround the market. Concepts of God as dominator which belong to older social formations such as feudal, imperial, and tributary systems still appear in market ideology as a necessary element by which the dominant class explains to itself why it is and should be dominant.

Political theology has claimed that the reformation of church and the transformation of society depend upon the transformation of prevailing God concepts in church and society. Since God concepts have epitomized and borne the West's apperception of power, authority, and freedom, theology's peculiar contribution to the critique of domination in the modern world is a criticism of the God concepts of its own tradition and church practices and of the hidden or patent, consciously or unconsciously held God concepts in public expressions of power.

Liberation theology also denies the liberal theory of knowledge and power.[24] Liberation theology argues that solidarity with the poor and oppressed is the means of thinking theologically, for it is the only way that does not mask reality with the stubborn blindness and insensitivity of the liberal theory to those who suffer from the market arrangements. The praxis of the oppressed seeking to become free from the ideologized structures of oppression uncovers the actuality of power in society.

Political theology and liberation theology in North America, however, need to be enhanced by what we may call "politico-economic theology." Does not a thoroughgoing critique of the political ideologies of the market society and a mode of doing theology in the suffering and liberating praxis of the oppressed require a deeper critique of some premises of the market system itself? The principal issue, I submit, is the degree to which theology and church should accept the claim that there is no domination in market economy itself. Much of the largely uncontested moral justification for our economic arrangements rests on this assumption. *If* there is domination in market/production relations themselves, then the *nature* and *logic* of capital should also be the subject of theological criticism. Theology then would have to engage more directly in the issues of political economy and in a political critique of economic domination. This is not to suggest that theology should shift its attention exclusively to political economy. It is rather an attempt to help church and theology in North America become conscious of the economic functions of their belief, worship, organization, and mission in society. Theology would need, first, to unmask the claim that God is absent in the market economy by showing the presence of dominative God concepts in the ideology of the market society and, second, to point to the presence of the living God of Israel and of Jesus Christ in the struggle of those who suffer economic, political, and cultural domination.

It is generally understood that the way human beings think about God will determine the way they think about about themselves. It has been characteristic to think of God in terms of mastery and thus to ground the rulership of human beings over others. This political function of theology in traditional society has been noted by many theologians since Augustine. But in our time it is scarcely recognized by theology and church that the view of the human being in market culture provides a similar ground for rulership and mastery.

The fundamental theological issue is that the exchange, production, and work relationships of *costly choice* do not in theory or practice issue in livelihood for all. Nothing is of such importance and yet so veiled as the fact that livelihood is involved in economy. As we have seen, "livelihood" traditionally was the fundamental meaning of *oikonomia*. Its own precluding of livelihood is the fact that liberal theory consistently overlooks. Market theory offers liberty by failing to include livelihood within exchange relationships. Politico-economic theology will ask about ways in which the market fails to allocate what is necessary to life and will point out the lack of freedom and equality in a market system in which everything is directed to the accumulation of wealth.

While maintaining and enhancing the liberal tradition's democratic discourse of rights, we should reject liberalism's private-public partition. It is claimed that private control over productive property is the only effective way to limit the power of the state, but, as we shall see, such private control is itself one of the basic reasons for economic dependency in our society and in the global economy. Private, unaccountable control of productive property prevents many people from participating in the shaping of their own and the community's future. It is urgent then to consider the cost of maintaining an order based on accumulation through exclusive property rights alone.

Because the livelihood of individuals and communities is involved in economy and because economy expresses socially consequential power, the sphere of economy should also be public, that is, it should fall in the realm of democratic accountability. This does not mean by any stretch of the imagination giving up market mechanisms and many other advances in modern economy. But it does mean learning how to discern those spheres of economic power that must be made accountable to popular will. This will require a social order that values the democratic accountability not only of state power but also of the exercise of property rights. This would require the democratic control of investment and production as the precondition for the democratic control of the state. Maintaining traditional forms of representative democracy and personal rights, we should find ways of blocking the market so that other logics of distributing social goods in other spheres can be employed.

This will require a new model of economic growth. Growth should not be based on infinite needs and acquisition leading to an ever-widening appropriation of nature for the sake of accumulation of wealth as power. Rather growth should be a deepening of human capacities for the service of human development within community. Moreover, learning governed by the exercise of personal rights in community will necessitate new forms of social power independent of the state and the corporation. It will require that we stress workplace and community empowerment instead of the expansion of the unaccountable collectivities of state and corporate power. A just political economy will reject the notion that some have unlimited power to choose while others remain dependent. The individual should be understood as an intrinsically communal being. A commitment to democratic culture demands participatory forms of political action and social practices in institutions and communities.

A politico-economic theology devoted to the criticism of the ways God concepts are used relative to the processes of democratization and socialization has to engage the presence of authority and coercion within production and exchange relationships, despite the fact that modern economic orthodoxy has argued that authority is absent from such relationships. There are God concepts assumed in the nature and logic of the market society that function to justify the prevailing view of reality behind the market logic. They are God concepts that are congruous with the universal reach of the market logic. Even though they do not normally occur in public discourse, they are nevertheless entailed in the description of the necessitous human being. They are typically God concepts that have been used traditionally to ground authority politically, and thus they mediate the domination of older social formations, in radically different forms to be sure. Hence, despite what is normally assumed, the culture of economic theory also makes use of hidden God concepts. The arguments that ground the "market reality" are utopian and ideological in character. God concepts serve utopianly to define the persons who are candidates for liberty and ideologically to sanctify extramarket conditions that exclude some from what it takes to enter exchange relations and thus from livelihood.

The market claims to be free of domination. Is this claim true?

ROOTS OF
DOMINATION IN THE MARKET

By "domination" I mean in the first place unaccountable power to command and control the behavior of others. In the second place, following Michael Walzer, I mean the ability to determine the logic of distribution in a sphere beyond a social good's own proper sphere of distribution.[25]

The assumption of the liberal theory of liberty that domination is eliminated by market arrangements is false. Domination enters into exchange and production relationships by means of the determination of property and work. So dominant is the market regime that the logic of distribution within the market controls many, if not all, of the other spheres of distribution within the market society. What are the roots of this domination and how have they been systematically masked?

In order to see what is distinctively new in market society, it is important to note that capital is not a material thing, goods, or money, but rather a social process. It is a "web of activities." A crucial factor in the shaping of the social formation of the market society is that wealth is understood as an "expansive value" instead of the traditional "use value."[26] What characterizes surplus in a market society is that wealth is used not as an end in itself but as a means for gaining more wealth. The capitalist form of extracting wealth is an *expansive* use of surplus, that is, it is the utilization of surplus to increase the power of a dominant class. The regime of capital is the "form of rulership we find when power takes the remarkable aspect of the domination, by those who control access to the means of production, of the great majority who must gain 'employment'. . . ."[27]

Furthermore, in the market society wealth "inhabits things only transiently."[28] We speak of capitalist wealth only when there is a continuous "transformation of capital-as-money into capital-as-commodities, followed by a retransformation of capital-as-commodities into capital as money."[29] No object of wealth is an end in itself but rather only a stage of a never-ending cycle of expanding metamorphoses. The fundamental logic or trajectory of the market society, then, is the process of the accumulation of wealth. The nature of capitalism is the sublimation of the drive for power into the drive for capital.

Whereas in precapitalist societies wealth was generally associated with prestige (with the exception of military and some religious concentrations of wealth), in the market society wealth is a social category inseparable from power. What distinguishes wealth from mere prestige goods is its power to mobilize activities of society, to enlist command and obedience on a vast scale. The ability to command comes from the rights of denying others access to the goods that constitute livelihood. These rights are basically property rights.

This gives rise to the decisive social relationship of domination in market society: the social dependency of propertyless persons who have lost access to means of livelihood. This relationship of dependency required the dissolution of older social formations, in particular the dissolution of the laws and customs that allowed peasants to retain a portion of the crops they raised and supported the workers's owning their means of production. The result was the disruption of centuries-old rights of direct access to the product of one's own work. In their stead came new rights by which peasants and workers could be legally excluded from access to what they needed to live and work.

Capital can exert its organizing and disciplinary influence only when social conditions make the withholding of capital an act of critical social consequence. Wealth cannot exist in a simple egalitarian society in which all have access to the resources needed for life lived in a customary way (although prestige objects can). Wealth, at least wealth as power, exists when and only when the right of access of all members of society to livelihood is denied, so that being able to control this access assumes life and death proportions.

We should note here the crucial corollary, namely, wealth can exist only when there exists a condition of scarcity. But what is meant by "scarcity" in the logic of the market is not an insufficiency of resources but rather an *insufficiency of the means of access to resources*. When we identify scarcity with the simple lack of things, we continue the masking of dominative power in capital.[30] The domination of capital will work only if the means of access to livelihood can be made scarce.[31]

At the center of this process is a social relationship between the owners of money and goods (the momentary embodiment of capital) and the users of these embodiments (who need them to carry on the activity of production on which their own livelihood depends).[32] The legal crux of this relationship is the *right of exclusion*, that is, the right of owners legally to refuse to allow their possessions to be used by others. The power wielded by capitalists is the power to withhold support, no matter how necessary to life that support may be. The right to withhold things from use for livelihood if their owners see fit constitutes their domination of and authority in the sphere of production and exchange.

But that there is domination and coercion in the market is precisely what is denied by the liberal theory of liberty. The mystification of capital's power happens first in the interpretation of market forces and, then, of human nature. The owners of capital, so goes the argument, cannot be deemed a ruling class of a system when they themselves are at the mercy of market forces. Thus domination within market relationships does not appear to the modern consciousness as domination. The new market arrangements emancipate society from harsher precapitalist modes of domination: slavery, serfdom, and the absolutist state. This constitutes an enormous ethical justification of capital. Domination by owners, always operating at a remove, seems a humane advance, since it does not derive from the use or threat of physical or spiritual punishment. There are no visible symbols of power that point to the capacity of capitalists to utilize force or inflict suffering on those who refuse to obey their commands, as is the case in the social relationship of soldier to officer, citizen to state official, or sinner to priest. This is so because owners of capital have no legal right to forbid their victims to move elsewhere or to appeal to the state against them. Implicit is the notion of voluntary submission to the commands of the owners of capital. When one submits "voluntarily," one cannot be said to be dominated.[33]

Where then is domination? The answer lies in the fundamental inequalities of social position, the respective capacities of each to supply their own livelihood or to have access to the household. Let us look at two principal ways in which the inequalities are enfleshed: property rights and wage labor.

The liberal argument assumes that private property, on which exchange rests, does not itself constitute a barrier to freedom and is, in addition, noncoercively established and perpetuated. But such a lack of coercion could exist only in the utopia assumed as the ideal set of market conditions, that is, that everyone already has something to exchange freely. Market theory offers liberty not only, as we have seen, by failing to include livelihood within exchange relationships but also by refusing to recognize the conflict by which people have obtained what they exchange. How much one can accomplish and how effectively one can protect oneself through exchange in large part depends on what one owns and can offer in exchange. The market means of control limit liberty to those who are a party to exchange. They ignore the effects of transactions on persons not party to them. Free exchange does not leave non-propertied people free. "And if the move from collective to private ownership is imposed by strong men who forcibly take the lion's share of the assets, clearly no simple argument leads to the conclusion that subsequent exchanges among them, however free, make those who have little property free."[34] If property rights are already assigned, it does not follow that exchange supports one's freedom unless one owns much.[35] Livelihood is involved in exchange, and those who already own grossly unequally distributed property can exclude those who have no claim to what can be exchanged.[36]

Exchange has been justified as a way of taking seriously the human sin of greed. The exchange relationship is supposed to use avarice to good purpose. But this assumes that no one will take advantage of trying to control the control mechanisms themselves. The market cannot control human sin. Some people are in a better position to control the control relationships.

Labor is the other primary dimension in which the dominative power of capital is present. Although classical economics argued that one of the great virtues of the market was that it forced people to work through the pressure of *hunger* or the enticement of *gain,* the ideology identifying market with liberty introduces a distinction at this point: Liberty is abridged only when a person is compelled to work by another. If people are compelled to work only by the impersonal requirements of the system, it cannot be said that they are being forced by human authority. So, it is claimed, there is no coercion, no domination, within exchange situations of work. Impersonal coercion is not authority and does not threaten freedom. It is as if one would say, whatever happens within exchange is acceptable because it has been *chosen.* Authority one *chooses* cannot coerce.

It is assumed that everyone equally enjoys freedom from impressment. Both the employer and the employee have the right of refusal (exit) that protects each from the coercive use of his or her property (capital or capacity to labor). *This is the essential political foundation of capital and its essential moral justification.*[37] This freedom from impressment is an important, though extremely narrow, definition of freedom, but it does not mean an equality of entitlements. Owners of labor and owners of capital, it is assumed, confront one another in the market place on equal footing. What belies this is the ownership of the product.

Of greatest significance in the relationship of domination and yet the least evident factor is the way profits arise within the unique relation between capital and labor. Surplus is derived not simply from the activity of exchange but, more decisively, from production. Liberty of exchange relations may function in distribution, but the authority of control functions in work relationships within the production site. The rules of market exchange do not control production. The key institution is wage labor: "The peculiar mode of allowing workers access to resources that only comes into being after the dependency of labor has been historically established."[38] The owners of labor resources have no legal claim to their product; it belongs to the owners of capitalist resources. In this way the workers maintain the right of exit but lose the essential right to make choices about their lives and the community in which they live.[39]

Freedom depends on the character of alternatives, so avers orthodox theory.[40] Exchange best supports freedom when every person can choose among offers that do not greatly differ in value from each other or can choose not to enter exchange at all. How can this requirement be met? The theory of market exchange claims that coercion can be prevented when "no single act of exchange is greatly more advantageous to either party than other available exchange opportunities."[41] In such a circumstance one can prevent being coerced by refusing an offer without suffering great loss. This argument makes liberty depend on *competition,* that is, the situation in which "everyone is able to escape coercion at the hands of any one buyer or seller by turning to another."

If this is the case, however, poor labor markets throughout the world are therefore a negation of freedom.[42] Livelihood is at stake in market systems. When people have nothing to offer in their pursuit of livelihood except their labor, they must depend on jobs alone to protect their freedom in the market. They are vulnerable to coercion when jobs are scarce and insecure. When livelihood is involved in exchange, the employer can coerce the employee. Anyone who has a job to offer can coerce a job applicant. "Only in a market system in which all persons are provided, through money income, with a generous basic livelihood whether they work or not would these coercive possibilities in exchange vanish."[43] Hence, unemployment compensation and other security and welfare programs are, according to the logic, *necessary* to freedom in the market.

We have shown that domination exists in modern market arrangements. Market arrangements ruled by absolute exclusive property rights and wage labor are not free of power to coerce and thus cannot be free of politics. Coercion enters exchange relationships by means of the determination of the actual relationships of property and work. Economic dependency is no less an antithesis of a community of free people and thus of democracy than personal political bondage. Whatever the value of the liberal argument that market exchange enhances democracy, it is also true that unaccountable control and domination within market exchange deters democracy.

Market theory, however, asserts that whatever happens in the market has its justification because of human nature.

The Acquisitive Human Being: Justifying the Process of Accumulation

Orthodox market theory claims that the process of accumulation is autonomous, that is, it has a systemic, self-correcting logic. The forces that limit the amassing of wealth are rooted within the process itself. Capitalists's efforts to acquire wealth are subordinated to the objective requirements of the market, that is, the purchases of usually unknown buyers. Accumulative momentum is constantly held back by the pressures of the market. Production and exchange follow the wants and needs of consumers. This claim is a central way in which domination is masked. For it can then be idealistically claimed that the capitalist, forced to accept the costs and price levels imposed by the market, is without any power whatsoever.

This is the historic apologia for capitalism: The needs and desires of the public must be satisfied in order to gain wealth. The system must necessarily cater to the material appetites of the population. In an act of awesome imagination it is thereby assumed that the process of accumulation necessarily abides by socially imposed limits. Neither the origin and character of these appetites nor their moral significance for society is dealt with.

But everything now falls back to the procrustean bed of the whole theory: human nature. Everything in market arrangements is based on human nature, which is incorrigible.[44] This human nature justifies the restless and insatiable drive to accumulate as well as the resulting domination within the market. The process of accumulation expresses nothing that contradicts human nature. Human nature contains the hidden forces that drive the market.

This is the source of the "economic illusion" that profit and equality, the amassing of wealth and justice, cannot be chosen or happen simultaneously.[45] If society cannot have both, then it should choose what emerges undeniably from human nature: the drive to amass wealth. The myth is that enough profit will eventually bring about the improvement of everyone's situation, which, factually, is an illusion elites continue to teach despite evidence to the contrary.[46]

God Concepts in the Market Assumptions

Although orthodox economics, as a moral principle of its scientific character, refuses to reflect "God" in its domain, it cannot be doubted on close inspection that economists make representations of another level of reality. They point to a "netherworld," a "beyond" of hidden forces, which is full of assumptions grounding the market mechanism.[47] These "forces" are like the *deus absconditus*. They are known somewhat in the way the God of the cosmological and teleological proofs was known, that is, by argument from effects in the drives and institutions of the business world to their presumed cause. How these forces bring about structuring in the economy is never explained; they are felt as *result*. They must be obeyed because the laws of the market that reflect them result in incontestable positive knowledge and prediction, for example, laws about the flow of money and the productive and purchasing power of the economy. Neoclassical economists speak of these forces as religious people speak of the numinous, for these mostly unexamined premises entail a "transcendent" destination of capital not of its own making. Though they must be held on faith, economists are sure of the allegiances of thought and action required by these God concepts. These forces or structures or laws reside, unalterably, in human nature.

The market may be considered free of God and thus of all authoritarian influences. But the working of the market depends on coercive conceptions once applied to God but now given as presuppositions of the market human being. A reflection of the market conception of the human being can be found in the ancient concepts of God. It is at this point that the conflicts over the character of God have such crucial bearing on the economy.

There is a similarity of the "netherworld" assumptions of the liberal market logic to the God concepts that belong to older social formations, God concepts that themselves were rationales for domination. Attributes that denote domination within the market are residues of Western conceptions of divinity that still function as uncontested assumptions in our society. These concepts at one time justified the unlimitedness of political rulership. They did, nevertheless, function to set limits on the economy. They gave clear boundaries to wealth and its accumulation. Now, applied to the nature of the human being, they justify the unlimitedness of the power which is formed through the process of accumulation in market society.

A certain kind of God concept or authority center is needed outside the bounds of market mechanisms to provide justification for exclusive property rights and wage labor. God is rendered in such a way as to make God's freedom a whim. God chooses, elects, and determines according to an atomistic sovereignty, and

God little regards those that fall outside God's contracting. Such a requirement can be met by a God concept that identifies divine freedom with claims to exclusive property and thus the ability to make choices about atomistically determined preferences. It is a view of a God who does not stay in relation with those who have not expressed preferences (who have nothing with which to express a preference in exchange). The authority symbolized in such a God concept must then be applied to the notion that existing property rights are immutable and inviolable.

Furthermore, such a God concept must function to authorize contractual relationships within labor markets and justify nonentitlement to what it takes to live for those who fall outside the labor contract. God concepts are needed to rationalize not only the liberty to enter exchange relations according to one's desire but also to dismiss or justify the costs (suffering) that result from exchange relationships or that are incurred outside exchange relationships.[48] Such a God must be incapable of suffering human pain. This, I submit, is a depiction of authority and power found in many traditional pictures of God as dominator. It is a God concept that publicly justifies the relationships of dependency that exist within market relationships. It is a concept of God that is increasingly widespread in our culture as an analogue to what Bowles and Gintis call the "neo-Hobbesian accommodation" (in place of the Keynesian accommodation of property and personal rights) and to the Trilateralist theories by which democratic rights are increasingly sacrificed in order to prevent the spread of basic human rights.[49]

Out of these considerations three God-economy correlations emerge:

First, the God concepts at work in precapitalist economies point to God as plenipotent being. Divine being is defined to serve mastery. In the classical metaphysical doctrines of God there was a prevalent tendency to think of God not as three persons united in one *community* but as one simple, undivided being behind the Trinity. This monistic conception of God yielded a constellation of divine attributes that are still very much alive and effective in economic life today.

By way of the *via negativa*, classical theology defined God's transcendence over against the human experience of immanence. If, for example, we experience ourselves and the world as finite, we posit of God infinitude. According to this method God is said to be infinite, immutable, indivisible, immortal, independent and self-sufficient (having aseity or having no needs), and impassible (incapable of suffering). The God defined in this way does not go outside of himself and does not have relations with other beings, for he is self-sufficient. He has no needs outside of himself. This being does not change or suffer and therefore cannot love but only be loved. This being does not change his mind or repent and therefore is incapable of forgiving. He does not suffer from death. This God is a radically individual being, a *monas*. Christian doctrines of God have often grounded or protected these divine attributes instead of reflecting the history of God in Jesus Christ and Israel. Thus many of the classical views of the Trinity, even though they work against subordinationist and modalist doctrines of God, end up with a conception of God as absolute ruler of the world and hence refer more to Plato's "maker and Father of the universe" (*Timaeus*, 28c) than to the God of Israel and Jesus.

Certain divine attributes had been in process of clarification for centuries prior to Christian theology through the Homeric poetry and Greek enlightenment philosophy. Behind these attributes, in their uncritical poetic form or highly abstract philosophical form, was the political impulse to unity and centralization of power and authority, that is, theorizing that reflected and legitimized imperial rule. These attributes of infinity, immutability, immortality, aseity, and impassibility in their extremity describe the emperor, the ultimate property owner, whose divinity is his expansive power to dispose property. They are the political attributes of domination. They are the set of attributes that constitutes *dominium* and *imperium*, which are at the heart of many historical and contemporary notions of economics, especially property. God as absolute "owner of the world" is a theological key to Western politics down to the seventeenth century and in a hidden way remains a key to economics in our time.

The freedom of God has traditionally been denoted as God's having no need of the creation or of human beings, as God being self-sufficient and totally beatific within God's own life. This formalistic concept construes God's freedom as absolute freedom of choice. But this view of freedom is akin to the concept of the absolute power of the disposal of property found in Roman law and reconstructed in the modern world by John Locke and others. Freedom is sovereignty of owning. *Those who own are free to rule.* Freedom can only belong to the absolutely sovereign deity and to the sovereign *homo politicus*. The dominative character of many traditional Christian doctrines of God was that their logic of divine freedom was the ground for slavery, the patriarchal family, "skin privilege" and other forms of master-servant relationships.

We should note that the metaphysical notions of transcendence, which pictured divinity in terms of the absolute rule of the emperor, did have a value, namely, they provided human economy with a sense of limit. We shall argue against thinking of God on the model of the emperor's rule, but we should nevertheless be aware of the loss of the sense of limit in modern economic anthropology because of the eclipse of ancient metaphysical notions of God.

The second correlation results from the elimination of such a God in the market revolution, for this God concept was the ground of political rulership by which limits were placed on all transactions.[50]

Eliminating such a God concept seemed to be required to make way for an anthropology adequate to a market economy. Theory was reduced to practice, namely, the practice necessary for the market to function. All human relations were resolved into relations of the market. The market psychology of the "economic human being" led to a new image of personality.[51] Whereas God had once been thought of as the transcendent, ultimate "maximizer," now the human being takes over the attributes of "infinity." The human being is now viewed as an infinite acquisitor, an infinite appropriator, an infinite antagonist against scarcity, and an infinite consumer. The human being is naturally infinitely desirous. This is human nature, which, according to the official doctrines of market society, cannot be changed. And thus all possible economic theory and practice must be measured by the opportunistic human being with a constant sense of scarcity and urge to competition and maximization. In market anthropology it is assumed that the unlimited human capacity for production/creativity grounded in progress overcomes absolute scarcity.

Is the imperial God we have described dead? When Aristotle's physics collapsed, it is argued, so did Aristotle's metaphysics and therewith the metaphysical God. But the death of this God may have been declared prematurely. Even if the essence of this imperial God were dead, its attributes are still very much alive in the modern market concept of the human being. Once the metaphysical attributes are no longer applied to an eternal essence, they are reappropriated by the human being. Divine attributes in the classical concept of God, stripped from their metaphysical moorings in the divine *ousia* (being), are now lodged in the market definitions of the human being. They become the substance of a concept of the market human being, an anthropology without limits.

The market human being becomes an uncritical reflection of the emperor deity. The human being as producer of growth and efficiency and as rational calculator of costs and benefits has to have unlimited power to dispose property. Now it becomes natural to think of the human being as possessing the infinite attributes of God. The "imperial" attributes remain but with no limit or horizon. The human being as "owner of the world" is the key to the basic behavioral assumption of modern economics—rational utility maximization.

Domination in the market is justified by attributes of human nature that are derived from older concepts of God. Divine attributes are implicit in the conception of the human nature that grounds the market logic itself. The attributes by which God was said to rule are now in a transmuted way the attributes by which some human beings are said to gain power and prestige justifiably through their economic activity. This is the netherworld of market exchange and production. Put it to work and the nature and logic of capital will ineluctably result.

The God concept at work in the context of the modern market theory and practice is at first functionalist and then nihilistic. Pure choice is now seen as sheer potentiality. The God of pure choice makes possible the human being who is constituted by pure choice. The decisive factor is that the older power and authority attributes of God have been assumed by the human being. God is merely the ground of the possibility of these attributes in the human being.

If God is empty, then God can be merely a cipher of the regulatory principles of the system. Franz J. Hinkelammert comments on the nihilistic tendencies of Michael Novak's doctrine of God:

> Knowing that the idea of a God who is fulness leads to the
> demand of as full a life as possible here on earth, Novak
> infers the idea of God as emptiness, since he can then infer
> also an empty life. The suffering of this emptiness is then
> presented as a necessary sacrifice. The totalization of the
> total market leads quite logically in this direction. . . .
> In reality God becomes a nihilistic God, hiding and
> revealing—at the same time—the nihilism which
> undergirds the political position of the total market.[52]

This way of conceiving God clears the decks for assumptions about the human being, society, and nature that are radically different from the biblical and traditional metaphysical conceptions of these realities. Within the market economy and increasingly within market society God became merely the condition of human freedom, the ensemble of "invisible forces" that ground liberty. God is present by guaranteeing God's absence, or God is absent in order to assure the presence of divine attributes in the human being. This is the culmination of the modern assumption that God is known merely in terms of God's effect on the world and the human being. God is not thought to have a life of God's own or to be affected by or suffer from the world.

In the end the invisible forces are the needs and drives of the human nature. Masked, however, is the fact that the divine attributes lodged in human nature lead to the older result: *Those who own are free to rule.*

A third way of speaking of God renders God with the biblical traditions and thus speaks of God as the promiser, as the one who makes covenants, as the one who dwells with human beings and sides with the poor and oppressed, as the one who is immanently present in the creation and as the one who is God precisely by constituting God's power in these ways. The human being is uncovered in the *oikonomia tou theou,* in which God is present for the sake of human livelihood, indeed, for "life abundant." This is the way God's *oikonomia,* the gospel, renders God.

The Trinity is the view of God that arises out of, interprets, and through constant criticism protects the gospel's rendering of God as the communal relationships of Father, Son, and Holy Spirit, which come to expression in the history of Jesus Christ. The doctrine of the Trinity may be understood as a kind of logic of God's economy that creates access to livelihood by the gifting of God's righteousness, which is God's power for life. The Trinity will therefore be a means of demythologizing God concepts that undergird utopian and ideological depictions of exchange and production. Trinitarian views of God's freedom and power should be set over against claims made about liberty, property, and work according to the modern rules of exchange and production based on the market view of the human being.[53]

During the same period as the rise of the market society in the West the Trinity came to be regarded a pure speculation. But "Father, Son, and Holy Spirit" is not a compendium of metaphysical subtleties or abstract theological concepts. Rather it is a proper name. The critical function of the Trinity as the name of God is that it identifies *which God* we mean when we pray, worship, and devote our lives. Not all gods in our society are the same. Not all God concepts point to the same reality. Trinitarian language is the church's way of identifying the God who has claimed us.

"God" can be a conundrum or a help, a threat or a promise within the sphere of economy only if God is named, only if we specify which God we mean. If we leave "God" as the formal, empty concept that it is before being filled with the content of a concrete history, then God can be almost anything that a particular socioeconomic system would like to call divinity. "God" can be, for instance, the extrapolated values of efficiency, economizing, or maximizing that form the ideals of modern economy. "God" can serve as justifier, legitimizer of the economic system. Christian worship sets out to make clear that God is radically different from these extrapolations, from economic values writ large.

The Trinity came and comes from the church's primary experience of God in Jesus Christ and the Holy Spirit. Who God is we know from the history of God's righteousness with the world. Who God is we know through the story of Jesus, which is continuous with the story of Israel and ultimately includes the creation and the eschaton. In the first place the Trinity is a formula for understanding and living the story of Jesus. Everything that can be said of the Trinity emerges from the relationship among the Father, Son, and Holy Spirit in the story of Jesus. Theological statements of the Trinity should be judged by the story of Jesus. The Trinity is a name for God's economy in Jesus. "The Trinity is thus the conceptual framework for understanding that the history of Jesus crucified and raised is the history of God."[54]

We should look to the speech habits and liturgies that are immediate interpretations of this experience of Jesus and the Spirit as embodying a primal Christian logic and rhetoric. Trinitarian language, for example, embodies the church's calling out to God in prayer. We pray to the Abba/Father in the name of the Son through the power of the Holy Spirit. The Trinity brings us into the drama of the history it points to.

The trinitarian name is found at the heart of Christian worship and liturgy because it is the chief way of identifying which God we worship and give allegiance to. "The doctrine of the Trinity comprises . . . the Christian faith's repertoire of ways of identifying its God, to say which of the many candidates for godhead we mean when we say, for example, 'God is loving' or 'Dear God, please'. . . ."[55] The initial objective of every worship act is to make clear which God, among all the offers and claims of deity in our religiously drenched society, we are giving allegiance and obedience.

The character of the triune community is not empty infinity but rather faithfulness to the love that is God's being. God gives Godself not out of emptiness or sheer potentiality but out of the fullness of God's being, which is God's love.[56] God's freedom is not constituted by God's exclusive property owning but is the realization and expression of God's love. This love is not pure expansiveness but has the character of self-giving seen in Jesus Christ. God's passions precede God's actions and determine who God is. God's love is God's freedom not to forsake God's character. God's freedom is God's ability to remain faithful to God's love. The human being who lives within the *oikonomia tou theou* will live not in search of infinity and therefore immortality but will correspond as the *imago Dei* to God's freedom to keep God's promises.

The God who justifies scarcity (of the means of access to livelihood) and the apathetic elimination of all suffering with others (as interference with impersonal acquisitiveness) must be a God incapable of suffering. The God known in Jesus and Israel, on the contrary, is not impassible but rather suffers and identifies with those who suffer.

The God who justifies rights to exclude others from livelihood must be a self-sufficient *monas* that possesses itself. The God known in Jesus and Israel, on the contrary, is not a radical individual of pure choice but is a community constituted by the relationships of persons with peculiar characteristics and tasks. Each is constituted by his/her reciprocal relationships to the others. There is no domination of others and no principle of hierarchy. Each has distinctive identity and work, but, except for these, they have all things in common.

The God who justifies the separation of the worker and his or her product must be one which coerces the labor of a slave. The work of the God known in Jesus and Israel, on the contrary, does not coerce the other in an ends-means relationship but is the free gifting of God, which serves life and invites the free response of the other for the sake of the life of the community. God is not an individual maximizer.

Life in the church of Jesus Christ should make plain that human beings are fully responsible for all social relationships in which they enter. The process of accumulation as a totalizing process cannot remain legitimate without the use of God concepts that contradict the integrity of God as the triune community and force human beings into a stupor of irresponsibility for their social relationships. Faith, hope, and love in and within the community of God are thus inherently questions of political economy, first within the church's own economy and then in its presence and witness to the public household. Living in these modalities presses Christians to a public conflict over political economy and to a struggle with God's character as Economist.

Chapter 4 | # God the Economist

RYING TO PERCEIVE GOD AS CONSISTENTLY as possible as the triune community known in Jesus Christ opens up, we have argued, the possibility of recovering forgotten biblical metaphors for God. There is good reason according to the biblical traditions to render God "the Economist." This may at first shock the sensibilities, since, as we have seen, we ordinarily want to keep God as far separated from the so-called dismal science as possible. We should not call God Economist for shock value, simply to create an easy and uncritical correlation. We do not intend "God" to be a cipher for the cluster of values that could be called democratic capitalism or democratic socialism. Rather the divine metaphor Economist should be ruled by the naming of God in the biblical traditions, as is the case with all metaphors by which we render God. The ways in which God is the Economist are determined by God's self-uncovering in the biblical narratives.[1] Calling upon God as Economist allows us to see more clearly aspects of God's life that we have repressed or forgotten.

By speaking of God as Economist we mean to retrieve repressed aspects of the naming of God in the biblical traditions as well as suggest fresh ways of conceiving economy in our time. While the meaning of *oikonomia* is extensively present in the biblical traditions in connection with God language, the conception of God the Economist is of course by no means present or uniformly understood in all of the biblical traditions. Yet in many of the traditions, as we have seen, the creation is pictured as God's household and God as the Economist who has made Godself responsible for the life of this fragile household. God's history with the creation is the divine economy.

The political metaphors for God found in the Bible and throughout antiquity have been predominant in the Western traditions. God as Ruler, King, Judge, Governor, or Legislator sounds appropriate to the Western ear. We are used to thinking of God with the language of politics. In the broad sweep of the Western tradition, though not in the modern world, things political have been considered of higher value than things economic.

Already in antiquity it was thoroughly problematic to refer to God as Economist, since the *homo economicus* was qualitatively inferior to the *homo politicus*. In short, an "economist" was a household servant, one who was by definition unfree. An economist was what our culture has termed a "steward." The English word "steward" is derived from the Middle English *stigweard* or *styward*. A styward was one who kept the pig pen in the summer so that the household would not starve in the winter. *Styward* became *steward*, which signified one who cared for the livelihood and survival of the household. *Steward* nicely catches the ancient significance of one who lived an economic existence rather than a political existence.

It made sense to refer to God as a political being because God in the Greco-Roman culture was by definition absolutely free. God could be called a "householder" or a *pater familias* (father of the household) because householders were free persons and thus capable of living politically. In antiquity only those who possessed property could leave the economic sphere, in which the necessities of life were produced and reproduced, and enter into the free public space of the polis. Politics was to rule economics, the householder was to rule the household, as the mind rules the body or the man rules the woman. To speak of God as an Economist would have denigrated the divine attributes that made God freely omnipotent and omnipotently free. God could epitomize political existence but could not be associated with economic life.

In the modern world, *economist* is connected with power gained through the market. Given the fact that our culture generally regards economy as more important than politics, it will perhaps be possible for many in our time to appreciate the notion of God as property-owning householder. We shall argue, however, that the biblical traditions speak of God (1) as householder in radically different ways than either antiquity or modernity would construe that word, and (2) as Economist in the ancient sense of the word, namely, as household servant. In both senses the biblical perspective on God as Economist would seem scandalous not only in antiquity but also in modernity. But it is precisely this different perspective on God and economy that the church has to offer today in the struggle for a more humane economy. To call God the Economist means that the God of Israel and of Jesus Christ is fundamentally identified through what God does in relation to household building and management. Calling God Economist is in no way meant to denigrate God, but rather to express God's life and work with biblical concreteness.

The biblical names of God are characteristically narrative descriptions, or, rather, they are short formulas of the peculiar narratives that depict God's relation to human beings and the creation. The trinitarian formula "Father, Son and Holy Spirit" points to such narratives. It is a name, not a metaphor. Metaphors alone cannot convey the *whoness* of God. When we name the Triune God this way, we are giving a narrative description of the God we know through the peculiar history of Jesus, a history embracing the story of Israel and the universal future of the creation. This name comes from the history of an irreplaceable person, Jesus, that governs the appropriateness and use of metaphors for God. The triune name of God signifies who God is; the metaphor Economist is one among many metaphors that seek to uncover and flesh out who God is and to imagine the new world God is seeking to create through God's power of redemption.

Within the all-encompassing horizon of creation as household, the economy of God, most briefly put, is the distribution of God's righteousness.[2] *Righteousness* in the biblical traditions, in the first instance, is not a moral, anthropological term. Nor can it be reduced to a forensic sense. Righteousness refers to God, the "righteous one" (Isa. 24:16), the One who does "steadfast love, justice, righteousness in the earth" (Jer. 9:24; cf. Jer. 23:5; Ps. 15:1–2). Righteousness is the expression of God's being in what God does. *Righteousness,* which appears in all strands of biblical literature, can very often be translated "God's power for life," though the mode of life-giving may be different in the various traditions. God's righteousness means God's power to create/liberate life out of the power of nothingness (*nihil*). God's economy is fundamentally about God's struggle with death, the power of the *nihil.* Will the cosmic household live or will it fall victim to God's enemy, death, which seeks in every moment to disrupt the distribution of righteousness in the household and thus to close out life? This is the pervasive question of the biblical traditions.

This struggle can be seen in the great economic acts of God: the exodus, the creation, and the resurrection. Each economic act calls forth corresponding economic acts on the part of God's own economist, the human being.

The exodus is the initiating event of Israel's history in which through the act of righteousness God calls the people of Israel out of the death which is slavery. The event is thoroughly economic. The first truly historical question of Israel is in whose household and in what kind of household it will live. Israel's history begins in the household of slavery. Israel lives in Pharaoh's economy. Israel comes to know God through its history of struggling to conform to God's economy, which is a household of freedom. In Israel's memory it is a long and complicated story.

Its post-exodus memory is that one of Israel's children had been a great economist in Pharaoh's household. In the "land of afflic-tion" Joseph, the lowly Hebrew, is blessed by God and elevated to great heights. As Pharaoh's economist, Joseph manages the food stores so well that he redeems the nation from famine. His eco-nomic work leads to his being called "the lord of the land," for, the Egyptians say, "You are like Pharaoh himself" (Gen. 44:18). The exaltation continues, as it would for any economist who solved our economic problems today: Joseph is "father to Pharaoh and lord of all his house and ruler over all the land of Egypt" (Gen. 45:8). All the earth came to Joseph, the great economist, to buy grain (Gen. 41:57). The livelihood of many depended upon him, not least Jacob and all his family.

When his brothers are finally confronted by the well-disguised Joseph, he gives a stirring definition of a true economist: "God sent me before you to preserve life. . . . And God sent me before you to preserve for you a remnant on earth, and to keep alive for you many survivors" (Gen. 45:5b, 7). The work of an economist is preserving, keeping alive. The biblical traditions treat Joseph as the first great economist, on whom "all the earth" was dependent and whose economics meant survival.

And, yet, according to the story, Joseph laid the groundwork for the economic conditions under which the descendants of Israel suffered. His economic power grew into massive political power. He used famine as a way of centralizing power, gaining control over the land, and creating a labor force. The Scriptures present a fairly sophisticated account of the economic processes that led ultimately to the affliction of God's people. In some senses it is as insightful as the analyses of modern political economists.

In the midst of extreme famine the people came to Joseph to buy food. When their money had run out, he required them to pay with their cattle and flocks and asses, their means of livelihood and work. And when money and stock were gone, he required their land and work in exchange for food. "Why should we die before your eyes, both we and our land? Buy us and our land for food, and we with our land will be slaves to Pharaoh . . ."(Gen. 47:19). "So Joseph bought all the land of Egypt for Pharaoh; for all the Egyptians sold their fields, because the famine was severe upon them." And then comes that most ominous report which sets the stage for God's history with us to the present day: "The land became Pharaoh's; and as for the people, he made slaves of them from one end of Egypt to the other." To whom does the land belong? To whom do human beings belong? Without money, without livestock and tools, without land, the people had only themselves and their labor to sell. Joseph's management of Pharoah's economy had certainly been successful at first. But its logic became inhumane. "Economic miracles" often lead to conditions in which some become masters of the many, in which some exclude others from household.

The narrator of Genesis goes on to make a telling observation about the relation of Pharaoh's economy to the religious cult. "Only the land of the priests he did not buy; for the priests had a fixed allowance from Pharaoh, and lived on the allowance which Pharaoh gave them; therefore they did not sell their land" (Gen. 47:20–22). Here is expressed the suspicion prevalent throughout the premonarchal and prophetic traditions that those in charge of the economy and those in charge of the religious cult are mutually dependent on each other. Economic oppression cannot exist without its religious justifications.

Thus does the tradition have to come to grips with a bitter irony: The conditions of slavery that the children of Israel were to suffer were prepared by a son of Israel. The greatest economist succumbed to a household management that seemed to promise life but ended by serving death, an economy of slavery. Israel could not expect ever again an "economic miracle" from an economist the likes of Joseph. Since Joseph, Israel and the church have pondered the question, Is there a management of the household that does not lead to slavery?

"There arose a new king over Egypt, who did not know Joseph" (Exod. 1:8). Now the Israelites were integrated into the economy of slavery. The taskmasters "made the people of Israel serve with rigor, and made their lives bitter with hard service, in mortar and brick, and in all kinds of work in the field; in all their work they made them serve with rigor" (Exod. 1:13–14). The mighty Joseph once dreamed up the economic design of the storehouses. Now

Joseph's people build the Pharaoh's storehouses as slaves. To be a slave means to be excluded from the household while providing the life conditions for others in the household. Since Joseph, the household of Israel and the household of Jesus Christ have been suspicious of storehouses and storehouse economies.

The Israelites, as chattel of Pharaoh's management of the household, yearned for a new household and a new way of distributing what it takes to live. But their yearning did not mean that they readily accepted the economic work of the God of Israel. In fact, they resisted God's work of liberation from Pharaoh's household because God's economic work was strange even to slaves who, hating Pharaoh's household, had nevertheless come to believe that it was an unchangeable destiny.

But to be faithful to the narrative of God's economy, we should not speak of these slaves as if they were our ancestors. We were they. "Once *we* were slaves." That is the beginning of our story. There is no other economic fact so important to us. We first came to a knowledge of the Economist while we were yet in Pharaoh's economy of slavery. The stench, the chains, the whip, the separation from our children, the lack of freedom to move and decide our future—these are the things we remember when we ask how we first came to know the Economist God.

This God cannot be defined with the metaphysical abstractions of infinity, immutability, immortality, self-sufficiency, and impassibility. This God is not the high and uplifted dominator. According to Aristotle, the essence of divine being was his reflection upon his own perfection throughout eternity, which Aristotle took to be the characteristic male act. This God has no needs outside of himself and thus has no need to go outside of himself. He is not able to suffer with others. Faith in a divine being defined with these characteristics is eros. Such faith is a constant endeavor to rise up and partake of the divine perfections.

The liberating Economist God defines God's life in radically different terms. Not abstracted beyond human suffering and need, the Economist speaks this way: "I have seen the affliction of my people who are in Egypt, and have heard their cry because of their taskmasters. I know their sufferings, and I have come down to deliver them. . . ." (Exod. 3:7–8b). Thus begins the theme of God's habitat with God's people. This is the God who dwells among the slaves, who makes God's home among the forsaken so that they can come out into a new home of freedom. This God has a domicile in a people who are no people. Such incarnation is attested by people of the Bible to be the ground of their future.

How is this Economist known? Moses, yet another but exceedingly reluctant economist in God's dealings with Israel, confronts the strange phenomenon of the burning bush that is not consumed. Out of it comes first the promise of God's dwelling with God's people, Immanuel. Then, on the basis of this promise comes the voice, a command that Moses go to Egypt and free the Economist's people. Moses' immediate reply is, "Not on your life!" For one thing Moses has already been to Egypt; he knows firsthand the harsh repression of Pharaoh's political economy. He couches his refusal initially in the terms of his unworthiness. But then, crafty theologian that he is, Moses argues against taking part in the Economist's work for a just economy by claiming insufficient knowledge of the One who commands. "If I come to the people of Israel and say to them, 'The God of your fathers has sent me to you,' and they ask me, 'What is his name?' what shall I say to them?" (Exod. 3:13).

But this is not simply an abstract and evasive theological query. Moses wants to know how it is possible to speak of the liberating Economist in the midst of the Egyptian economy. How can a life-giving counter-Economist be known in an economy determined by death-serving systems from which only a few benefit and which even slaves see as a destiny to be endured?

Moses bargains that if God will provide a fully constructed ontology of God's being by which Moses can make fully explicit to the slaves who and what is guaranteeing their liberation, perhaps he would consider going on the mission. Then comes God's answer in the form of a truly enigmatic utterance, "I am who I am" (Exod. 3:14), which could also be translated "I am becoming who I am becoming" or "I will be who I will be." God answers to the effect that Moses will not get a fully worked out ontology of God's being in advance. He will find out who God the Economist is only by following up God's *promise* ("I have come down to deliver them") and God's *command* ("Come, I will send you to Pharaoh that you may bring forth my people").

God's promise and command will send Moses into the place where God is working for a new household for God's people. There in the midst of this struggle for a new economy, there through the particulars of this historical situation, Moses will find out who God is. The Economist God will be known insofar as one takes part in God's economic work. There is "a complex moral and psychological realism in biblical narrative because God's purposes are always entrammeled in history, dependent on the acts of individual men and women for their continuing realization."[3]

The great event of liberation is leaving the household of hated slavery. The name of God becomes a narrative description of God's economic act: "I am the one who brought you out of Egypt, out of the house [economy] of bondage" (Exod. 20:1). God appears first and most centrally in God's history with Israel as one who liberates from a household or economy in which God's people cannot live. God is Economist as the One who brings us out of the economy of bondage. God does not appear as a landlord, or a land speculator, or a real estate agent. God appears as one who liberates slaves from a household where people cannot be fully human. God the liberator Economist is set over against Pharaoh, the pretended owner of all the land, and even over against Joseph, who became the instrument of the economy of slavery.

Yahweh's exclusive right to or claim on the household of Israel is based on his liberation of them from the house of bondage (LXX = *oikos douleias*, Exod. 20:2; Deut. 5:6, 7–21). "And you shall remember that you were a slave (*oiketēs*) in the land of Egypt and the Lord your God brought you out. . ." (Deut. 5:15). This God is interested in a new household whose distribution will make for life against death. This God stands against all justifications of slavery, against making people commodities for the economic process. This God wills to create an economy of freedom.

From now on, "Unless the Lord builds the house, those who build it labor in vain" (Ps. 127:1). Israel's history becomes a history of the destroying and building of the household, according to the righteousness of God (Jer. 31:28, 40:7, 42; Amos 9:11).

This liberator Economist demonstrates faithfulness by doing economic acts of righteousness. Going before the people, Yahweh "does a righteousness," the Scriptures say, by providing the people with manna in the wilderness or with water from a rock in the desert. Succoring and nurturing God's people, God makes home for them in uninhabitable places. "Yahweh's House" refers often to the cultic tent or the Temple in Jerusalem.[4] But it also refers to dwelling in or with Yahweh as the One who takes in the "resident alien," Israel. In God's "courts" or "tent," or under the "shadow of God's wings," God is Economist as host who gives the hospitality of life, that is, as the One who provides everything that is needed for the life that is not subject to slavery.

THE TORAH KEEPER AS ECONOMIST

Those who have been redeemed from the death of slavery are called to live in co-respondence to this liberating Economist who will create a new household, a household of freedom. They become economists as "Torah keepers." How shall the people of Israel live in the household of freedom without falling again into slavery? The answer to this question is God's gift of the Torah. The Torah is a kind of "political economy" that is yet alive for us. That we are unable to see this immediately is due to the modern dualisms, including the law-gospel dualism, which have become second nature to us. We have left God's law behind us, first, because we have assumed that it has been superseded by God's grace, and, second, because we thought the modern I-thou relationships coincided better with the contractual exchange relationships of the market society.

Both assumptions are wrong. The Torah assumes and includes God's grace. Furthermore, Israel's ancient conception of the Torah offers a better framework for genuinely valuing the pluralism of our society than do the depleted schemes of ego-alter which have debilitated our imagination.

Israel's very existence is Torah-existence. Torah is the essence of the covenant that invites and commands a human ordering of life. "Living by Torah is Israel's grateful response to the covenant of grace made with Israel at Sinai by its Redeemer and Creator. The covenant is of grace because it is a gift of God's free love and is accepted by Israel as such. Living by Torah is by no means the way into this covenant; it is rather Israel's response to the gift of covenant. It is how Israel lives because of its election, and that election is God's free gift."[5] God's mercy is the means by which the true Torah is distinguished from the false law.

It is important to emphasize the creative and redemptive aspects of God's Torah. The Torah is God's power to create an economy of life on the basis of the costly liberation that God has graciously enacted for God's people. The law as God's gift is God's power to protect life. The law builds common expectations within the plural context of the community.[6] The future is guaranteed not by I-thou contract but by the binding agreement of the community. What is required for promise-keeping is that all put each other under obligation. It is not that two individuals can guarantee what each expects. Rather, the realm of life created by the Torah, that is, the multiple relationships of the community, which are all subject to God's intention of life, is the guarantor of all expectations within the community.

Life in God's household of freedom, then, means living in obedience to God's way of distributing righteousness. Keeping God's Torah economy is life; disregarding God's Torah economy is death. Those who live in the exodus community, in the household of freedom, learn in covenant faithfulness what the Torah requires in the distribution of what it takes for everyone in the household to live.

Torah means guidance for the life of righteousness in God's household. The Torah intends to ground laws that defend the poor, for it is only in defending the poor and weak that order and justice can be realized in society. "Laws favoring the weaker members of society demonstrate the ethos of the exodus experience wherein Yahweh delivered helpless slaves. . . . Poor and weak Israelites were given the identity of brothers and sisters to encourage society to care for them."[7] The laws that spring from the Torah are meant to preserve the political and economic equality that Yahweh means to create as deliverer of Israel. The Torah rests within the framework of Yahweh's promise that poverty will cease (Deut. 15:4–5). The fact that Israel rooted the defense of the poor in theology (that is, in regard for God's being and acts) rather than in the mere concern for order explains why its laws sought to afford greater protection for the poor than did those of Israel's neighbors. This ethos is in conflict with the political, economic, cultural, as well as the religious dimensions of the Canaanite perspective on reality. The recalling of Yahweh's economic acts in the festival of Passover, the spring festival of Weeks, and the fall festival of Tabernacles brought into being a decisively different economic reality than comparable festivals in Canaan. The economic ethos of early Israel can be summed up as follows:

> You shall not wrong a stranger or oppress him, for you were
> strangers in the land of Egypt. You shall not afflict any
> widow or orphan. If you do afflict them and they cry out to
> me, I will surely hear their cry; and my wrath will burn, and
> I will kill you with the sword, and your wives shall become
> widows and your children fatherless. (Exod. 22:21–24;
> cf. Deut. 24:17–18)

The Covenant Code (Exod. 20:22—23:33), the Deuteronomic Code (Deut. 12–26), and the Holiness Code (Leviticus 17–26) all protect the endangered livelihood of the weak. They picture what is necessary for all of God's people to have access to the household, to what it takes to live.

The motive for God's defense of the poor, the stranger, the orphan, the widow, and the needy is made transparent throughout the legal codes: Yahweh himself liberated Yahweh's people when they were strangers and oppressed; therefore Yahweh's redeemed people should show the same compassion toward the homeless ones in their midst (Exod. 22:21; 23:9), for to be homeless means to be subjected to slavery. It is as if Yahweh says constantly, "It cost me so much suffering and grief to bring my people out of the economy of slavery, I will not tolerate that they be again submitted to slavery." God's economy is based on and enfleshes God's own suffering love.

The question of interest on loans is a good place to begin. The legal codes of the Near East (for example, those of Hammurabi and Eshnunna) allowed enormously high interest rates. Israel seems to have been alone in condemning interest. "If you lend money to any of my people with you who is poor, you shall not be to him a creditor, and you shall not exact interest from him" (Exod. 22:25; cf. Deut. 23:19–20). The problem with interest is that it leads to poverty and to various forms of slavery. Israel's experience was that interest was a means by which the needs and rights of human beings were violated, with the result being life-denying poverty:

> And if your brother becomes poor and cannot maintain himself with you, you shall maintain him; as a stranger and as a sojourner he shall live with you. Take no interest from him or increase, but fear your God; that your brother may live beside you. You shall not lend him your money at interest, nor give him food for profit. I am the Lord your God, who brought you forth out of the land of Egypt to give you the land of Canaan, and to be your God. (Lev. 25:35–38)

Even when the introduction of a trade economy seemed to require interest on loans, the Torah laws placed strict regulations on the use and abuse of surety for loans. "If ever you take your neighbor's garment in pledge, you shall restore it to him before the sun goes down; for that is his only covering, it is his mantle for his body; in what else shall he sleep? And if he cries to me, I will hear, for I am compassionate" (Exod. 22:26–27; cf. Deut. 24:6, 10–13; 15:7–11). Claiming collateral in a way that would destroy a person's access to livelihood cannot be allowed in God's economy. The Torah sets limits on the exclusion of the poor by restricting the right of creditors to seize that property on which the poor depend for existence.

The reason interest on loans was so crucial for God's household was that it so often forced people to sell themselves into slavery. When people are claimed as property this destroys the household Yahweh has intended by precluding Yahweh's own claim on Yahweh's people. "For they are my people, whom I brought forth out of Egypt; they shall not be sold as slaves. You shall not rule over him with harshness, but shall fear your God. . . . For to me the people of Israel are servants; they are my servants whom I brought out of the land of Egypt: I am the Lord your God" (Lev. 25:42–43, 55). God's people, liberated by the power of Yahweh's love, may not belong to anyone else. Insofar as interest on loans leads to impoverishment and slavery, Yahweh's own claim on Yahweh's delivered people is denied and the economy of freedom is obstructed.

In a society that runs on credit, loans, interest, debt, and collateral this household rule may seem quaint. But it does not take much sympathy to notice that the lives of persons, families, and communities are still disastrously torn apart by the system of interest. For example, farm families who lose their land because they cannot repay their loans are thrown into the hidden slaveries of our society. The resulting disruptions to the public household are immense. It takes generations to create a farm family with the patience and grace to live in symbiosis with the land. Myopic corporate agribusiness that pounds the soil and poisons it with chemicals in order to gain quick profits threatens the land with death. If the land dies, even those who thrive in the business districts of the cities will also die. Only an economy that serves a household of freedom will resist also the oppression of the land.

Even if slavery should exist among God's people, the practices of slavery followed by Israel's neighbors may not pertain to the household of freedom. The slave is to be treated like a wage-earning guest (Lev. 25:40) and is to be released after six years (Exod. 21; Deuteronomy 15) or fifty years (Leviticus 25). The life of a slave is set on a par with that of a free Israelite (Exod. 21:20–21, 26–27).

Further ways in which the Torah provides for distribution within God's household of freedom in order to prevent the return to a slave economy are gleaning rights, traveler's rights, and the poverty tithe. The poor are given access to God's economy of life through the right to share in the harvest. "When you reap the harvest of your land, you shall not reap your field to its very border neither shall you gather the gleanings after your harvest.

And you shall not strip your vineyard; you shall leave them for the poor and for the sojourner: I am the Lord your God" (Lev. 19:9–10; cf. Deut. 24:19–22; Lev. 23:22; Ruth 2). In the seventh year the vineyards and orchards are to be left untended not only so that that ground may be rejuvenated but principally so that the poor may benefit (Exod. 21:24; 23:10–11). The Deuteronomic law extends the law of leaving sheaves and fruit beyond the seventh year to each harvest time (Deut. 24:19–22). It even permits the poor to enter the field before harvest, although the hungry may merely satisfy their need and may not take advantage of the owner of the field (Deut. 23:24–25; cf. Matt. 12:1–8). These laws prevent the poor from begging for their survival and show that God's claim on redeemed slaves constitutes their right to the means of life. This right supersedes the right to land and produce.

Gleaning rights are not voluntary acts of charity of the rich toward the poor; they are the poor's right to livelihood. Isaiah responds to Israel's refusal to recognize these rights in this way: "The Lord has taken his place to contend, he stands to judge his people. The Lord enters into judgment with the elders and princes of his people: 'It is you who have devoured the vineyard, the spoil of the poor is on your houses. What do you mean by crushing my people, by grinding the face of the poor?' says the Lord God of hosts" (Isa. 3:13–15). From the Holiness Code comes Jesus' quotation: "You shall love your neighbor as yourself" because of who God the Economist is (Lev. 19:18).

Crucial to God's economy in the household of freedom is the law of the tithe. The tithe exists for the sake of the poor's access to livelihood (Deut. 14:22–29). We often think of the tithe in our time as a means of supporting a religious institution. But the tithe is rather a means of building up the household by making certain that no one is excluded from the livelihood of the household. The tithe is for the poor; it belongs to them by God's right. The reason for tithing is the same as the one repeated for other household codes: "You shall remember you were a slave in Egypt and the Lord your God redeemed you" (Deut. 24:18, 22). Even if the poor are always present, "You shall open wide your hand to your brother, to the needy and to the poor in the land" (Deut. 15:11).

The tithe is Torah household redistribution of God's power for life; it is also the way in which the work and productivity of the household is blessed: "At the end of every three years you shall bring forth all the tithe of your produce in the same year, and lay it up within your towns; and the Levite, because he has no portion or inheritance with you, and the sojourner, the fatherless, and the widow, who are in your towns, shall come and eat and be filled; that the Lord your God may bless you in all the work of your hands that you do" (Deut. 14:28–29; cf. Deut. 26:12; 16:13–15). The distribution of God's righteousness for the poor is constitutive of God's blessing of the whole household.

Hospitality is a central way in which God builds the household of freedom. The abundance of the feast (Passover, Booths, and Tabernacles) is meant for sharing with the stranger and sojourner, as well as with the widow, the orphan, and the servants. Those who intend to live in the household of life against death are "Not to harden your heart or shut your hand against your poor brother but you shall open your hand to him, and lend him sufficient for his need, whatever it may be" (Deut. 15:7–11). Almost all of the prophets are concerned with the replacement of hospitality in God's household by empty worship and malicious feasts. Isaiah connects the worship of God and hospitality for the poor and stranger:

> Is not this the fast that I choose: to loose the bonds of wickedness, to undo the thongs of the yoke, to let the oppressed go free, and to break every yoke? Is it not to share your bread with the hungry, and bring the homeless poor into your house; when you see the naked, to cover him, and not to hide yourself from your own flesh? Then shall my light break forth like the dawn, and your healing shall spring up speedily; your righteousness shall go before you, the glory of the Lord shall be your rear guard. Then you shall call, and the Lord will answer, you shall cry, and he will say, Here I am (Isa. 58:6–9; cf. Isa. 1:12–17; Amos 2:6–7; 5:21–24).

True worship is living the economy in which God invites into the household all those who are excluded by being denied God's gifts for life.

The Torah works against the disharmony of class and of great discrepancy in wealth through several institutions: the Fallow Year, the Sabbath Year, and the Jubilee Year. In God's Torah household the amassing of wealth cannot be justified in the face of the poor who are excluded from what gives them life and future. One can neither take nor withhold from others what they need to contribute to the life of God's economy for God's people.

The Jubilee Year of the Holiness Code, closely kin to the Sabbatical year, adds a further provision which makes it the most radical household command of the liberator Economist. Every forty-ninth year Yahweh requires the following so that the household of freedom will not succumb again to slavery: (1) slaves are to be freed, (2) debts are to be canceled, (3) the land is to lie fallow, and (4) the land (wealth or access to livelihood) is to be returned or redistributed to its original holders (Lev. 25:23–24). Even if the Jubilee year cannot be proved to have been practiced, it has been remembered by Israel as what Yahweh desires in the *oikos* of freedom.[8] The blowing of the Jubilee horn (*shofar*) in the story of Joshua is the symbol of what brings down the rotten economy of Jericho.

THE CREATOR ECONOMIST

When later on the poets attempted to declare Israel's faith that this One, the redeemer from the economy of slavery and the sabbath Economist of the household of freedom, is also the creator of everything that is, they used the assumptions and forms of the exodus story to depict the creation.[9] Through God's word and spirit of righteousness God calls everything that is out of the *nihil*, out of the power of nothingness, chaos, and vanity. From the very beginning God's economy is a struggle with the power of death and chaos.[10] The household itself (creation) and everything that is in it is the result of this householder's power for life.

The creator-householder is to be praised for victory over the power of the *nihil*, a victory that brought the creation into being. As creator the Economist makes space for the household of the creation. The creator Economist declares the household of the creation "very good" but not yet perfect. The household (cosmos) is still and was from the very beginning yearning and groaning for the freedom of the children of God (Romans 8) which will come when death is utterly destroyed by God's righteousness (1 Corinthians 15; Revelation 22). God's economic work is not completed with the original creation, but is only begun.

THE IMAGE OF GOD AS ECONOMIST

The human being is first of all a creature. That is, the human being stands in solidarity with everything else that has been called into being by God's word of righteousness. The ideology of growth through technical mastery of nature has forgotten this primal reality of the human being. Our creatureliness entails givens, limits, and boundaries. An economic system that does not recognize that the human being is a part of nature and that if nature dies the human being will too, is not worth supporting, for it will give no hope for the coming generations, much less the long-range human future of human beings and nature.

But the human being is more than simply a part of nature. The biblical view is that we are not only creatures sharing finitude in solidarity with all other creatures, but that we are also created in the image of God. Corresponding to the creator Economist is the "image of God," who can also be called economist. The "image of God" has traditionally been thought of as a piece of divine being or as the immortal soul. In later anthropologies the image was reduced to a human possession that separated the human being from the rest of the animals, such as the ability to reason, the capacity for laughter, the use of a flexible thumb, or sexual intercourse in all seasons. But there may in fact be no ultimate biological *differentium specificum* separating human beings from other creatures.

In God's economy the only thing that separates the human being from the rest of the animals is that the human being is called into being in order to keep God's household. Being human is an economic commission to join God the Economist in distributing righteousness so that the world may live. What does separate us from the rest of the creation is that we are called to be God's representatives, God's economists, collaborators in representing and obeying God's will for the creation.

The metaphor of the "image of God" comes from the Near Eastern practice of the emperor putting in the hand of the ambassador a medallion with the emperor's image on it and saying to the ambassador, "When you go to the outlying country or a foreign land, show this: This image is my commission, my authorization of you to represent my will." Thus the work of God as Economist is to be reflected in the work of the human being as economist for the creation. To be a human being means to be sent as God's economist to live and work for God's will for the creation.

For the Christian faith this being created in the image of God, this being made God's economist, is the ground of human rights. To be a human being is to be authorized to represent God's economy for the household of the creation. This imaging/sending is a claim of God on every human being. Thus every human being has a claim on whatever is necessary to fulfill this task of being human. Whenever what is necessary for this task is denied a person, his or her very humanity is being denied, distorted, and ruined.

Human rights are necessary to answer the creating/calling of every human being by God and are thus the basic requirements of the dignity of a person. Among those rights, among those divine claims that God is making for every human being, are food, clean water, clothing, shelter, human intimacy, education, and meaningful work. Our society is enormously regressive in not recognizing these needs as human rights. The sin that produces the evils of our economic systems is sometimes the pride and sometimes the sloth by which we prevent some people from having what is necessary to be God's economists, that is, to be human.

The most fundamental survival principle for an alternative economic system is that every person have economic and political rights. The land and all of its fruition is a gift of God which is meant to be used as the means of God's righteousness, as a means toward the fullness of the life of all of God's children and of the whole creation. To be human means to have a right to a life-giving share of the world's resources so that one can serve God's life-giving economy for the creation.

THE RESURRECTION
GOD AS ECONOMIST

The victory over death for which the whole creation is groaning has already begun in Jesus' resurrection from the dead. God's acts of righteousness in the exodus and the creation lie behind the New Testament view of the resurrection. Through the Spirit of righteousness (Rom. 1:3–4; 8:11) God the Father calls the Son out of his bondage to death. Thus the Economist comes to be known as the One who "gives life to the dead and calls into existence the things that do not exist" (Rom. 4:17). The greatest reversal of all is that the "regal house" that would last forever (2 Sam. 7:8–16) is now based on the exalted risen one who is none other than the crucified, humiliated one. The resurrection Economist is enfleshed in the poor man Jesus and in him identifies with the poor.

When the New Testament comes to the point of making clear the saving significance of Jesus' liberation from death for the whole household, it speaks again in terms of creation. The resurrection is not just a private occurrence in and for Jesus; it is the beginning of the "new creation." Thus the resurrection has significance for the whole household/cosmos. The resurrection sets in motion the peculiar history called mission in which the Holy

Spirit through baptism creates persons whose lives are given over to God's work of distributing righteousness to the whole creation. This righteousness under the conditions of history has the shape of the cross.

THE *DIAKONOS* OF
JESUS AS ECONOMIST

Corresponding to and created by God's act of raising the crucified Jesus from the dead is the disciple, the *diakonos,* the martyr of Jesus. The person who is baptized into the Triune name enters God's economic history with the world. His or her life is given over to God's distribution of life through the "standing up" (*anastasis*) community, the resurrection community. The heart of this community's life is the eucharist, the act *par excellence* of the distribution of life. Those who live from the table of God's household are no longer simply advocates of those who struggle to live without what is necessary for life; they have become brothers and sisters of these people.

The salvation of the world is taking place through the identification of this God with the weak, the foolish, the low and despised, even what is dead in the world (1 Cor. 1:20–31). The economy of this God is to provide righteousness, the power of life, to those who are most threatened with death, poverty, oppression, and sin.

The interpretation of these three "economic acts" of God comes principally from the Mosaic trajectory.[11] If the primary economic role of God in these traditions is seen as "householder," the trajectory nevertheless aims at the astounding fact that God becomes the Economist in the sense of housekeeper, homemaker, the steward, the diakonos, or the household slave.[12] The epitome of this claim is found in Jesus who, "though he was in the form of God, did not count equality with God a thing to be grasped, but emptied himself, taking the form of a [household slave, *doulos*] . . ." (Phil. 2:6–7). God overcomes human mastery by becoming a slave. God overcomes the scarcity of what it takes to live by becoming the Household Slave, by seeking to distribute to all what it takes to live and live abundantly. God opens up the household which has been closed to the homeless by becoming the Economist.

God in Jesus performs the lowest and dirtiest work conceivable by taking upon Godself the sin and evil of all human beings. This is household economist work which only God as household Economist can do. And it is not only sin and evil that God takes on but also the result of sin and evil, death itself. God overcomes death by taking death into the divine communal life. Thus the center of God's economy is found in the cross of Christ. "For the love of Christ controls us, because we are convinced that one has died for all; therefore all have died. And he died for all, that those who live might live no longer for themselves but for him who for their sake died and was raised" (1 Cor. 5:14–15).

The Gospels narrate the story of Jesus as the announcement and distribution of the righteousness of God's reign. The heart of Jesus' message is, "Seek first the Kingdom of God and his righteousness" (Matt. 6:33). In distributing bread, freedom, a new name and identity, peace with nature, and faith and hope Jesus enters into a controversy with his own people over the meaning of righteousness, a controversy which leads to his crucifixion by the Roman authorities in the name of Caesar's economy. The controversy has to do with God's economy. How does God distribute the power of life? Does it come through self-righteous keeping of the law, amassing wealth, controlling property, the right cult? The proclamation, ministry, and death of Jesus show that God's economy is the gifting of righteousness through God's own self-giving. In Jesus Christ God is seeking to call into being and sustain an *oikos* in which all of God's creatures will have access to life.

TRANSFORMATIVE CORRELATION OF GOD AND ECONOMY

We turn now to a closer look at the economy which God is seeking to create out of the reality of the resurrected crucified one and its correlation with the economy of the Greco-Roman world. It is widely accepted that *oikonomia,* the management of the household, "provided a traditional mode for the discussion of the roles, relationships and responsibilities which characterized the governing of life in the larger social arena of the polis, namely, its *politeia.*"[13] As John Elliott argues, "In the focus upon the household and community as *oikos* of God we have a striking example of the correlation of social reality and theological reflection, of theory and practice."[14] Early Christian movements radically transformed the Greco-Roman concept of the *oikos.* Because the political and social reality of the Greco-Roman world was largely conceived and based upon the *oikos,* the Christian revisioning of the *oikos* had vast implications for the whole of social and personal life in antiquity. In order to see what is at stake in this transformation we should examine first the theoretical basis for the Greco-Roman *oikos* as found specifically in Aristotle.

Although it certainly contains humane aspects which should be retrieved, Aristotle's economics also demonstrates the oppressive characteristics of the *oikos* in the Greco-Roman world. It reflects the racism and sexism that were built into the Greco-Roman definition of the household. The household is understood as the place where the basic necessities of life are met. Once living is taken care of then living well in the *polis* can be pursued. But by definition not everyone in the household is a candidate for living well. This is possible only for the one who is truly freed by the *oikos*, namely, the *pater familias*, the householder, the owner of all household property.

The freedom of the householder is grounded in and constituted by his possessing and disposing property.[15] Freedom is dominance through owning the means to livelihood. Slavery and subordination mean having access to livelihood only through the sufferance of the *pater potestas*. The other members of the household, slaves, women, children, tenants, workers, assistants in crafts and trade, were all defined as unfree because without property and without property because unfree. The hierarchy of the Greco-Roman *oikos* entailed domination and subordination in its very definition.

How did the early Christian movement transform this conception of *oikos*, even as it took over *oikos* as the dominant organizing principle of its social situation and theological thought?

It can be mentioned first that these movements agree with the Aristotelian starting point that scarcity should not be an assumption of the household. The *oikos*, analogous to the land and the basileia, means access to life. The *oikos* of God is a gracious gift of God's righteousness, God's power for life. God's gracious goodness gives enough, more than enough, for everyone in the household to live abundantly. *The question* of economics, Will everyone in the household get what it takes to live? is referenced not to scarcity but to the righteousness of God which makes possible the sharing of the household's store. In any case the work of God the Holy Spirit is to subvert any *oikonomia* based on scarcity. The reason for this is that scarcity as a starting point will always produce an *oikos* in which some are excluded from the means of life.

Elisabeth Schüssler Fiorenza fills out the picture of how the Jesus movement and the earliest Pauline missionary movement subvert the *oikonomia* of Hellenistic Roman society.[16] The Jesus movement is a socioreligious reality within Palestinian Judaism.[17]

It does not totally reject the validity of Temple and Torah as symbols of Israel's election but offers an alternative interpretation of them by focusing on the people itself as the locus of God's power and presence.[18] Integrating prophetic-apocalyptic and sophia theology, Jesus' praxis and vision of God's rule of righteousness is directed toward the household of Israel. The reality of the *basileia* transforms the *oikos* of Israel. Its peculiar character is that everyone in Israel is invited into the *basileia oikos*.

Jesus claims the *basileia* for three distinct groups: (1) the destitute poor, (2) the sick and crippled, and (3) tax collectors, sinners, and prostitutes. The table community of Israel's household is now to include women and even notorious sinners. The "scum of Palestinian society" constituted the people among whom Jesus proclaimed and enacted the presence of God's rule of righteousness. The distinguishing factor of all of these people is that they had been denied access to *oikos*, to livelihood, to the family of Israel's God.

Jesus' intrusion into the dominant religious ethos of his people created a new household in which there was equality of discipleship. The invitation of the gospel is not simply to receive access to the livelihood of God's righteousness but to extend that access to those people of Israel who had been shut out of God's household. The right that the gospel gives is not the right to dispose property but rather property in God's household, the right to be included in God's own economy, which is the source of life. A discipleship claim on access to God's economy entails the responsibility of giving access to livelihood to others, namely, "the least of these, my brothers and sisters."

Jesus' proclamation subverts structures of oppression by envisioning different household relationships in which *all* persons of Israel are welcomed by God's gracious goodness. Those who do the will of God, who live the gracious goodness of God, come together as the disciple-family of Jesus and form a new "household" (Mark 3:31–35). The new discipleship community overturns the claims of the patriarchal family and forms a new familial community, one that no longer includes the role of *pater familias*. Jesus' saying, "Whoever does not receive the *basileia* of God like a child (or "little one") shall not enter it" (Mark 10:15), is not an "invitation to childlike innocence and naiveté but a challenge to relinquish all claims of power and domination over others."[19] This saying challenges those who are dominant in a feudal society to become "equal" with those who are powerless. Structures of domination are not to be tolerated in the discipleship of equals. The sign of true leadership in the community is solidarity with those who are "slaves and servants."

Elliott has shown how the *oikonomia* of the early church, the *oikos tou theou*, functions as a means of God's good graciousness in bringing the poor and marginal into God's economy. He argues that the addressees of 1 Peter are called *paroikoi* and *parepidēmoi*, sociolegal terms for describing the limited status and rights of foreigners or strangers in Greco-Roman society.[20] "Included among the *paroikoi* were slaves, serfs, and those constituting the multitude of the déclassé and the homeless strangers who lacked citizenship either in their previous homeland or where they currently resided."[21] In contrast to the *homo politicus* or full citizen, the *paroikos* was the *homo oeconomicus* who provided the work force and economic base of society. The Christians addressed in 1 Peter were "strangers, aliens, unrooted transients, dangerous nonconformists. They were despicable fanatics, lowly slaves, 'Christ-lackeys,' obsequious advocates of humiliation."[22]

The message of 1 Peter is that the household of God offers these homeless people a home. Their name is now "the ones shown mercy" (2:10). The Petrine response to *paroikia* (homelessness) is *oikos*. Through God's mercy strangers experience "infamilialization." Access to God's *oikos* depends neither on property nor on the incentives of hunger and gain. Access to the *oikos* is given by the gracious goodness of God. Hunger and gain are eclipsed as incentives to enter the economy by the *plērōma* of God, which negates scarcity. Access is at once God's gracious invitation and one's acceptance of the responsibility of returning the hospitality of God's economy.

In the early Christian movement, therefore, there is a qualitatively different God-*oikos* correlation than in the economics of antiquity and modernity. In the Jesus movement and the early Pauline missionary movement God takes the form of a household servant, a homemaker, and thereby radically subverts the patriarchal hierarchy that excludes some from livelihood. In the case of the Asia Minor Christians addressed by 1 Peter God is a householder who invites all who are homeless into the household of life.

A transformative God-economics correlation, through solidarity with the victims of a dehumanized *oikos*, will disclose and criticize the false infinity of the God concepts prevalent in market definitions of reality, that is, the domination of the property-owning God, and will engage in the praxis of the *oikos*-creating, homemaking, God. It will do this by retrieving the symbols that imagine a different *oikos* from that defined exhaustively by the market arrangements. It will question the biblical and church traditions about the character of God's power, which can actually convert the interests, values, worship, law, and organization of North Atlantic Christians, so that they can work publicly for an access to livelihood for those presently denied access.

Among other things, this will mean working for a change in property rights. It will mean questioning the narrow notion of absolute exclusive property right as the sole meaning of property. And it will mean moving toward a broader meaning of property that will embrace the right not to be excluded from what it takes to live and to fulfill the calling to be God's economist, God's image, and God's disciple.

Chapter 5 | # God and Property

OR ISRAEL AND THE CHURCH, AS FOR much of the human race, property has been one of the thorniest problems of communal existence. Evidently the distinction between "mine and thine" is as old as the history of human beings. History attests that property is necessary to human existence, and just as clearly it shows that property has issued in misery and dehumanization. Human beings cannot live without property, and yet they can hardly live with it. Property is a primary way by which a community decides who will be admitted to the household and how its members will relate to each other.

The mystery of property is its connection to power, on the one hand, and to authority, the justification of property, on the other hand. Property always has to be justified, for all forms of property can potentially lead to the dehumanization of life. While force can maintain a certain perception and practice of property for a time, it will prove insufficient in the long run. That property is so closely related to power and authority is the reason that it is so closely related to God concepts. In the West concepts of God have been the epitome term of power and authority and thus an available foundation for the justification of property. The prevailing model or paradigm of property will often reflect the prevailing perception of God and vice versa. The history of property is the history of human power and authority and thus in many ways the history of the way human beings have conceived and worshiped divine power and authority. No matter how sophisticated the moral and social philosophies behind it, the ultimate justification of property has required ideologies that depend on God concepts at work in a society's public morality or civil religion. The ideologies that justify property have become the measure of everything in our society.

THE PROMISE AND THREAT OF PROPERTY: FREEDOM AND MASTERY

It is difficult to grasp the meaning of the word *property,* in part because our ordinary usage of this word refers to things, whereas in the legal and philosophical traditions it refers to rights to things or their use.[1] Property in this sense is a reference not to objects, such as a house, a piece of land, a television set, or an insurance policy but to "claims on" these objects. The etymological root of property (*proprius* = one's own) points to the relationship between a person or thing and what is properly possessed. We may speak of a spectrum of property: there is property as personal characteristics, there is personal property, and there is productive property.

When we speak of property in the most basic sense of properties belonging to persons or things, property is then a means of finding order. People or things can only be identified by their properties or attributes. Theology is familiar with this sense of "property" in referring to what is distinctive in God with the words *propria* or *propriatates.* We refer to the color green as a property of leaves or refer to showing respect to elders as a proper way of behaving. Property in this sense is a way of identifying or describing a mode of being of a person or thing. The language of property by which we speak of the passive properties that identify persons and things is mostly unproblematic, though even the wit or the green eyes of a person can be used to dominate others. It is another matter when we speak of active property, property connected with the human will.

Property begins to become excruciatingly complicated when it signifies (1) the liberty one needs in order to be himself or herself over against external powers, or (2) the justice by which what one needs for life and life abundant is distributed. Property gives rise to the modern conflict between liberty and equality, freedom and just distribution. How can we distribute in such a way that will not destroy the freedom of individual persons? How can we protect the free will of individuals in a way that does not preclude equality, that is, the equal access of all persons to what they need for their lives and what they need to contribute to the lives of others? As soon as these questions are raised, property becomes both a promise and a threat. Property promises home, but it also threatens homelessness.

The great promise of property has always been that it would give the human being freedom. Having property means not being left defenseless against the capriciousness of overlords, nature, and fate. It means that one does not have to depend on others for livelihood. It means that one is less likely to be subordinated and reduced to servitude or made a client. The Western consciousness remembers the long struggle against lords, kings, and states and how property rights have been an essential weapon against those whose rule entailed claiming all things of value for themselves. Property is the promise of protection against despotism. Thus in the history of civil society those who have property are also said to possess liberty, independence, and responsibility.

But if the promise of property is liberty and security, the threat of property is domination. Property and dominion seem married. Freedom gained through property as *dominium* (Latin for both rule and ownership) often is the means for denying the freedom of others and even their right to what it takes to live. Those who gain their own freedom and guarantee their own future through property are often prone to deny property to others. Property is the threat of mastery. Thus arises the question about the just distribution of property.

Consequently, we can observe an enormous difference in kinds of property. Property that is *access to life* is vastly different from property that gives one the *power to exclude and hence control others.* Property that makes one independent is qualitatively different from property that makes others dependent. The one is a means of realizing one's vocation as a human being; the other is potentially a means of destroying the humanity of others and one's own humanity. The one is the means of entering the household; the other is the means of the privileged to exclude others from the household. The deep ambiguity of property is that it can mean both power for life as inclusion in livelihood or power for death as exclusion from livelihood. Property promises freedom, but it also threatens to destroy human dignity.

The biblical traditions are replete with this ambiguity about property. An abiding hope of God's people is that there will be a time in which people "shall live in the houses they build, and eat the fruit of the vineyards they plant; they shall not build houses for others to live in, or plant for others to eat" (Isa. 65:21). Far from doing away with property, the Bible emphasizes the necessity of property as claim on what people need to be God's economists.

But the biblical traditions also know about the ruthless violence connected with property. The household of God remembers Ahab's attempt to annex the land of Naboth. Naboth will not give the inheritance of land to Ahab for money or exchange because the land belongs to God (1 Kings 21). The sulking Ahab is addressed by his wife, Jezebel, with one of the most telling questions in our memory: "Do you now govern Israel?" The implication is that the powerful should be able to determine property rights.

Jezebel arranges for the murder of Naboth by inciting the false charge that Naboth has cursed God and the king. The claims to and conflicts over property almost always entail God and patriotism, atheism and national betrayal. In North America atheism equals communism and communism equals atheism, and they both are epithets slung at those who have suspicions about the way the powerful define property rights. The monetary system of the United States, the way we exchange, protect, and increase our property, is stamped with an appeal to its ultimate authorization, "In God we trust."

Once property has been authorized by divinity, it is something that can no longer be questioned. Property then becomes axiomatic, so foundational that everything else has to be thought in relation to it. The law of property is like the law of God. To question the sanctity of property would be to question the sanctity of God. One reason that it is so easy to lose hope for making the fundamental changes that are necessary to the survival of the world is that property seems to be sacrosanct, beyond all questioning. Poverty, hunger, unemployment, enormous discrepancy in wealth, war, depletion of natural resources, and destruction of the ecosphere all seem insuperable problems because their solutions seem to contradict or undermine the most sacred assumptions about property.

Jezebel to Ahab: "Arise, take possession of the vineyard of Naboth the Jezreelite, which he refused to give you for money; for Naboth is not alive, but dead" (1 Kings 21:16–17). Elijah to Ahab: "Have you killed, and also taken possession?" (v. 19) Killing and taking possession. This is a theme that the human race seems bent on playing out over and over again. It is dimly discernible in contemporary economic theory:

> The essence of property right is the right to exclude, and an organization which has a comparative advantage in violence is in the position to specify and enforce property rights. In contrast to the theories frequently advanced in the literature

of political science, sociology, and anthropology, here the key to understanding the state involves the potential use of violence to gain control over resources. One cannot develop a useful analysis of the state divorced from property right.[2]

Ahab to Elijah: "Have you found me, O my enemy?" Elijah responds, "I have found you, because you have sold yourself to do what is evil in the sight of the Lord. Behold, I will bring evil upon you, I will utterly sweep you away, and will cut off from Ahab every male, bond or free, in Israel; and I will make your house like the house of Jeroboam . . . for the anger to which you have provoked me, and because you have made Israel to sin" (1 Kings 21:20–22). The Economist is zealous about how property is defined because it makes all the difference whether and how the Economist's people will live.

Property as Right:
Inclusive and Exclusive Property

While some theories of property portray it as a universal reality, ontologically given and never changing, it is actually the case that property is historically determined according to the power that authorizes and is authorized by the community. Property has a history and must be made open to history. Its meaning and function have varied widely.[3]

If in human history there have always been kinds of property, there has certainly not always been what is thought of in modernity as absolute *exclusive* private property.[4] Most primitive communities are built collectively on some form of communal ownership or use of those things necessary for sustenance. When human beings give up their exclusive dependence on hunting, gathering wild vegetation for raising domestic animals, or the cultivation of the soil, there arises the problem of how resources can be used equitably for the benefit of the whole group. An exclusive claim on what has formerly been communal property (such as, hunting grounds, beasts, cattle, or granary) appears together with the privilege of some community members over others. When a person or group gains exclusive control over valuable objects, two problems for social existence arise. The first concerns the privileges and benefits that flow to the owner from exclusive *use* of property. The second is the power that *control* of property beyond what is needed for one's personal needs puts into the hands of one person or group over others. The privilege and power of property thus raise in an acute form the social problems of property: "Inequality in the satisfaction of the needs of life, and a growing gap between the governors and the governed through the power that the former exercise over the latter."[5] Property that entails power over others inevitably raises the questions of distributive justice and liberty.

Traditionally, property rights were derived from essential human needs. Property was a claim on what it takes to live. The institution of property has always been justified ultimately in terms of the right to life, whether that be understood as the "good" life, the "fully human life" or merely bare existence. This has always meant, at least, the property in one's daily bread and the other consumables necessary to maintain life. The principal and obvious justification for property is that human needs cannot be met without the institution of property, that is, a claim on access to what is necessary for livelihood.

Does every human being have an equal right to life? If this is granted, it can be demonstrated that everyone requires such a claim on the means of life and access to the means of labor as will ensure the continuance of his or her life.[6] And if we mean a genuine right to life, we are referring to more than a right to bare physical existence. We mean an equal right of access to such means of life and means of labor as a public household can provide according to its present ability to produce goods.

Thus most societies have agreed that the equal right to life requires personal property rights of two kinds. The first kind is some property in consumable things needed for survival. This must be an exclusive private right, that is, the right to exclude others from the food, shirt, toothbrush, and bed I use. Some form of exclusive property seems to be basic and necessary to human life. Indeed it is probable that objects such as clothes, beds, and personal ornaments have always been considered as belonging to a specific person and no other.

The second kind of personal property is a claim on the means of labor, that is, the resources, the land, and capital, access to which I need in order to use my gifts and my capacities. This need not be exclusive property. In fact, it can be another kind of personal property, that is, the right not to be excluded from using or enjoying some resource or good. If the first property is a claim on the means of life to ensure continuous life, a right to *living*, the second property is a share of *living well*. This is a personal right not to be excluded from use and enjoyment of what it takes to live life in the community or the polis. It can be a legal right not only to life but to a certain quality of life. It is a right not to be excluded from household, from livelihood.

From Aristotle down to the seventeenth century property was said to include these two kinds of rights, though the latter right to a quality of life was extremely limited because human beings were assumed to have unequal value. In the classical and medieval world private property was a function of the master-slave relationship. Slaves and serfs were not considered fully human.[7] Only those who were capable of a fully human life (free citizens) needed a property right that would exclude others. Of course, the former, the right to the necessities for maintaining life, was easier to justify than the latter. Property in land, capital, and revenue (that is, the right to control more than what I need to maintain life) means also power to control the lives of others. This kind of property, therefore, has always required greater justification.

The Modern
Threat to Inclusive Personal Property

The theoretical presupposition as well as practical result of throwing everything, including human energy, into the modern market under the assumption that the market would now replace custom, prescription, and political authority as the means of allocating resources, labor, and rewards was a new view of property. As a result, the meaning of property has been drastically narrowed in modernity. The most momentous change was the loss of the traditional inclusive property right.

The kind of property necessary to the logic of the market is the right of an individual or corporation (natural or artificial individual) to exclude others from some use or enjoyment of something. Only exclusive rights can be marketed. The right not to be excluded from use or enjoyment of something cannot, by its very nature, be marketed. This second right virtually dropped out of sight.

All rights in material things and in one's labor had to be converted into private property, the right to buy and sell, to dispose of or alienate. An exclusive right merely to use and enjoy something was reduced to property as an exclusive right both to use and dispose of a material object. In comparison with earlier senses, property became a right "which is not conditioned on the owner's performance of any social function."[8] This narrowing of the meaning of property meant an enormous increase in the function of property as a means of controlling the lives of those who, without property, are dependent for their livelihood on those with excess property.

Modernity was faced with the dilemma of how to conceive and justify these new demands for property in the market. Once the equality of human beings in capacity for a fully human life was postulated by the modern liberal tradition, a new ground for private property in land and capital was required.[9] This Locke and the other first-generation liberal theorists provided in the "labor justification of property," which became the "case for an individual right of unlimited appropriation."[10] Before turning to Locke's argument, let us look at the traditional understanding of God's property in creation/nature, stretching from the Torah to the seventeenth century, as articulated by the early Christian theologians.

The early church theologians had to relate what they understood to be the biblical perspectives on property to the actual structures of property in the Roman Empire. They lived not only within the "household of Jesus Christ" but also in the "household of Caesar" which determined the public character of property. Rome, a former agricultural society transposed into a "complex multinational commercial empire," developed the notion of the *dominium ex iure quiritium,* a concept denoting unrestricted right of control over a piece of land and the air or sky over it.[11] Private property as complete right of control over things movable and immovable was made the bedrock of all other economic interests and was increasingly reserved to the patrician class. The accumulation of large land properties, the *latifundia,* in the hands of a few owners created the social inequalities that made property an instrument of domination and provided the few the power to exploit the many.[12]

The emperor was viewed as the property owner *par excellence.* [13] The emperor's political power was constituted by his property claim, at least symbolically, on the entire realm. As we have seen, the classical properties of God describe what it takes to possess and dispose property, that is, to be the emperor. The question for the early theologians was whether exclusive private property was to be given a ground in divinity or nature.

The answer was that, far from justifying exclusive private property, God, the source of all possession, gives to all human beings a common property in nature to be used equally by all for the satisfaction of needs.[14] "The earth was made in common for all. . . . Why do you arrogate to yourselves, ye rich, exclusive right to the soil?"[15] Did God unjustly distribute the necessities of life to human beings unequally? With one accord the church Fathers answer no. If

God intended to give the necessities of life to all people equally, this meant that private property was neither natural nor inevitable, neither religiously valuable nor necessarily socially meritorious. If there are no poor by nature or by God's design, the disparity between rich and poor could only have happened through exploitation, expropriation, extraction, and dispossession. With obvious allusion to the Quiritarian property law, Ambrose says, "For all the world has been created, which you few are trying to keep for yourselves. For not merely the possession of the earth, but the very sky, the air, and the sea are claimed for the use of the very rich few. How many people can this air feed which you include within your widespread estate?"[16] The root of accumulated wealth must be injustice.

There is a relationship of causality between the rich and the poor.[17] Avarice must be the cause of human need if indeed there is abundance even for the birds who do not sow. Human society takes a right common to all and transforms it into an exclusive individual right. The conventions of positive civil law which established private property were justified only because human corruption made instruments of social domination necessary to preserve law and order. This meant that property rules determining exclusive property were a human fabrication. They have no eternal grounding in God. Property rules may be just, or they may be unjust, and if they are unjust they should be changed.

The early Christian theologians' view of property as based on God's universal claim to the creation represented the general view up to the seventeenth century when Locke attempted once again to give exclusive property a grounding in nature. Locke set out to "show how men might come to have a property in several parts of that which God gave to mankind in common, and that without any express compact of all the commoners."[18] Locke began with the traditional assumption that all human beings own nature in common by the divine will. But Locke interprets this commonality in a negative way. Things belong to no one in particular and each shares the common right to take what he or she needs without getting the consent of others. What people take out of nature with their labor becomes theirs. Because a person's body is exclusively his or hers, the right to that with which the labor of his or her body is mixed is an *exclusive* right.

> Though the earth and all inferior creatures be common to
> all men, yet every man has a "property" in his own "person."
> This nobody has any right to but himself. The "labour" of his

own body and the "work" of his hands, we may say, are properly his. Whatsoever, then he removes out of the state that Nature hath provided and left it in, he hath mixed his labour with it, and joined to it something that is his own, and thereby makes it his property. It being by him removed from the common state Nature placed it in, it hath by this labour something annexed to it that excludes the common right of other men.[19]

Locke thus resurrected the old claim that private property is an institution of nature, not of social convention and human laws. Human beings are constrained to maintain the law dictated by nature; property rights should be thought of in the same way as the natural rights of life and liberty. But then in midstream Locke reverses his logic. By establishing a monetary system and a code of positive law Englishmen had agreed, argues Locke, to the possibility of taking more than one needed.[20] "Locke began by saying the natural right of property was the equal right of every man to acquire by labor the necessities of life; in the end he implied that it was the right of each man to keep what he had, however he had acquired it and whether he could use it or not."[21] Locke began by saying modern property rights had been instituted by natural law; he ended by asserting that they were superior to law. Government, having been instituted for the preservation of life, liberty, and property, is bound to hold them all inviolate.[22]

Lawrence Becker has discerned within the liberal perspective on property four general theories justifying private property: (1) the Locke-Mill version of the labor theory, in which entitlement comes from the laborer producing something that would not otherwise have existed; (2) the labor-desert version of the labor theory, in which a laborer who produces something of value to others is said to deserve some benefit for it; (3) complex arguments of utility in terms of economic efficiency or political and social stability; and (4) the argument from political liberty, which claims that the inevitable acquisitiveness of human beings cannot be prohibited without ruining all liberties but nevertheless should be regulated, a system of private property rights being the only justifiable way of regulating acquisitiveness so as to maintain liberty.[23] On the basis of these general theories of justification absolute exclusive property became a fundamental assumption of social organization. The liberal theory of property changed the individual right not to be excluded.[24] The most fateful postulate in all of these justifications of the new notion of private, alienable, exclusive property was that human beings own or possess themselves and their labor. A new conception of the human being, the self as private property, resulted. How does this view of the human being function economically?

When land runs out, relatively few persons have property in land and working capital. But if I and no one else owns my labor, then I have a right to sell my labor as a commodity. In fact, I must sell my self-possession, my right to myself, in order to survive. Those without land to work or capital have to pay others for access to it by giving over control of their capacities and some of the product of their labor. "Those who had no land lost the right to the product of their labour. They lost also the possibility of their labour entitling them to a property in what they had mixed their labour with. They lost, therefore, the effective right to that which they needed in order to be fully human."[25] It is essentially, as we have seen, the story of our way into slavery under Pharaoh (Genesis 47). The problem in the liberal property theory is that for many of those persons who must sell their labor the property right derived from essential human needs is denied by the property right derived from labor.[26]

Property as an exclusive right both to use and dispose material things is bound to result in inequality of wealth and power.[27] Not everyone is equal in skill and energy. Exclusive and disposable property rights lead to some getting more than others. The more one gets the easier it is to get still more. This results in a constant transfer of part of the powers of the non-propertied to the propertied. Many persons in a market society upholding this right will be constantly submitted to the threat of inhuman existence. Moreover, when this logic of exclusive property right is transferred to other spheres of society or when it converts other social goods into power and privilege, we form a public household that excludes forms of property, such as gift, which are essential to human dignity.

TRINITARIAN REFLECTION
ON GOD AND PROPERTY

Theories justifying property became the most important cultural determinants in European and North American society. Officially, God was to be removed from the determination of property; in actuality certain God concepts have remained crucial to the justification of property that does not support the meeting of human needs or the strengthening of community, that is, the justification of the concentration of the power of property in the hands of the few.

When the attributes of God as Emperor are applied, in a highly attenuated sense, to the human being under the conditions of the market society, they describe what is required by the modern conception of exclusive private property, namely, the ability and right to possess, use, manage, gain revenue from, devise, hold a perpetuity to, consume, waste, alienate and destroy property.[28] This notion of exclusive alienable property and the ideologies connected with it are at least in part grounded in the concept of God as exclusive owner. Behind the modern concept of absolute exclusive private property are the market anthropological notions which reflect three classical assumptions about God: (1) God is a self-possessor, (2) God is the exclusive property owner *par excellence;* and (3) God's freedom consists in the power to dispose property.

Although subordinationist and modalistic interpretations of the Trinity have been made to support views of God as Emperor, the doctrine of the Trinity has always potentially entailed the criticism of doctrines of God built on the emperor cult. Politico-economic theology is faced with the task of criticizing the elements of domination in the classical concepts of God as emperor and their absorption into modern economic anthropology. We turn now to some concrete instances of this critique.

God as Self-Possessor
and the Social Doctrine of the Trinity

The doctrine of God in Western teaching has often conceived God as a self-possessor, a self-proprietor.[29] Behind the three divine persons is the absolute being, a simple, indivisible, self-sufficient individual. God's absolute existence is in and for God's self. With Augustine the West came to think of the Trinity on the model of the radically individual human being who constitutes himself, is proper to himself, and is property of himself. On this model God exists for God's self, God is proper to God's self, and that means God's self is the property of God.

The description of God as a simple, undivided, atomistic essence is the description of the human being as private individual in our economic life today. It is the theological background for the statement C.B. Macpherson deduces from his exhaustive historical study of economic anthropology in the modern world: "The individual in market society *is* human as proprietor of his own person

. . . his humanity . . . depends on his freedom from any but self-interested . . . relations with others"[30] In *About Possession: The Self as Private Property*, John R. Wikse comments similarly:

> Where human identity is defined by subjectivity, inward-ness or interiority, the experience of being deprived of intimate and enduring associations and relationships with others is discounted and is transformed into the meaning of freedom. This is the freedom and privilege of the *bourgeois* individual, fearfully suspicious that others will deprive him of his possessions, including himself. . . . To be able to think of oneself as "living property" means the logic of socioeconomic relationships has penetrated the psyche. . . . Subjectivity understood in this way is intelligible in terms of private property, as a hidden, private relationship: the self's ownership of itself.[31]

To conceive of myself as my ultimate property which I must protect at all costs is to make me unable to give myself away to the other and to recognize the other's right not to be excluded from what he or she needs to live abundantly.[32] The *homo Americanus* is the private individual, who is absolute, exclusive owner of himself or herself. Economic freedom comes to mean having no claims laid upon oneself by others. It is the freedom to view oneself as one's own property. It is the freedom to make oneself and remake oneself and thus to be "on the make." It is the freedom not to have to suffer when the other suffers. It is the freedom to serve one's own self-interests. The possession of self as property and property as self prevents the formation of human community.

A critical retrieval of the Trinity today in relation to the current problems of property should reconstruct the social doctrine of the Trinity. It would emphasize that God is not an indivisible, self-sufficient individual. God is not a self-possessor. God is rather a community, a community of persons united in giving themselves to each other and to the world. God is not a closed self, acting autonomously without regard to impact on the community as when God is worshiped as an absolute private property owner. The Triune God is the inexhaustible life that the three persons share in common, in which they are present with one another, for one another, and in one another. There can be no simple notion of self-possession because God is a community in which persons find their distinct identities in mutual relationships of self-giving. As we shall see, God "has" God's self precisely in giving God's self away.

The social doctrine of the Trinity maintains the distinctiveness of the persons as well as the unity of their community of love. From the perspective of the social doctrine of the Trinity the ecumenical church should be engaged in a criticism of both individualistic and collectivist concepts of property. The abiding contribution of the Western trinitarian tradition is the translation of the Greek *hypostasis* into *persona,* thereby meaning a distinct person with unique characteristics and a nonexchangeable individual existence.[33] It has served in the West as a background for an emphasis on personal dignity and freedom and for the great tradition of legal and civil rights for individuals. But personalism defined by henotheistic/imperialistic conceptions of God also served the rise of Western possessive individualism.

The Western cult of the individual is in consort with the self-possessing, property-mastering God. In this sphere social relationships are less primal and often subordinated to the individual. The result is that the rights of the individual to possess property eclipse the right of the individual not to be excluded from access to the means to life and access to the means of labor. Those excluded by lack of property from community lose the right to fulfill their calling to full humanity.

There is an expanding double standard in so-called free market societies: an egalitarian political system that dispenses rights equally but harnessed to an nonequalitarian system of economic distribution. In this context the community is so little emphasized that it shrivels up and all persons become individuals in exchange relationships. Individuals become commodities to be exchanged in supply and demand ratios.

The abiding contribution of the Eastern Orthodox trinitarian tradition is the definition of God's unity in terms of the bonding love of a community or family. This gave rise to the communal doctrine of the Trinity. The Cappadocians contributed the best perception of the unity of the community of distinct persons in their concept of *perichōrēsis* or mutual coinherence. According to this doctrine there is no absolute exclusive right of any person in the divine community. Rather, everything is shared except each person's personal attributes and peculiar commissions.

This emphasis on community has been a fertile ground for Eastern communitarianism: the idea of a just provision of the basic necessities of life so that all human beings can have fundamental access to the means of labor. But communitarianism set in the atmosphere of pantheism becomes collectivism. In this tradition the rights of the community are emphasized over against the individual person. Often economic rights are not extended in such a way as to become personal democratic rights. The person is not given the right to develop, express, and offer to the community his or her own particular characteristics, gifts, and calling.

The Christian social doctrine of the Trinity does not sacrifice either personality or sociality. Mutual coinherence of persons means that personality and sociality arise from each other and subsist in each other. We are who we are in relationship to others. To be human is to be a social being created for God's own *koinōnia*. The *koinōnia* of the church should be modeled after the *koinōnia* of God's own life.[34]

In the Jesus movement the rule of God's righteousness embodied in communal relationships defines property. The secret of property in the *basileia* economy has to do with the relationship of those within the household. Household relationships come first, then the definition of property. In our society property is defined as the premise; then household relations must conform to requirements of property abstractly defined. Human relationships are subservient to property. The communal relationships within the Jesus movement and the primitive community of Acts 4 lead to different forms of property. Karl Polanyi designates these forms "reciprocity" and "redistribution" as over against the modern market form of property.[35] These forms of property also lead to abundance and often to a more equally divided abundance. If according to most social standards Jesus and his disciples seem poor, they were certainly not abjectly poor. They had what it took to live, and to "live abundantly."[36] For the household of God the tendency of property to create domination is to be overcome in oikic relationships of mutual self-giving, in which possessions are used for the realization of God's will in the community.

The self-giving life of the trinitarian community of God is a criticism of the self as private property. Human possession, whether it be personal attribute, personal property, or capital, is basically a means to nurture koinonia. Hence under whatever arrangements of ownership, the primary communal purpose of human goods ought to be safeguarded. Property is not only a right against community but also a right to the life-giving powers of community. Ownership is a means of fulfilling our calling to be God's economist through community with God, other human beings, and nature. Property is a function of the community, a performance of a social function. Ownership is a responsibility. Property entails the necessity and protection of community.

No one actually lives as an atomistic individual in the economic sphere. The megatrends vision of a nonpolitical, ever more individualized future existence in an information-based society is a utopia that masks the increasingly collective control of those who have property in high-tech structures and organizations.[37] Technology increasingly makes our existence associative or collective. The only question is, What kind of associative existence shall we have? Bureaucratic, totalitarian, democratic? And that can be answered only by a political economy that treats as its first concern the relationships of those within the public household. But it is precisely the basic tenet of "possessive individualism" that prevents even the recognition of a public household.

God's Mode of Possessing: Property as Gift and Commodity

If God is not a self-possessor who dominates by excluding others from access to what is necessary for life, then it is also true that God's mode of possessing cannot be the model or justification for understanding all property as absolute exclusive property. What, then, is God's ownership like? How does God possess? On what basis does God have a right to the creation and the possessions of God's creatures? Traditional teachings about the divine have made God a heavenly landlord, lording it over his property. But this does not correspond to the scriptural narratives of God's redemptive and creative work.

God has a claim on the creation and all creatures not as maker (labor theory of property) or owner (first occupancy), but rather as creator and liberator.[38] At the heart of God's act of liberating/creating is God's suffering and self-giving.[39] God's work of suffering is the source of God's claim in, that is, God's property in creation. God brings the world into being through God's costly struggle against the power of the *nihil*. God has suffered for the creation and will not allow it to fall into vanity or be alienated. The creation is properly God's because God's power of righteousness makes its life fundamentally a gift of God's grace. No one else, including Pharaoh, has the power to suffer and prevail against the power of nothingness. Thus no one else has the right to everything in creation, which is yet subject to death and must yet be redeemed from the threat of nothingness.

God's owning is not grounded in self-possession but rather is self-giving. The mode of God's possessing is giving, not the hoarding by which human beings claim dominion.[40] "The Author of nature and the Provider of all things exercises his absolute dominion by continually giving us all the riches of the earth. . . ."[41] It is the character of this God to give Godself to us and with Godself all things (Rom. 8:32). God's self-giving is the font of human livelihood in community. The early theologians speak often of the inner trinitarian life in which there is a sharing within the community of God as well as God's sharing of Godself with God's creatures.[42] The commonality of human claim to God's goodness in creation is based on God's self-giving for all. God owns by giving.

This leads us to reflect on the way God's mode of property comes to expression in the Jesus movement. The history of God's righteousness is the history of God's property, that is, God's life-giving right to the creation. "Seek first the righteousness of God" (Matt. 6:33) is the ground for Jesus' considerable teaching and praxis concerning property. Living in and proclaiming the presence of God's rule of righteousness, Jesus was engaged in the work of opening up God's household in which God's righteousness was to be distributed to all. His movement embraced an expansion of property rights to all who were denied access to the economy that God desired for Israel. The economic strategy of the Jesus movement was consonant with what was required to give a claim on what God promised for their lives to the poor, the outcasts, the lame, the sick, and the ritually unclean.[43] The gospel is a gracious offer of a claim on God's goodness, a property in God's power for life.

The life of the poor with their suffering is not an ascetic ideal, nor is it in harmony with God's will. Poverty is not from God. God intends daily bread sufficient for all of life's needs, even for the unrighteous and ungrateful (Luke 6:35). Jesus seeks to live life in a new community in which the needs of one person are met by the gifts of others, where there is a common sharing of possessions according to need, where a supportive community suffers and rejoices together, and where one can trust God without fear or anxiety over earthly needs.

God builds God's household by breaking down the conditions of inequality between God's people. Wealth is a problem when one is wealthy before the others are. The problem is *differentiating wealth,* the condition in which some are poor while others are rich.[44] The early Christian theologians deplored the fact that under the institution of private property the rich could live luxuriously while others were reduced to dehumanizing poverty. "It is absurd (*atopon*) that one man live in luxury when there are so many who labor in poverty."[45] The discrepancy of wealth and poverty distorts human community and thus ruins the purpose of property which is to serve human community.

Much of Jesus' teaching and life is about the right use of property. Jesus affirms possessions as good gifts of God necessary to human life. No ascetic, Jesus rejoices in life and accepts the goodness of God's creation, including some of the things only money can buy (seemingly in opposition to John the Baptist and the Qumran community). Jesus describes his own ministry as a time of festivity. His chief image of God's coming household was that of the eschatological feast, where joy reigns and the Messiah and all the redeemed share in abundance (Luke 14:16–24; 15:11–24; 16:25; 22:18).

Jesus' affirmation of the possessions necessary for life is reflected in the church tradition. The early church theologians did not condemn possessions as such. Clement of Alexandria was fairly typical in teaching that material goods were gifts of God provided by God's gracious goodness. Absolute renunciation of them cannot be made an end in itself. Yet when property is treated as an end in itself, it destroys the life of the household. What God gives for us to claim must preserve God's claim on it. All property is obligated.[46] It is obligated to meeting one's basic requirements of life and to keeping God's command to love neighbor by which God seeks to build an economy open to those who have no property claims.

This begins with the redemption of the household members from the hold that possessions have on them.[47] Nothing should be allowed to blunt the radicality of the word about freedom from possessions. It is the irreducible framework in which we must wrestle with our relationship to property.

God's way of owning creates the freedom from possession embodied in Jesus. The story through which we come to know the Triune God focuses on the "poverty" of Jesus and his disciples (Luke 9:3, 58; 10:4). Jesus spent his entire public ministry as an itinerant teacher, without permanent residence or occupation and "no place to lay his head."[48] He led a possessionless life. Not only was Jesus himself poor by most external measurements, he also spent most of his ministry in the midst of the poor. One cannot build a theology on these facts. But neither are they irrelevant to the church's economy and its mission in the public household today. The household of God will not be established unless the righteousness of God gives entrance to the poor. Jesus causes the greatest offense by offering home to the marginal people, the homeless and sinners, and by offering good news to the poor and the exploited. The new blessing of the New Testament has to do with not taking offense at such a one who gives home to the homeless (Luke 7:23).

Jesus' call of his disciples into this new household seemed to require a total relinquishment of their possessions. This is true not only of the fishermen who "left everything (*panta*)" (Luke 5:11) and the Twelve and the Seventy who left their homes and lived in constant fellowship with Jesus but evidently of every potential disciple: "Whoever of you does not renounce all that he or she has cannot be my disciple" (Luke 14:33). Instead of martyrdom the call to relinquish one's possessions is, in some instances, the supreme test of discipleship. Such total abandonment is obviously an imitation of Jesus' life. But what should we make of this? Are we who depend for life and security on our property not stupefied by the notion of giving up our property?

In the first instance Jesus' command to relinquish property claims carries forward the older traditions' focus on idolatry. The way we relate to our possessions embodies our response to God and neighbor. The biblical traditions make plain that all possessing has a proclivity toward idolatry. An idol is a possession that we trust to give us life and power, something we authorize by our possession. It is possessed by us to do our bidding. The worship of an idol causes us to take on the character and attributes of the idol and in the end makes us do the bidding that has become reified in the idol. The mystery of idolatry is that persons reflect what they possess. Idolatry is being possessed by a possession and thereby refusing God's claim on oneself and shirking one's responsibility toward others in the community.[49] Idolatry is the loss of freedom. Property can be instrumental to freedom, but it can also mean the destruction of freedom.

But Jesus is not trying to do away with property. The command to give up possessions is not an attack against property, if by property we mean a claim on something necessary for life. Even the most radical statements in the New Testament about property do not argue against property in the sense of what it takes to enter God's economy. Only in comparison with notions of exclusive private property would one think that the New Testament is trying to destroy every sense of property. Rather, what is at stake is Jesus' understanding of property as gift as opposed to property as commodity.

It is increasingly difficult in our culture to understand and practice gifting because the market *oikos* teaches us to reduce all our property to commodities. We understand property as that which can be kept, held, controlled, stored, displayed, priced, consumed, or destroyed by the owner. Thus much of our lives is absorbed in counting and pricing what we own, for we assume a property has value only if it is a candidate for selling. Even our family "gifting" at Christmas often takes on the character of the exchange of equally valued commodities, and disappointed expectations of renewed life can easily lead to sullen and depressed relationships. What is lost when commodity relationships replace gift relationships?

The character of a gift is that it always has to be on the move. But when everything is counted and priced, wealth ceases to move. As Lewis Hyde has shown, the Puritans gave the epithet "Indian giver" to Native Americans who thought a gift should stay in motion, that it should be continually gifted. The character of a gift is that in some way it is passed on for the enhancement of life in community. Hyde suggests that "White man keeper" might be the proper epithet to denote our instinct to remove property from circulation.[50] A commodity is something that has been taken out of circulation. It ceases to circulate in service of the enhanced life of the community. The instantaneous, twenty-four-hour-a-day stock market gives the illusion that property is moving when it is actually accumulating in ever-greater heaps but touching fewer and fewer people.

Gifting is usually not a matter of simple reciprocity. Gifting is circular. Three or more are involved. This can be seen in primitive societies, but it is true in ours as well.[51] Every gift calls forth further gifting, and the giver and recipient cannot always be easily traced. Gifts literally cease to be gifts if they are not used, if they are not constantly consumed, if they are not relinquished. When gifts are sold they change their nature. As is demonstrated in countless fairy tales, our choice is to keep the gift moving or to be eaten by it. Our property can devour us if we hoard it. God the Economist seeks to keep the gift in motion.

Market exchange and gifting generate different kinds of relationships. The exchange of commodities aims at a stasis or equilibrium. When I buy a hammer at the hardware store, I exchange what is considered equal value for the hammer. I pay in order to balance the scales. In the transaction there is neither motion nor emotion. I and the former owner of the hammer part company, confident that neither owes the other anything. The whole point is to keep the balance, to make sure that the exchange does not consume anything or involve one person with the other. The point is that consumer goods are to be consumed by their owners, not by the relationship or transaction.

In gift-giving, on the other hand, an imbalance is created that causes momentum and creates new relationships. Gifts obligate. Persons in older generations used to respond to a gift by saying, "much obliged." Now one seldom hears this in our society, for we do not want to be obligated. But the fundamental logic of the economy of God is that Jesus Christ is the *charis* (which means both gift and grace), the unexcelled generosity by which God has gifted us with God's own life in order to redeem us from the nothingness of death, and that this gift is what obligates, moves, and empowers our lives for serving life against death in the world.

Accordingly, at stake in Jesus' command to relinquish possessions is not simply a life free of possessions and their hold on human life, a freedom offered by many philosophies. Rather the issue is entrance into God's *basileia* economy. By gifting what one has, one becomes free for the new life of the kingdom and the discipleship of Jesus. Radical freedom for gifting is possible because of God's radical provision of God's righteousness.

The meaning of Jesus' command about relinquishment of possessions is that a gift property perishes for the person who gives it away; the exchange itself consumes the gift. That something will come back to the giver is not the condition of the gift, though the character of gifting is that something does come back and also goes further. In the final analysis the question of property is the question of life for all those whom God is inviting into the household. Property as commodity perishes for the one who gifts so that all people in the household may have property, that is, a claim on what it takes to live and live abundantly. The renouncing of possessions for the sake of the livelihood of all in the *basileia* is epitomized by the widow who gives all (Luke 21:1–4; cf. Mark 12:41–44). The rich bring large Temple tithes for the poor, but they give only out of their surplus. The widow drops in an offering of only two copper coins. "Truly, I tell you this poor widow has put in more than all of them; for they contributed out of their abundance, but she out of her poverty put in all the living she had." Even though she is one of the poor and under the protection of Yahweh, she holds nothing back. She shares unconditionally with the poor. For the sake of others she gives her livelihood and thereby enters into the new property claim on the livelihood of God's household.

God does not expect the relinquishment of possessions without anything in return. The notion of the saint who renounces all simply for the sake of renunciation is foreign to the Scriptures.

The relinquishment is made for the sake of and on the ground of God's *basileia* righteousness. In return for the gifting of self and possessions for the sake of God's economy of righteousness, Jesus' disciples receive manifold treasures in God's *basileia* household *in this age* and eternal life in the next age. Gift property has a bountiful future.

God's Freedom as Property Right or as Love?

A critical retrieval of the Trinity in light of the dehumanization resulting from property defined only as private and exclusive requires that we work toward a new understanding of God's freedom and our freedom. For much of the theological tradition God's freedom has been viewed as God's unlimited power to dispose property. Out of the notion of God's freedom as mastery of property has come the modern possessive individualistic notion of freedom as free choice. Nothing is worshiped more extensively in the God concepts of our society and churches. This concept makes property the fountainhead of a liberty without restraint. Can God's freedom be made a paradigm of such liberty?

Traditionally absolute divine lordship has been construed as absolute freedom. That God is free to do whatever God likes, including disposing God's property according to God's whim, is taken to be the essence of God's lordship and sovereignty. When God's freedom is conceived as mastery, the image of God, conceived as the male human being, also understands his freedom as mastery.[52] In the West this has been manifested in terms of the white male's mastery of nature, women, people of color, and his own body.

The biblical narratives, however, do not speak of God's freedom as the power of exclusive and alienable ownership. God's freedom is not free choice. God's freedom is God's love. The notion of God's freedom as "free choice" based on ability to dispose property denies God's nature as love. God:

> does not have the choice between mutually exclusive
> possibilities. . .between being love and *not* being love.
> If he is love, then in loving the world he is by no means
> 'his own prisoner'; on the contrary, in loving the world he
> is entirely free because he is entirely himself. If God is the
> highest good, then God's liberty cannot consist of having to
> choose between good and evil. On the contrary, it lies in

doing the good which he himself is, which means communicating himself.[53]

God cannot just will and do anything imaginable. God limits Godself through faithfulness to God's promise. God's self-limitation
through God's promise is the reverse side of the full freedom of
God in God's love. God's freedom consists of God's communicating immanently and economically the love that God essentially is.
The unity of the Trinity as the love expressed among the persons of
the community negates the notion of God's freedom and unity construed as property ownership and disposal.

The biblical narratives picture property construed as sheer freedom to be a threat not only to individuals but most especially to the
community.[54] The notion that property is simply a matter of the
individual's free choice creates divisive wealth and uncaring relationships. "Woe to you that are rich" (Luke 6:24–26). In a culture
such as ours in which property is the measure of the possibility of
happiness, the biblical woes sound menacing or quaint. The woes
announce the great reversal of God's justice and the reverse side of
"good news to the poor" (cf. the prophetic oracles of judgment, e.g.,
Isa. 1:4–5; 5:8–23; Amos 5:18; 6:1; Enoch 5:7). Though the rich
prosper now, the coming rule of God's righteousness will bring an
end to their present status of privilege and prosperity. The filled
and the laughing are not charged with gross injustice or dissipation;
they simply will have no part of the coming joy of God's household.
Unable to live economically with the weeping and the hungry, they
will be excluded from eternal life.

A vivid illustration of the coming reversal and the need of
repentance for irresponsible use of property is the story of the rich
man and Lazarus (Luke 16:19–31). The clothing, mansion, and
daily feasts of the rich man contrast with Lazarus's miserable
existence. Lazarus reflects the social poverty of the common people of the land. Every detail makes vivid the misery of poverty.
Lazarus scrounges the waste from the daily feast of the household. His emaciated body is covered with sores, which dogs continually irritate. Propertyless, he is excluded from the livelihood
of the household. But, not even decently buried, Lazarus, whose
name means "God helps," sits at table with Abraham in God's
eschatological household.

Properly mourned and interred, the rich man experiences the
hell that the poor Lazarus had known in his lifetime. The great
chasm is fixed. God's justice turns everything upside down. The
Economist has "scattered the proud in the imaginations of their

hearts, he has put down the mighty from their thrones, and exalted those of low degree; he has filled the hungry with good things, and the rich he has sent away empty" (Luke 1:51b–53). Can the rich as rich avoid the eschatological reversal? Not without repenting whatever in their lives makes them hoard themselves and their possessions.

The essential character of property is its law of *use* (*usus fructus*). Ownership cannot mean the free choice to do anything one wants to do with property. There can be no such thing as absolute ownership. Property is for use, not holding or hoarding.[55] To be possessed justly, property must be used according to its nature to meet human needs and create human community.[56] God has given human beings authority to use possessions according to these purposes.[57]

Using property justly means the rich are accountable for meeting the essential needs of the poor from their surplus wealth.[58] It is God who has entitled the poor to what they need for life. This led to a harsh conclusion by the early church theologians: The rich are in jeopardy of being thieves. If you claim as your own what is common (*koina*) by right, it is clear that you are forcibly taking what belongs to another. Not to share one's resources, the refusal to take part in redistribution, is robbery. According to Augustine, "The superfluous things of the wealthy are the necessities of the poor. When superfluous things are possessed, others' property is possessed."[59] The poor have something like a just lien on the surplus property of the wealthy.[60] Thus if the rich have more than they need and the poor are in urgent need of goods like those the rich possess, the rich have a compensatory obligation in justice to bestow from their surplus goods what is needed to sustain the deprived.[61]

Redistributing possessions is thus basically an act of restitution. "Not from your own do you bestow upon the poor man, but you make return from what is his."[62] According to Aquinas the poor person under the stress of need could be justified in stealing from the rich.[63] Thus does the tradition uphold the original Torah prohibition of property arrangements by which the rich steal from the poor what is the poor's by God's intention.[64]

Property is meant to serve the livelihood of others, not their domination and exploitation. This is the basic reason that the Christian tradition through the Reformation condemned the injustice of usury. Basil, Aquinas, and Luther all point to usury as a way of enslaving the borrower.[65] Through the payment of interest the borrower often contracts a voluntary servitude for life. Usury damages the community because of the "unlimited bosoms of the rich" (Basil).

TOWARD A REVISION OF PROPERTY: THE INCLUSIVE RIGHT TO LIFE AND WORK

We have seen that property is extremely complicated. We should not assume that property is of one kind throughout history or that one theory of property can dominate all others. Property is not determined by nature or fate. It is a human arrangement, a community's way of regulating the management of its possessions and resources for the sake of the life of the community.

Property is the occasion for massive struggles between liberty and equality, efficiency and justice, the right to possess and the right not to be excluded. The major justifications of property in the modern world (labor, utility, and liberty) favor the liberty of the individual to accumulate wealth without limit and without accountability for its use. Exclusive property claims are freighted with moral significance as the bulwark of the sacred notion of liberty, but they can easily eclipse the rights of those who do not measure up to the standards of liberty as defined by white, male property owners. The results of exclusive, alienable private property contradict one of the basic justifications of property, that human needs cannot be met without that institution. The limited view of property cannot be justified on its own grounds. The ultimate justification of property is still that it serves the fullness of life in community. Whatever the appropriateness of exclusive private property for commodities in market exchange, new forms of property have to be devised for our time that reflect the centrality of the right to be included in the livelihood of the community.

In order to do this we shall have to retrieve the broader view of property in the tradition. This entails scrutinizing the way in which property has assumed divine attributes. We have seen that Christian faith relativizes property by taking away the divine attributes accorded property.[66] Faith removes the claim that property is "eternal" or that property is as immutable as the laws of nature. Faith sees property as a function of God's will for human beings and the creation, not as a determinant of God's will. Also necessary is criticizing the God concepts that lie behind the view that all property is exclusive and private. These concepts lead to a notion of the human being as self-possessor. They form human beings who are unable to give themselves away but rather hoard themselves as their greatest and last possession. Becoming like commodities, such human beings value themselves according to what they own. The ability to control and dispose property becomes the material meaning of freedom.

We have seen that property understood exhaustively as the absolute right to exclude dehumanizes persons and communities. In opting for the narrow sense of property our society set property rights in opposition to democratic human or personal rights. "We have made property so central to our society that anything and any right that are not property are very apt to take second place . . . it is only if the human right to a full life is seen as a property right that it will stand much chance of general realization."[67] If the human right to life is a property right, then exclusive, alienable private property, as the sole definition extended across the broad range of property, is clearly inconsistent with one of the first principles of a democratic society: the equal opportunity to use, develop, and enjoy whatever capacities each person has.

The first step toward regaining a broader view of property is to see that property has essentially to do with social relationships that embrace the right not to be excluded from what it takes to realize one's commission as a human being and the gift/calling to serve the life of the community. The church should engage in a critical retrieval of property as the right of each person not to be excluded from whatever it takes to be in life-giving community with other human beings and with nature and in those relationships to serve God's will for the creation.

Property should be understood as a personal right not only to some exclusive property but also to some nonexclusive right of access to what a given society has accumulated. This would constitute a broadening of the meaning of property to the old concept of personal property in one's life, liberty, and God-given capacities.

In the first sense this would mean an equal right of access to means of labor, that is, the accumulated capital of society and its natural resources. One of the most realistic descriptions of many people's property has come to be a right to revenue. The first right to revenue is the right to earn an income from the exertion of one's gifts, if one is self-employed, or a right to a job, if one is a wage earner. This is not a right to exclude someone else from something, but it is increasingly seen as property.

A second sense of inclusive property is the right to income not currently earned. Such an income is not related to work but rather to what is needed for life. This is a right to an income from the whole of society's production. It includes income not only from investments and pension rights but also the variety of money and services provided by the state, such as health services, aid to children, unemployment benefits, and old age benefits. The latter would also include income provided by a negative income tax and guaranteed annual income.

Such a revision of property would mean holding to the traditional conviction that property is much more a right to the use and enjoyment of gifts and talents than merely a right to things and revenues. Before the market society converted us to consumers, we knew that life is for doing, gifting, and the practice of virtue rather than just getting or maximizing.[68] Views of property that destroy or prevent community submit us to what Alasdair MacIntyre calls Nietzschean moral solipsism.[69] However unlikely it seems in present arrangements, the right to an abundant life of action realizing one's gifts can be made a personal property claim that society will guarantee for each person.

This means that a new understanding of property is wrapped up with a new understanding of work and needs. Property, divorced from work, the means of livelihood, and from response to human need is not related to the life and future of the community. We may go on behaving as insatiable acquisitors and consumers. Our vision of the good life may remain simply the acquisition of ever more goods for consumption. But it need not be so.

Chapter 6 | **God and Work**

O HOUSEHOLD WILL SURVIVE WITHOUT work. Unless what is necessary for human life is made available by human effort we cannot even speak of an economy. Work, moreover, far from being simply the means of producing what is necessary for life, is also a means of access to household and a means of shaping the household. Thus a community constitutes itself in answering the questions, Who gets what kind of work? Who owns the tools and product of work? The way a community understands, distributes, and controls work will decide who will have access to livelihood and how the members of the household will relate to each other. How a community or society views work affects profoundly every person in it.

God concepts, albeit highly secularized in the modern world, have grounded and modeled society's prevailing concepts of work. Work is a central theological issue because nowhere are the relationships of authority and subordination more apparent than in the relationships of work. Work is the most immediate way in which human beings dominate and exploit each other. And those who would control other people through work must be able to control what a society teaches about the value and meaning, the incentives and control, and the distribution of work. The church's teachings about God, full of rationales of authority and subordination, have been available for social understandings of work and for selective use by those who would control work.[1] Richard Baxter recommended employing the godly servant because he would "do all your service in obedience to God, as if God himself had bid him do it."[2] Peter D. Anthony remarks, "The engagement of God as the supreme supervisor was a most convenient device; a great part of the effort of modern management has been aimed at finding a secular but equally omnipotent equivalent in the worker's own psyche."[3]

THE AMBIGUITY OF WORK

Work, perhaps even more than property, is profoundly ambiguous. For millennia human beings have blessed and cursed each other through work. Positive and negative views of work accompany each other, often in the same person. On the positive side, work has been extolled as the single way in which human beings can find meaning and purpose in life. The promises of work are that it justifies a person's existence, it proves a person's salvation, it gives a person value and dignity, status and security; it guarantees the future; it gives an upper hand over the competitor; it creates the self and the self's world. With such promises work is bound to be extolled. In the United States, especially during election times, political parties vie to elevate work as the reason for America's success in the world. And as for the individual, if he or she is willing to work, there is no reason success will not ensue. Every American, it is assumed, is born with the inclination to work with enthusiasm and devotion.

On the negative side, work has been connected with animal needs and denigrated as a dehumanizing distraction from the higher pursuits of the human soul. Work destroys what is peculiarly human. Work promises nothing but bare survival and that with considerable pain. "In the sweat of your face you shall eat bread . . ." (Gen. 3:19). This is the recognition of those who lead lives of hard work but never expect to find fulfillment in it. It requires only mild objectivity to see the inequities, brutalities, and exploitation of work in the global household. Studs Terkel caught this assessment in the Introduction to his book *Working*: "This book, being about work, is by its very nature, about violence—to the spirit as well as the body."[4]

The paradoxes of work abound. Some say work is the deepest satisfaction of their lives and has made them who they are; others say work has destroyed their health and their family life.[5] Some say technology has overcome backbreaking work; others say machine work and the division of labor have caused social fragmentation and boring and demeaning work.[6] Some say work is the great democratizer; others say workers have had ever less participation in shaping their own work and determining how the resources and product of their work are controlled.[7]

Some say all honest work obtains dignity; others say there is an enormous discrepancy between different kinds of work, not to speak of income from different kinds of work. Some say hard work will allow one to get ahead; others say this is true only for a very few, and often their getting ahead does not have much to do with the quantity and quality of their work. Some say work secures their future; others say their work is the most insecure thing about their future. Some say work has its own built-in assumption of progress; work will make things better. Others say progress is built on the backs of those who have to work with no prospect of benefiting from progress. Some say work is the way to enjoy the immense benefits of the capitalist society. Others say that working for capitalism spreads the effects of exploitative work relationships like a cancer into every dimension of life.[8]

So there appear to be two deeply opposed views of work. Work, on the one hand, seems to be a curse such that it would be better for people to fold their hands and cease all human activity. On the other hand, work seems to be a blessing associated with the use of work's product and with satisfaction in accomplishment.

While the ambiguities and paradoxes of work are lived out in human relationships hour by hour, what everyone can agree upon is that work has to be done. Whatever value we put on it, human existence is dependent on work, even if some "fortunate" people succeed in escaping from it. But who does it and under what circumstances and with what effect are questions which human beings have always disputed. Only one thing seems fairly certain: There will be a difference in perspective between those who do work and those who control work. The average life span for a migrant farm worker is forty-nine years, as compared to seventy-two years for the average American. Work will be regarded differently by those who do hard, dirty, and grueling work and those who do self-determined and satisfying work. And, of course, work will appear differently to those who have no work and those who take their work for granted.

In our time unemployment, underemployment, lack of meaningful work, and inequality in the distribution of hard work lead the list of problems with work, especially in view of the strong ideologies of work that still reign officially in our society. People are told that they are nothing if they do not work, but at the same time they hear that 6 to 8 percent unemployment will be considered normal or desirable in our economy. In recent years one might read front-page headlines declaring the administration's conviction that those who do not work are not "entitled" to what it takes to live and in the next column an announcement that two hundred thousand jobs are being eliminated in the automobile, steel, or other industry. How is it possible for a societal household to say both things: (1) Those in the household who do not work will have no dignity, and yet (2) there is not enough work in the household for everyone to do? It is possible because of ideologies of work.

IDEOLOGIES OF WORK AND
A TRINITARIAN VIEW OF WORK

Historically, there seem to be two choices: coerced work or ideologies of work that convince people to work "voluntarily" or so cover up the dehumanization of work that it can be tolerated. Ideologies of work seek to make hard work, underpaid work, or lack of work seem legitimate in a divided society. Seeking at all costs the cooperation of subordinates, work ideologies keep us from remembering what in the tradition would make us conscious of the suffering of people from work in the present. Their purpose is to make the existing shape of work seem universal or axiomatic, whereas they actually serve specific interests in a historical context. The most successful ideology is one that is not recognized as an ideology. The church's doctrine of God has sometimes aided the camouflage of work ideologies, making them seem common sensical assumptions, generally agreed upon.

To become free from dehumanizing ideologies of work requires that we remember the biblical narratives of God which open up a new praxis of work and criticize the God concepts that shore up the prevalent ideologies of work. Politico-economic theology should seek to detect the theological components of work ideologies and to ask whether they serve the will of God as known in the history of Israel and in Jesus Christ or whether they serve the dehumanization and alienation of human beings through work. To do this, theology should ask about the work of God as known in the triune community's uncovering in the history of Israel and of Jesus. In the biblical traditions work is filled with theological content. It is the epitome of the doctrine of salvation. The human distortion of work makes God's work of redeeming human work necessary. God's work is against domination and exploitation through work. It is against individualistic, noncooperative, falsely motivated, and unjustly distributed work.

The Market View of Work

In our society ideologies have appeared predominantly in connection with the developing market view of work. According to the market view the purpose of work is to produce goods or services in return for money which in turn is spent on goods and services. It is held that people work harder in order to get more.[9] This view assumes that the best way to distribute work is through market mechanisms. That one earn money to buy goods by entering the market distribution of work is basically all the market demands.

But these simple rules of the market are not sufficient to explain the massive suffering that results from work, including being shut out of the work market. For those who have no work or have demoralizing or underpaid work, there must be some justification supplied by ideology. Moreover, as soon as complex industrialism was introduced, such a calculative connection to a job proved insufficient to motivate the kind of skilled work required. Market theory requires a degree of commitment to work that it is incapable of commanding. Thus there was a need for ideologies of work that could support the performance of labor as if it were an absolute end in itself. This is not a "natural state of affairs" and can be achieved only through an "arduous process of education."[10] The problem has been to produce ideologies of work compatible with liberal economic doctrine when in fact imperatives to work that remain within the terms of the market logic prove repellent to subordinates.

Let us consider some principal points of the ideologies of work and set over against them some trinitarian perspectives on work.

Should everyone have a right to humanizing and remunerative work? If labor is made a commodity and distributed according to market rules, then some people will be left out of work. The market view of work will therefore require ideologies that make it appear reasonable that some people do not have work and that some people have degrading work.

Should work be cooperative? Early on, Adam Smith saw that the division of labor at the heart of modern industrialism would make cooperation almost impossible. He did not, however, see the worst consequences: the anomie caused by persons being separated into minute functions and tasks and the alienation caused by the social division of human beings by interest and class.[11] The market view of work will thus require ways of justifying the necessity of alienating and anomic industrial work.

Should work take place in a democratic environment? In the modern workplace efficiency has been the dominant criterion of work. This has led to harsher discipline and bureaucratic control of workers and less participation by workers in the decisions that affect their work and the disposition of the product of their work. Thus ideologies have been constructed that try to motivate workers within a hierarchical situation that robs them of freedom to participate in the shaping of their work.

Should work be motivated by regard for the community? According to Adam Smith, cooperation was to be provided not by a benevolent regard each for the other's welfare but rather through self-interest. The resulting moral principle of selfishness is a process of demoralization unprecedented in history. When fear of losing one's job is the whip with which employers extract greater work effort, work destroys community rather than supporting it. This necessitates ideologies exalting the individual at work in isolation.

A Trinitarian Perspective on Work

A trinitarian view of God as the economic community of righteousness will provide us with the hermeneutical keys for understanding biblical perspectives on God's work and human work as well as a critical focus on the ways certain theological emphases on work have been used ideologically in the past and the present.[12] We shall again draw on the focal doctrine of *perichōrēsis,* now applied to God's work. The life of the triune God pictures the economy of work that God is working to bring into being. The Trinity is the church's teaching against domination through work. What is the character of God's work?

The first thing to be said is that each person of the Trinity engages in *distinctive personal work.* Each person of the Trinity is described in the narratives of Jesus/Israel as working. Each makes a specific contribution to the divine economic work in and for the world. On the basis of these narratives we can also speak of the peculiar work of each person within and for the divine community itself.

The tradition has usually identified the work of the Father as creating, the work of the Son as redeeming, and the work of the Holy Spirit as creating anew. Or, more immediately focused in the story of Jesus, we could say that the Father does the work of sending, the Son the work of being sent, and the Holy Spirit the work of empowerment of the mission of the Father and the Son. No person of the divine community is left without distinctive work. Each has a name, a reputation, a dignity, a place within the community of work. The Trinity is a criticism of all systems of work that exclude some people in the household from distinctive personal work.

Second, the Trinity engages in *cooperative work*. Traditional views of the triune persons tend to emphasize the Father as being the exclusively active person and the other two persons as being acted upon or simply doing the bidding of the Father. The work of the Holy Spirit is especially de-emphasized.[13] But according to the scriptural narratives the whole community is involved in each work, event, or process of God. The Father does not work as an isolated individual; every work the Father does is in cooperation with the Son and the Holy Spirit. The same is true for the Son and the Holy Spirit. They each contribute their own work to creation, redemption, and new creation. Thus the second hermeneutical key is the *co-work* of the persons of the triune community. God's work is the cooperative work of the three persons of the community of righteousness. Each person's distinctive work coinheres in the work of the other members of the community, that is, each person's work cannot be done without the cooperation of the others. God's work is thoroughly communal or social work. The distinctive work of one member of the Trinity is made possible by the cooperation of the other members. Their freedom is to communicate themselves to each other in love. What of themselves they give up in work they find again in the fullness of the community for whose life they work. The Trinity is a criticism of all structures of work that atomize the worker by separating his or her work from the other members of the community, the worker from the product of his or her work, or working classes from nonworking classes.

The third hermeneutical key is the *equalitarian work* of the triune community. While the three persons of the Trinity have their own work, the work of no one of them elevates that person higher than the others. Traditionally the Father's work has been given ascendancy resulting in a hierarchy or stratification of work within the divine community. This in turn has given justification to an authoritarian order of subordination for human work. The master-slave relationship has found a justification in the notion of the hierarchically arranged work of God. But the fact that the Father initiates the work of the triune community does not mean that the Father's is a higher, more valuable work.[14] The Trinity is a criticism of all forms of work that incur relationships of domination.

The fourth hermeneutical key is the integration of the Triune community's work through the *self-giving* love of each other. The work of each is done for the life of the community. The motivation and incentive of the triune community's work is the fullness of life of the other and the redemption of the creation. God works for the sake of God's faithfulness, for the sake of keeping God's promises and thus showing God to be God. God's work is aimed at the fulfillment of what God has promised. God's work is the expression of God's faithfulness.

This calls into question all human attempts to integrate work through coercive means, such as state laws, or through dehumanizing incentives such as poverty or the drive to unaccountable accumulated wealth. The unity of God's work is not gained by the uniformity of being or a notion of self-possession but by the suffering of each person for the other and for the creation. The work of love is the unifying and integrating of God's work. Life-giving work is suffering love. The Trinity is a criticism of ideologically defined motivations and incentives of work. All ideologies of work stand under judgment by the integration of God's work through suffering love.

God's work is personally distinctive, cooperative, equalitarian, integrated by love, and faithful to God's promises.

We turn now to three major tendencies detectable in modern ideologies of work: the (1) degradation, (2) exaltation, (3) redemption of work.

THE DEGRADATION OF WORK

The first tendency is a negative view of work found in the ancient and modern aristocratic denigration of work, the romantic exaltation of leisure, and the degradation of the worker. Christian teaching abets this ideology when it separates the Holy Spirit from the economic community of the Trinity. The Holy Spirit then becomes a subjective dynamic that can be used to justify, with a view of a God who does not work and suffer, the advantages of some people who do not have to work. Such a narrow pneumatology serves the claim that human life can be filled with meaning only when it can transcend work. This spiritualizing tendency, in turn, plays into the hands of attempts, pervasive in every society, to distribute hard work to degraded people.

Does God work? This is a crucial question, for the denigration of work and the degradation of the worker in both antiquity and modernity are supported by the view that the gods do not have to work.[15] That is what makes them gods. The virtue of the life of the polis is connected with the freedom of the gods from work. Only those who live beyond the realm of the necessity of work can be considered virtuous and hence rulers of the *oikos* and "guardians" of the polis.[16] Thus the *pater familias,* the male householder, is free, like the gods, to leave the realm of necessity and lead a life of decision-making in the polis. Those left behind, slaves, artisans, women, and children, simply reflect the meaninglessness of labor.[17] Not corresponding to such divine virtue, they are merely *metics* or "living instruments" for producing subsistence and repro-ducing life.[18] To be unfree is to be condemned to work; to work is to become unfree. Work defiles, and whoever is defiled has to work.

Even in our highly developed society this divinely based dichotomy between work and virtue is still enormously influen-tial, especially as regards the question of who will do hard work. Harvesting crops, collecting garbage, mining coal, caring for the sick and aged, cooking, and cleaning are socially necessary, even if we try to hide such work. It is still assumed that degraded work should be assigned to degraded people. As in antiquity, this work is increasingly being done by foreigners. It is impossible to keep completely outside the household people who do such nec-essary work, without which the household would not survive. But they remain something like strangers in the household, always viewed as lacking in worth. Feminist critiques point to the experi-ence of estrangement through work that many women have in their own homes as well as in their work outside the home.[19]

Christian theology sometimes supports this aristocratic disdain of work and worker by picturing God as resting throughout eter-nity. God makes the world as a designer makes a machine and then steps back to relax for eternity. It is as if God lives in a permanent sabbath. Those favored by God should live free from work and enjoy the divinelike leisure that befits their inherent goodness.

This spiritualization of the doctrine of God as the leisured supreme being also lends itself to the modern search for the mean-ing of life in leisure and against work. Romanticism and idealism maintain that life can be fulfilled only beyond work. These move-ments are full of nostalgia for the golden age in which work did not kill the human spirit and did not produce inequality. There is a longing for immediate communication with nature, for contemplation, for simple pleasures in noncaste communities. We encounter such views in the utopia of Thomas More, the criticisms of Morris, Ruskin, and Southey, and the Emersonian strains of American literature. Some modern theologies of leisure and play have also echoed to a certain extent the negative view of work.[20] They look upon the human being as a creature of the expression of being in play rather than work.[21] They essay a "life ethic" instead of a "work ethic." They distrust work to produce meaning in life, especially the increasingly narrow sense of work in the industrial society. They also claim that in a society bent against "full employment" it is better to develop an ethic of "full life." Thus they look for positive and creative nonwork alternatives to both employment and unemployment.

A different kind of negative approach to work welcomes technology as the only means to liberation from hard work. By mastering nature technology is supposed to free us from the struggle for survival in nature and increase our leisure for cultural pursuits.[22] Here we encounter the romantic notion that machines and human freedom will be reconciled, at least in the sense that machines will deliver human beings from the work that prevents them from being reconciled with nature. But our modern experience has been that machines save people from only some kinds of hard work and often from work that people actually like to do.

Much is to be gained from these critiques of work and appreciations of leisure and play. But it is a mistake to overlook the consequences of the denigration of work and the exaltation of leisure. Extreme theologies of freedom play into the hands of ideological justifications of unemployment and distorted forms of work. The exaltation of leisure as the meaning of life leaves open the claim that it is permissible for some people not to have meaningful work or for certain people, by their very nature, to deserve dirty work. Leisure is not sufficient compensation for lack of work or meaninglessness in work. Leisure becomes unsatisfying to the extent that society's work systems become unsatisfying, and vice versa.

God the Economist Works

Even if the biblical traditions, as we shall see, have their own negative perspectives toward work, they do not denigrate work and degrade the worker.[23] The reason for this is God's own work. It has to be said, over against every attempt to make God a workless supreme being, that according to the biblical narratives God the Economist works. God the Economist works to bring creation into being, to redeem creation, and to create all things anew.[24] There is also for God no work-free age at the beginning, even though God's work of creation seems relatively effortless. God is not the distant emperor or city-state king living the life of leisure while expecting God's people to do all of God's hard work. Human beings are not made, as in the Sumerian and Babylonian myths, to do the arduous work of the gods.[25] Rather, God is the slave-freeing Economist, the liberator from the household of bondage, and the builder of the household of freedom.

God's work of liberation and creation is the ground of an affirmative view of work. Work is neither condemned nor sacralized. Even after the expulsion from the garden, work itself is not seen as a cursed fate; rather hardship and difficulty that accompany work are the result of sin (Gen. 3:17–19). Work belongs to human existence and is commanded by God (Gen. 2:15). God's work, to be sure, is qualitatively different.[26] Human beings do not do God's work. There is a definite limitation to human work: It must be done within the finitude of the created order. Yet God calls the human being into partnership with God's creative work. Every human being, as the image of God, is called to correspond to God's work as he or she represents God's will to the creation. While human work cannot create something out of nothing, it can with imagination be similar to God's doing a new thing.[27] Work is the power to answer with effort God's call to be God's economist in God's household. That God the Economist works and that human beings are given their own proper work by God means that work in itself is not to be denigrated.

God the Economist Rests

God also rests. God's sabbath rest, however, is justification for neither the hatred of work nor the degradation of the worker. Workday and sabbath are not divided into sacred time and worldly time. The sabbath is not reserved for gods and aristocrats and the workday for slaves and laborers. It is in God's rest that the work of human beings finds its limit. For the human being, a finite creature, sabbath is first of all a limit to the toil, pain, and fatigue of work. "So then, there remains a sabbath rest for the people of God; for whoever enters God's rest also ceases from his labors as God did from his" (Heb. 4:9). The human being, unlike God, needs recuperation. "Sweet is the sleep of the laborer" (Eccles. 5:12). For the majority of people even in our society a Sunday afternoon nap is the margin against physical and mental exhaustion. Only the "surfeit of the rich," as Ecclesiastes says, prevents the sabbath scoffers not only from resting but also from understanding the need for rest among those who labor and are heavy laden. Without sabbath, work will destroy the human being. An economy driven to incessant work by the profit motive is an economy that is driving itself mad. Sabbath is a limit to the presumptions of work.

If God's creative work culminates in rest, it is not because God's energy is depleted but because only joy can fulfill God's creative work. God rejoices in God's work, not in its efficiency or finality but in its goodness: "And God saw everything that he had made, and behold, it was very good" (Gen. 1:31). The joy of the creator makes work meaningful. Joy in being limits work. Joy and glory, not work, have the last word. God yearns for the joy of God's economists in their affirmation of their being and work. Work is connected not only with a productive value but also with a representative, imaginative, and celebrative value of joy in being and festivity.[28] Life is a dialectic between the seriousness of work and the relaxed joy of being.

The relation between arduous work and its fruit is grounded in God's grace, which gives freely both the energy for work and its results (Ps. 65, 104). Thus sabbath is thanksgiving for this gift of the energy of work through which the earth has "yielded its increase" and "God has blessed us" (Ps. 67:6). Work and the benefits of work are to be offered back to God as acts of service and worship (Deut. 14:28–29; 26; Eccles. 38:25–39). Although the human being must work in order to bring forth the fruit of the earth and to keep the community alive, there is no "sexual or ecstatic connection between such work and its results."[29] Work is done for the sake of God's love of the creation. Work is thus demythologized insofar as culture and civilization develop from the creator's joy in work and not from the fire and *techné* given by Prometheus.

Jesus does not do away with the sabbath; he radicalizes it. Jesus announces to the household of Israel that it is called to live by the righteousness of God's sabbath at all times and all places. The sabbath is made for the human being and thus must be removed from every cultic attempt to separate it from the situations in which work destroys human beings.

The Torah and the Gospel grant to the human being sabbath time, redeemed time. The future-giving words of the gospel, "Do not be anxious" or "Do not be afraid," open up time no longer compelled by the drives of work. The sabbath gives time for the generations to remember, tell, reflect on the stories of God's work and rest and thus to create home. The household of God comes to know its past, its future, and its name in sabbath time.

The sabbath, therefore, is not simply a negative zone separated from work. That God commands rest, then, does not mean we can define the church according to modern understandings of leisure as vacation time, the "pause that refreshes." The Sabbath is not "Miller time." The church is not the cult of the private. The church is not the place and time in which one can do anything one pleases. It is the place where sabbath rest transforms work.

THE EXALTATION OF WORK

The second ideological tendency is the valuing of work as the means of the ordering and self-justification of life.[30] It is noticeable in the so-called Protestant work ethic and other perceptions of work in the market society. When Christian teaching isolates the Abba/Father from the economic community with the Son and Holy Spirit, there arises a model of the overbearing taskmaster who works capriciously to control the work of subordinates. These notions are the mainstay of ideologies of work that attempt to justify master-subordinate relationships. They uphold the "Father God" who works by fiat. This tendency also results in a model of the isolated, self-sufficient worker. The theological view that identifies God with the Father working alone as an absolute subject without feeling with others in the community correlates with the human being as absolute subject working alone.

According to Max Weber, the new economic situation of nascent capitalism required and was partially caused by what he called "the spirit of capitalism," which emerged, he argued, from the Protestant Reformation.[31] When the Christian "call" is secularized, vocation is attached to already existing social privilege, mostly that of civil servants and ministers. Since not everyone has a "position," the "class of the classless" is left out of the vocational ethos. Social stratification appears to be the result of divine will. This results in a hollow ring to the exhortations to work, not unlike those in Proverbs and Ecclesiastes, which assume work relations and conditions will always be as they are. The traditional emphases on work as the means of ordering society and enhancing communal participation thus gave way to increased stratification and individualism in work.

Puritan pastors called their flocks to a life of disciplined work as a way of reducing doubt about their damnation and as a sign to others of their salvation. Work as a necessity for survival or a means of bonding community gave way to work as something positive to do for one's soul.[32] Focusing work on the subjective means of affirming one's calling and election to salvation gave rise to a sense of sovereign individuality and the justification of one's life through proficiency.

The secularization of the doctrines of providence and salvation connects work with the internal laws of progress. Work is good in itself. Work is not fundamentally problematic. It does not need to be redeemed. Work can be affirmed without any dialectic of negation. The new perspective on work produced a radical inversion of the traditional values. People were now individualized and isolated. Each one was set in competitive struggle with everyone else.

The notion of God as Father-taskmaster or as a monadic worker provides justification for (1) laissez-faire and libertarian freedom of entrepreneurs to do anything they want without regard to the other's needs and desires in order to realize one's own interests; (2) paternalistic freedom to use the work of others for one's own ends under the disguise of fatherly concern and protection; (3) individualized freedom and power to make one's destiny exclusively by dint of one's own work and denigration of all those who lack the initiative to be competitive in work. These ideologies portray a view of work that coincides with the nature of the market society as accumulation of wealth.

Behind these ideologies is the faith that the mechanisms of the price system, not the state, can best fulfill the utilitarian calculus (pursue pleasure, avoid pain).[33] The "fate" in which the market mechanisms rest can be trusted to motivate the needed work. How? Fate provides poverty as the key to "persuading" people to work. Poverty is the reason for progress, for without the threat of poverty, people would not work. If you do away with the workers's poverty, you remove the workers's incentive to work and thus their sole means of bettering themselves. Since poverty is the motivation for work, it is also the reason for humanity's unhindered happiness and welfare.

The laissez-faire ideology of work is the most extreme in its support of hierarchical, individualistic, and egoistic modes of work. Even though entrepreneurs have generally recognized the advantage of moral responsibility inculcated in workers by the church, under the spell of laissez-faire they have freed themselves from moral restraint. Laissez-faire expressly condemns the interference of do-gooders because their good intentions always harm those they seek to help by ruining their only chance of getting out of poverty: self-restraint.[34] The old evangelical appeal that the poor could be reformed by emulating the upper classes is rejected. Laissez-faire ideology even drops out the religious motifs of deferred other-worldly rewards for work. The poor now have to be left to their own attempts to better their lives. Manufacturers gained from laissez-faire a sanction to do almost anything as long as it was not benevolent and well-meaning.

In the face of the brutalities of the laissez-faire view of work, paternalism seems more humane. Actually, paternalism is a harking back to the medieval network of dependent relationships. It gives to the superior a religious obligation to reward and punish, to care for and dismiss his employees and the right to expect their dutiful service. As does God the isolated Father who rules with an iron will, the owner has the unquestioned right to control the work and life conditions of his workers. For example, George M. Pullman gave a kind of security to his workers while taking away their dignity in their work and family life. He provided his workers with housing and minimal schooling and health care but in exchange expected not only unquestioning obedience in work but also compliance in his own conception as to how necessities of life were to be delivered. The dependent person, who is usually seen as dishonest and irresolute, owes the master work and respect in exchange for keeping him or her housed and generally fit. The motivation to work is the obligation to return the favor of the master. Paternalism has usually protected both servants and masters from the worst aspects of laissez-faire. But paternalism, however imperfectly disguised, is the appropriation of one human being's labor power by another.[35]

Laissez-faire and paternalism have been durable ideologies by which entrepreneurs and owners explain their actions to each other, but they convey such bleak and hopeless prospects for workers that they can serve as neither explanation nor motivation for the kind of work needed in a complex industrialized society. They are self-defeating for the purposes of industrialization. They create a dependent person without initiative, high skills, discernment, and ability to survive mobility.

In response to the deadening aspects of laissez-faire and paternalism ideologies the most influential and persistent work ethic in the modern world was developed. The success ethic is the individualized theory of progress writ small, in the life of the individual. In its less sophisticated form it is known by the name of Horatio Alger in the United States and by Samuel Smiles's *Self Help* in Britain. But even in its more complex ideological forms the premises are the same, and its essential features continue to appear over and over again in the defense of the advantages of the market household. The success ethic maintains elements from the Protestant work ethic, laissez-faire, and paternalism. Its ostensible intention, however, is to give work incentive to the unemployed or underemployed by convincing them that they are in charge of their own fate. In fact, through work they can break any fate under which they may seem to live.

Most notable in the success ethic is its pretension that poverty is no obstacle to the progress of the individual. Far from being connected with wickedness, failure, and damnation, poverty may even be a blessing and the opulent surroundings of the rich a social disadvantage. For success does not depend on traditional privileges of inherited wealth or even talent. Even the most poverty stricken members of society and the most repressed workers should take hope in what work promises. Positive belief in work and in self are sufficient for overcoming every obstacle. Work allows one to take personal responsibility for one's own well-being. Self-made people do not need to cooperate with anyone else. Like laissez-faire the success ethic contends that benevolence should be suspended, lest it impede persons from improving themselves through work.

The success work ethic hides the reality of class differences and dampens class conflict. By claiming the common background and common interest of the employer and the worker, it gives the appearance of being democratic and egalitarian. But it envisions no work of justice to redress inequalities. Injustices will be automatically wiped away, if indeed they are real, by work. Even if work brings success to a relatively few persons, this ideology of work offers a double advantage. It promises the prospect of material success and moral virtue for those who succeed by hard work; effort is good in itself, and if one only believes, it will eventually bring material rewards. But at the same time it strengthens the dependency and discipline of those who by hard work will nevertheless fail. Despite the fact that it crops up again and again in our society, the success ethic fails to convince the majority of workers to trust their work or their superiors' values to secure themselves and their families.

Thus, in face of the failures of the ideologies of the work ethic, laissez-faire, paternalism, and success through self-help, one might have to draw the conclusion that the market society is not capable of producing an ideology of work that will support the kind of intense work that capitalism requires. For the great majority of people incentives to work based on being taken care of or on success give way to the simple market demand to earn money to buy commodities and services. But as we have seen, this motivation alienates workers from their work and proves constantly insufficient to encourage the work of great energy and discipline required to meet the capitalist's own interests.

Let us summarize the ideologies that attempt to exalt work. Work justifies one's existence. Life is dependent on work and organized around it. Both the self-image and social recognition of the individual depends on his or her work and is measured by the results of his or her work. The meaning of life is dependent on the possibility of work and quality of work. The competitive vocational spirit readily accepts the fragmentation of work as natural and productive so much that it resists any reform of the work situation that would lessen its efficiency and productivity. The meaning of work is fixed ahistorically on the product. The product of work is not shared. Work is understood only as means to an end. This reduces the meaning of work to the working subject and brackets the communal and religious dimensions of work. The result of this view of work is that life becomes meaningless when one is unemployed or does work that is not regarded as valuable. In fact one is not entitled to the basic necessities of life if one does not work.

THE REDEMPTION OF WORK

The third tendency is the distinctively modern ideology of the redemption of work through work. It is found in the thought of Hegel, Saint-Simon, Marx, and Durkheim; it also suffuses much of Western managerialism, which uses psychology and sociology to restructure the worker's attitude and work situation. The Promethean ideologies of work exalt work to the highest conceivable dignity.[36] They draw on the content of Christian eschatological fulfillment and personal redemption as a source to criticize the inadequacies and brutalities of work practices. From the perspective of the Christian doctrine of God this ideological trend distorts the economy of life that God intends by extricating the Son from community with the Father and Holy Spirit. Modern Christology has often helped fill the ideological content of the Promethean ideologies of work. The isolated Son can become the model for *homo faber* and the modern messianism of work.

Hegel, making labor the subject matter of philosophical discourse, reached the opposite conclusion from antiquity. Work is not slavery; rather, it is the means of humanization. For Hegel the dialectic of work is the self-formation and emancipation process of the human spirit.[37] In work human beings create not just something according to an idea, but actually create their world and therefore themselves through work. In work one achieves individual identity by going outside of self and actualizing oneself in the world. I am, because I work. I am what I make out of myself.

According to Marx we express our humanity through artistic, theoretical, and technological work. Work is the revelation of one's hidden, inner self. Our cultural totality is the ongoing labor of men and women in history. Production is the foundation of the relationships, laws, ideas, and institutions of society. Thus the worker is of decisive importance in world history. Only because Marx's estimation of work is so high does he so radically criticize work as it exists in the modern world. People will not recognize their alienation through work until they have been asked to take their work seriously as their self-creation.

Marx argues that workers have become alienated because capital has dehumanized their relationship to work. Human beings have produced their surroundings, but they have been stolen from them. Human beings are important precisely because of their work, but yet work robs and impoverishes them. The market definition of work explained work and its dehumanizing relationships as self-interest. Such cold-blooded and calculated motivations make work meaningless and alienate the worker. In a sense the basic theory of capitalism cannot fathom alienation through work. How can a worker be alienated from work to which he or she has never been committed? The more the bourgeois society emphasizes a work ethic and work-based values, the more this alienation is intensified. The division of labor in machine production turns the worker into a "crippled monstrosity," "riveted to a single, fractional task," "working with the regularity of parts of a machine." The Marxian intention is to redeem work by changing the conditions and relationships of industrialization. How can we make the world a place in which work can be restored and made human? The answer: Remove the obstacles to zealous work which have been erected by capitalism.

Because human beings create themselves, their world, and their future through work, work must be redeemed at all costs. The messianic themes of God's work can be used for this purpose, but only if they are isolated from the creating and sanctifying work of God. When the Trinity is distorted in this way, we are left with the human become Promethean messiah in whose work rests the survival and salvation of the world. The human being takes back all the human excellences which have been projected on God. Now it is up to the human being to go it alone without God. The kingdom of God becomes merely a cipher for human effort or for human agreement with inevitable progress. But how in actuality is work to be redeemed?

In view of the failure of the ideologies designed to overcome alienation in modern work, both capitalism and socialism have turned to managerialism as a way of redeeming work. They agree that the problem is to overcome capitalism's impoverished appeals for work and the bleak picture of the worker's situation in work ideologies. Capitalist managerialism claims that the problem of capitalism is work; socialist managerialism claims that the problem of work is capitalism. The capitalist approach assigns to the manager the Promethean task of saving capitalism by redeeming work. The socialist approach to work assigns to the manager the Promethean task of redeeming work by fulfilling and transcending capitalism.

Managerialism under both capitalism and socialism follows the myth of the objectivity of science as a model for social theory and planning. It attempts to redeem work through the sophisticated applications of psychology and sociology to reconstruct the content of work and its relationships. The older work ideologies failed in their direct ideological appeals for devotion to work. But since they are not owners, it is claimed, managers have a better basis of authority for making appeals for work and cooperation. The impersonal scientific analysis of the situation can take the place of the boss. Furthermore, managers's decisions will never be "wrong" because their decisions are value-free. Managers, social scientists, and administrators can impersonally uncover correct solutions to problems and thus organize social life by organizing work. Management, like politics, becomes something like social physics. It takes on the unquestioned aura of a savior.[38]

Technocratization, rationalization, and efficiency under a managerialist guise, whether capitalist or socialist, do not solve the problem of work. The scientific control of work definitely carries social values. The dominative character of work can be changed only if these social values are submitted to criticism, not just by elites but by people at the grassroots. Work continues to serve the interests of those who control it, unless the relationships of those within the household are changed.

Sin, Evil, and Work

What does the economy of God tell us about why work must be redeemed? One important characteristic of some of the biblical traditions is that they look at work as a worker does. Israel's history with God begins with the stark reality of human bondage through forced labor. Work means "no freedom." In fact, much of Israel's history is lived under the conditions in which the product of one's labor is expropriated by another. One plants and another harvests. One builds and another occupies.

In the midst of societies that practice slavery as the will of the gods Israel stands out in asking why work leads to domination and exploitation. The basic answer is that bondage *through* work is ultimately based in bondage *to* work. Human work becomes destructive because of the sin of the working human being. God gives the human being an infinite capacity for love because God wants another who can love God freely and infinitely. This love of God is meant to be expressed also through the human being's work. The mystery of work is the power given to the human being to love God by serving life in God's creation. But this power for work is turned into the power to enslave. The human being misdirects this infinite capacity for love of God and invests it in self and things, in the power and privilege that will secure oneself. And thus the human being's God-given capacity for work gets caught up in an infinite love of what is not God. Distorted work is misdirected love. The very power God gives for work is also the power by which human beings set themselves over against God, destroy creation, and turn the human community into constant strife, fear, and anxious greed. Were it not for work human beings would not utterly distort life by making their own gods and their own counter-creation. By building their Babels they fool themselves into believing that there is no limit to human work. "Their land is filled with idols; they bow down to the work of their hands, to what their own fingers have made" (Isa. 2:8; cf. Rom. 1:25).

Thus the mystery of work is also its idolatrous service of death. Work, beginning with the work of Cain, is an attempt to escape death, but it ends up serving death. The most normal thing imaginable, work, becomes a threat to the creation because it threatens God's righteousness, which keeps creation in being. Work becomes odious. "What does a man gain by all the toil at which he toils under the sun?" (Eccles. 1:3). Work becomes a burden because the human being's household relationships with God, with each other, and with the creation have been spoiled. Work can no longer be done with innocence. In short, human work produces chaos and therefore work has to deal with the threat of chaos in creation (weeds and brambles) and in one's own heart (sweat and tears).

The human condition is that we depend infinitely on the capacity of our work. We expect that the products of our work will secure us. And yet we have the prevailing awareness that work can never accomplish what we expect of it; work can never finally secure us. Demonic powers gain control over us through our urge to make ourselves through work. Our idolatry gives power and authority over us to the products of our own work. The working human being is an anxious creature. We are neurotically coerced to protect our successes and products with our lives as though they constituted our lives. So we invest our livelihood in awesome weapons which, we wager, have the ultimate power to secure because they have the ultimate power to destroy the world. Nuclear weapons have become in our time the comprehensive symbol of the power of idolatrous human work. They are "the sacrilege set up where it ought not to be" (Mark 13:14).

Sinful work leads to the evil of work. Prideful work leads people to exclude others from their work and its fruits. The work of those who have property and power overwhelms the work of those without property and power. The powerful "work" in order to make the work of others produce riches for themselves. They "abhor justice and pervert all equity." Without even getting out of bed they manipulate the economic instruments for impoverishing others, "because it is in the power of their hand." "They covet fields, and seize them; and houses, and take them away; they oppress a man and his house, a man and his inheritance" (Mic. 2:1–2; cf. Amos 6:3–7). The work that supports the luxurious life of the "cows of Bashan," oppresses the poor and crushes the needy (Amos 4:1). This is a denial of the fundamental truth God's economists know about themselves: Once they were slaves and thus they may never enslave again. It is the abomination of abominations that Solomon builds the house of the Lord with the *corvée*, "forced labor" (1 Kings 9:15).

No one may "own" the labor of another person. But in our society we have become confused about this. When labor was made into a commodity in order to form a market in labor, we developed the simple notion that labor could be bought and sold. This is usually not said publicly, however, since it patently denies the dignity of the human being. Rather it is said that the employer buys the right to command the labor of another for a certain period; or that in exchange for wages the worker agrees to become obedient to the employer for a period of time. How different is this from the notion of owning the labor of another when the employer succeeds in gaining control over the consciousness, values, and family relations of the worker? And then we still have the thorniest question: If one cannot buy the labor of another person, how can it be justified that the employer gains the exclusive right to what the laborer produces?

God the Economist Redeems Work

God's economic work does not simply condemn, criticize, and relativize our work but also redeems the household from the dehumanizing work by which the members of the household want to lord it over each other and the creation. "All the work which the Lord did for Israel" (Josh. 24:31) was the work of redeeming Israel's own work from the power of death and sin.

God's redeeming work begins with God's creating work. God's work of creating has often been construed in tyrannical and mechanistic terms. But God's work is not that of a manufacturer who out of raw material "makes" a product by grasping and controlling. God, the single One who has power over the vanity of non-being, calls the creation into being through God's word of righteousness. God's work is not coercive but a passionate evocation of what does not exist to enter into God's grace and thus have being (cf. Rom. 4:17; Ps. 74:12–14; 8:5). Liberating everything that is out of the chaos of nothingness is a costly liberation, just as is that of the exodus and the cross. God's work is a struggle against the power of death (*mot*), the power of nothingness. The presence of night, storm, and sea symbolize the presence of the power of death from the very beginning of creation. Creation is no easy victory. Those who see God's work against death in purely effortless terms are already submitting the biblical narratives to ideological use. God suffers by experiencing the power of nothingness, which wants to hold all things captive to its emptiness.[39] God overcomes the recalcitrance of the *nihil* by embracing it. This work is dangerous and painful. It does not immediately issue in success. God declares that God's work is "very good," but not "perfect." God's work of creation does not end on the "sixth day." Nothing in creation is yet completely safe from death, the last and greatest enemy of God's household. God's work of creation continues every moment in God's liberating struggle against the power of death.

Transformed human work has its source in God's kenosis. "You have burdened me [caused me work] with your sins, you have wearied me with your iniquities" (Isa. 43:24–25). The passion story of Jesus is fashioned after the model of the slave of God in Deutero-Isaiah.[40] Here the language of the work of God refers to suffering, sacrifice, self-giving, emptying, free slaveship, and surrendering self. God's chosen one (*ebed Yahweh*) is a worker who carries our iniquities as a great burden (Isaiah 53). According to John the crucified Jesus speaks of his work being finished and his lordship over the world is pictured as happening in his divine slaveship for all (Philippians 2). God becomes the *metic*, the slave, and we God's free people. God is Lord of the household precisely by being the Economist, servant, of the household. Through the sacrifice of the Son God takes into God's own community the human death-serving work which is sin. This is God's grief work. Having the same mind as Christ, our lives are to be conformed to this self-giving work. Work is self-sacrifice. Love is the power and goal of work (1 Corinthians 12, 13).

Our work is useless in creating the righteousness by which we may stand against death and sin. God's work saves us from the attempt to justify and create ourselves through our own effort (Rom. 3:19–31; Galatians 3). The existence of the human being cannot be defined by work or made dependent on work, however necessary work is. God's gracious justification means that no one must justify himself or herself through work nor does anyone have to create or realize himself or herself through work. If that were so, the unemployed would be without rights and the handicapped unreal. We are able to work at our salvation with fear and trembling only because "God is at work in you, both to will and to work for his good pleasure" (Phil. 2:12). Being justified means no longer being dictated to by the demonic powers. Released from work as frenetic self-assertion, the justified person can enter into work as free service of God's grace (Rom. 12:1).

God's redemption of work is the possibility of radical transformation of the work relationships of the household and of its relationship to the Economist. Baptism is the sign of Christian work in God's economy. Those who are baptized enter into the Triune Community's history with the creation and thus are called to cooperate with God's work of building the *basileia* household of justice and peace in which all creatures will find home. Through baptism the Holy Spirit creates a new person with a new name and an open future and makes possible a work that corresponds to and participates in God's work of creation, redemption, and new creation. The primary vocation of the baptized person is to be "in Christ" and "in the Spirit" (1 Cor. 7:17) so that the world can trust in the *basileia* (1 Corinthians 14). "All work takes place for the Lord" (1 Thess. 2:12; 4:9–11; 2 Cor. 7:17), "for the sake of Christ" (2 Thess. 3:6; Acts 20:35, Col. 3:17). Abound "in the work of the Lord, knowing that in the Lord your labor is not in vain" (1 Cor. 15:58).

For Paul, being an apostle means being a "fellow worker" for the *basileia* (Col. 4:11). He carries all the marks of the servanthood of Christ (Rom. 1:1). Missionary and congregational work is described as the heaviest and most unpleasant work of a slave (*koros*). Proclaiming the gospel is a necessity (*ananke*) which he cannot escape (1 Cor. 9:16–17). When he claims that he has "worked more" (2 Cor. 11:23–25), he has in mind labors, imprisonment, beatings, mortal danger, persecution, slander, hunger, cold, theft, nakedness, and constant concern about the congregation. All are work for the *basileia*.

Because the *basileia* is present, the household of God can arrange its work relationships according to God's sabbath justice. The sabbath is equalitarian; it is common to all. It can't be purchased. The intention of God's sabbath is not simply to interrupt work or to make work possible again on the old terms; it is to end the injustices that come through work. On the sabbath no one can work, especially not one's manservant or maidservant, especially not one's beast of burden (Exod. 20:9–11). According to the Torah's demands for the Jubilee Year, which is a sabbath year, not even the earth can work (Lev. 25:1–7). Precisely in the here and now in which God's people live the sabbath breaks the exploitation as well as burden of work. God's life-giving justice reigns. The sabbath is a real, if partial, overcoming of the domination and destruction of human work. It is the fragmentary presence under the conditions of history of God's ultimate redemption of work. Every sabbath is a sacramental taste and a glimpse of God's coming triumph when in God's shalom the creation will bloom without the exploitation of work.[41] This does not mean that there will be no work in God's ultimate household of peace. The kingdom of heaven is not a retirement home in which people rock away for eternity. Rather, it is the reign of God's righteousness, in which work will be utterly redeemed and in which God's people will participate in the infinite joy of God's creative work. Thus the sabbath qualifies all work.

Far from eliminating the sabbath, Jesus therefore brings the sabbath into the workday, into everyday life. The sabbath is meant not only for rest but also for the surpassing joy of feeding the hungry, healing the sick, and making home for the homeless.

REDEEMING WORK

We have detected some theological elements of ideologies that justify dehumanizing practices of work and have criticized them according to the Trinity as the hermeneutic of the biblical narratives of God. Work ideologies make unemployment, underpaid work, isolated work, and degraded work seem tolerable. The work of God as known in the triune community's uncovering in Israel and Jesus Christ cannot be used to justify inhumanity in work.

We now ask what this trinitarian hermeneutic might offer in terms of orientation for new perspectives on work. If any expectation that work can be completely transcended is utopian in character, we can nevertheless speak of ways in which God seeks to redeem work under the conditions of history. What would liberated modes of work look like? How can the congregation as the alternative economy of God envision and demonstrate them? How can it practice "education for good work"?[42]

The Right to Work

Our view of work will not change significantly until we realize that work is not simply a commodity to be defined by workplace efficiency and distributed according to market rules. Work has to do with livelihood, with inclusion in the community, and with a sense of personal dignity and well-being. A humanizing economy depends upon the creation of meaningful work for every person who is able and wants to work. This is necessary for the formation of a community that can realize human rights and redistribute wealth. If work serves the socialization of the person, especially in an increasingly service-oriented society in which work takes place cooperatively, then unemployment threatens people with the loss of community or a kind of social death. Every person has a right to participate in the communal process according to his or her abilities with just compensation and means of deep satisfaction.[43] Work is a way of belonging to, sharing in, and contributing to the life of the community.

The market and its rules, though they are valuable in many respects, are on their own not capable of defining, motivating, and distributing work exhaustively. Other institutions of the community and the state must take responsibility for this as well. This inevitably raises the problem of coercion in work, though we have seen that, despite claims to the contrary, coercion also exists in the labor market. The inalienable right to meaningful work according to one's abilities presupposes freedom. When the market fails to provide work for all, some proponents of the market seem satisfied to allow state laws to coerce people to work. Workfare programs under the banner of "right to work" retain elements of such coercion. They are often thinly disguised measures to secure cheaper labor by tapping the pool of welfare recipients. It should not be surprising in a society that seeks dignity for all that persons will not accept just any job that is offered.

Without employment security, work is little more rewarding than a painful necessity. When a company lays off workers for the sake of greater technological efficiency or moves its labor market in search of cheaper labor costs, it should be held accountable to provide its share of the cost of creating new jobs and stabilizing the community from which it is removing jobs. Increased profits through automation or through the use of the labor platforms of Third World countries cannot justify the loss of communal cooperation, which is a higher survival value than increased profits.

From the Christian perspective work is fundamentally *diakonia*. Diakonic work is the daily work of Christians in the alternative economy of the household of God. The congregation should be the laboratory where baptismal work is learned. In the congregation part of the world is made into a witness to the power of the Holy Spirit at work and thus a challenge to the way the world organizes work.

The challenge of the congregation is to find diakonic work for all members in the congregation. One of the greatest debilitating factors of our congregations is that there are so many "unemployed" persons in them. Without work the baptized person is robbed of his or her ministry.[44] Within the calling to be in Christ, all are given special ministries, which are their gifts from the Holy Spirit (1 Cor. 12:27–31; 4:11). Almost every person, even the extremely disabled, can contribute some form of work. Prayer and simple testimony are also forms of work irreplaceably necessary to the life of the community. The gifts/tasks of each person are for building the household of God, which exists not for its own sake but for the sake of God's making the world into a home. Perhaps the most important gift we should look for in a pastor is the gift to discern the gifts of others. Pastors should have imagination and courage in discerning the gifts of persons and calling them into the work that is peculiarly theirs.

The alternative economy of the congregation should demonstrate to society how full employment can happen with noncoerced and satisfying work. Of course, incentives for work and reward systems in the church are quite different from those in the market economy. But such alternative incentives and rewards are precisely what the public household needs to see.

Incentive for Work

We have seen that market theory is incapable by itself to motivate humanizing work; the ideological incentives that are used for this purpose enhance domination through work.

In the congregation work can be understood as self-giving for the sake of participation in the fullness of life. Work is service to God and the human being. This is an incentive for work that does not serve the deadly compulsion to work as self-justification. Because God's *basileia* has come in Christ, work for the sake of the Lord receives a meaning that reaches beyond every human grounding of work. Work is a way of practicing patience as we are being formed, not certain of what we shall become. In the time of preparation, maturation, waiting, and anticipation work becomes very significant. If work is done as discipleship in the self-emptying Christ, then it reaches beyond all possible success to participation in the resurrection and the reign of God's righteousness. The true worth of work will be revealed only at the end time with the utter defeat of sin and the realization of God's glory in all things (Eph. 1:3–23; Matt. 7:24–27; 1 Cor. 3:10–15; 2 Cor. 5: 1–10).

The "more than enough" value of the messianic hope results in added effort, self-denial, and self-giving. Work receives a stimulus that moves people to invest more of themselves than is necessary and therefore to expect from work more than the earthly results would justify. The excess of expectations leads to the life of "going the second mile" depicted in Jesus' parables. This is the eschatological logic of the kingdom which market thinking gropes to explain.[45] This is work done not out of market assumptions of scarcity but out of the abundance of God's promise. Only out of such a sense of abundance can work be done in solidarity with and for the sake of the poor and oppressed, those who have been systemically excluded from the household.

Work in Community

The comprehensive meaning of work is active participation in the communal, social process. A new definition of work will have to go beyond the description of work as merely productive, wage earning, business, or professional. When we limit work to these definitions, the broader dimensions of work from which society actually lives remain invisible or repressed. Work is falsely defined unless we include reproductive or generative work. This includes all forms of familial and social service. The value of work has to do with increasing relationships among human beings and between human beings and God.[46] Destroying the community of work through relationships of domination and dependence dehumanizes work.

Redeemed work requires a complex participatory consciousness. New technological and organizational demands made on economic life are causing shifts from the production of goods to the production and processing of information and culture. This growing centrality of knowledge at the heart of economic dynamics contains the seeds of new kinds of domination through work. Those who are not given the opportunity to gain expertise in information and culture exchange are left out of the distribution of work. Workers from whom production and organizational information is withheld remain in a constant dependent relationship.

The only nondominative way beyond the destructive struggle of worker and management rights is genuinely shared authority and actual access to power on the part of all who work. Workers should have real influence over workplace relations and decisions. Meaningful participation in decision-making, whether by direct or elected representation, should be consistently available to each member, at least in the area of one's competence and concern. Top decision-makers should be ultimately accountable to and removable by working membership. And discipline of workers should be democratized by an independent appeals system composed of peers as much as possible.

Direct worker involvement in enterprise decisions is the best guarantee against armies of supervisors, producing nothing but grudging effort, and against costly unemployment leading to increased social unrest and crime. A highly democratic culture will not exist for long with highly undemocratic rules. Democratic rules shape actors who are capable of democratic participation. And without such democratic actors the culture and rules of democracy cannot be maintained and renewed. In fact, the future of democracy may be decided by the question of the democratization of the workplace. But there cannot be such democratic involvement without full sharing with employees of management-level information and management level expertise. Management cannot produce efficiency in work when profits are always put ahead of the community of work.[47]

The Equity of Work

Greed and fear become the work incentives if workers have no equity in working relationships or direct relation to the results of their work.[48] Democratic participation and work security lead to commitment and cooperation.[49] Equity in work depends upon workers having guaranteed individual rights, corresponding to political liberties. In the present-day workplace the problem of equity centers on status, pay, and share in the product of work. If individual return to workers based merely on the surplus they produce is considered the only way to guarantee efficiency, efficiency will always eclipse equity. Equity, however, is in fact the precondition for work that is both communal and efficient. The most momentous problem of equity now, as throughout most of history, is the question of the distribution of work's surplus. Equity in work requires fundamental change in the rules of production and of ownership decisions about capitalization, expansion, and diversification.

It should now be clear that we are not likely to change our praxis of property and work without an accompanying change in our perception and praxis of needs.

Chapter 7 | **God and Needs**

OD THE ECONOMIST WORKS TO BUILD households in which all of God's creatures can find home. Whether all potential members would be included in the predominant political economy of a time has always depended in large part on how it has understood human needs. What we think about needs shapes our beliefs and practices about consumption and about what, how, and to whom the goods of the *oikos* should be distributed. The praxis of economic justice is shaped by the character of needs. The character of needs is decisive for the *oikos*. The perceived character of God and the way human beings live before God will ultimately determine both the shape of needs and the means for meeting needs.

Sin is always at work in the way human beings define and satisfy needs. Our prideful conception and uses of needs threaten the household with inhumanity. Needs can be defined systemically in such a way that many people have no access to provisions for their needs while others are free to luxuriate in the imagination of one need after another. Some have no daily bread while others claim massive wealth to titillate their dulled senses and occupy their empty time. When in the same public household some live in luxury while others scrounge for the barest means of survival, a cancerous injustice is planted that will eventually destroy the entire household. There is no doubt that sin shows itself prominently in the needfulness of human beings. But sin is no excuse for the church to turn its back on God's own work to overcome our sinful distortion of needs.

The church in every historical epoch should enter into the public debates over needs and consumption and the distribution of

157

social goods. Up until the modern age it has usually done that. But in our time the church, like all other institutions, has been affected by a revolution in the language and experience of needs. The long tradition of true and false needs has been declared *passé* in our economy. In the past God language and metaphysics provided the framework in which society could articulate valid needs as opposed to destructive needs. But in the market society needs themselves have taken the place of God talk and metaphysics.

To the church is left the care of emotional or "spiritual" needs. Many churches also try to meet the needs of starving and homeless people on our city streets or in North African deserts. But they seldom question the meaning of needs in the public discourse of our economy, a discourse that has also invaded the life of the church, and the effect of that discourse on society. The church often simply assumes that it is a need-meeting institution and thereby lets itself be shaped by the public language and experience of needs. Whereas both capitalist and Marxist conceptions of needs based in nature steadfastly exclude God in formally defining needs, our economy nevertheless depends on God concepts to justify needs and patterns of consumption that are dehumanizing. Should not the church ask whether the public language of needs in our political economy has played a major role in shaping its worship of God, or whether its own understanding and worship of God plays a role in the way needs are officially defined in our society?

The church's public witness and its contribution to the question of needs in the global household should depend on the peculiar perspective on needs that the Triune God gives us. Needs arise and are met in the context of God's creating and sustaining a just household for God's creatures. Human needs are a dimension of God's righteousness in giving access to livelihood to all creatures. Life in the economy of the Triune God calls into question the way we perceive, name, and practice needs in our public household.

THE NEEDFULNESS
OF HUMAN BEINGS

To be human is to have needs. But what should we do with them? Can we control our needs or do they inevitably control us? Much of modernity answers that needs are so much the essence of human beings that, far from being controlled, they should be given free reign. The more needs we have, it is argued, the better life we will have. Needs are the impetus to vitality, productivity, progress, and success. As civilization progresses, needs proliferate, and this expansion of needs makes life fuller and more meaningful.

The premodern tradition, on the other hand, has generally viewed needs as the weakness and downfall of human beings. Desire, hunger, wants, and needs are what get human beings into trouble. According to Ecclesiastes, "The eye is not satisfied with seeing, nor the ear filled with hearing." Because of what Samuel Johnson called the "hunger of imagination" we are always able to imagine more than we have. And imagining more is tantamount to needing more. It is impossible to limit needs. If desire is not negated and needs severely limited, the hopeless effort to fulfill them will destroy human beings and their communities. Thus the ideal state would be to eliminate all needs. The philosophical traditions of the Greek Enlightenment and the religions of Buddhism and Hinduism recommend this prescription. So has Christianity at times.

Much of the West's tradition has emphasized the control of needs. For this purpose Christianity has traditionally joined in partnership with both transcendentalist and naturalist doctrines of true and false needs. The transcendentalist approach looks for a transnatural arbiter of needs. As did Freud in our time, Plato in the *Philebus* divided the human being into conflicting parts which must be governed by a transcendent monarchal principle such as *reason* or the *superego*. Both natural desires of the libido and culturally conditioned needs must be ruled. Whether a need is true or false depends on whether it is ruled by a transcendent common conception of the good.

The naturalist traditions of true and false needs, on the contrary, did not trust the cultural criteria of needs, including the monotheistic God depicted in classical philosophy, and thus inaugurated a distinctive criticism charging civilization with responsibility for distorted needs. A "natural" need, so argued the naturalists, is true, as opposed to those generated artificially, that is culturally or religiously.[1] Combining this with the Stoic ideal of self-sufficiency yielded the claim that the good person is one of "few needs." Virtue required minimizing one's chances for corruption by reducing one's needs to a physical minimum.[2] For monastic as well as ordinary Christians this remained a norm until the eighteenth century.

The naturalist tradition emerged again in the modern Enlightenment. Locke, Hume, Rousseau, Marx, the Utilitarians, Marcuse, Fromm, and, to some extent, Freud all return to the basic naturalist position of the ancient materialists, though of course with decidedly different outcomes. All look to some conception of nature, not God, as the governor of needs. Whereas the theological and philosophical traditions had regarded desire and passions as dangerous to the spirit, Locke called desire the basis of all human experience. "Natural passions," once considered unruly, were slowly changed into rational calculating interests.[3] Needs gradually became reasonable and, indeed, capable of giving order to life. Hume and later the Utilitarians replaced all metaphysical notions of God and the "dark melancholy" of religious transcendence with human need itself as the regulator of human life.[4] Everything that traditional metaphysics accomplished with the divine attributes could be collapsed into human need. In spite of our perplexity, claimed Hume, we find sufficient meaning in life through meeting our bodily and social needs, much more so than in metaphysical speculations. Daily life and morality could be organized and governed by needs. The traditional person "of few needs" was replaced by the individual for whom needs are the source of meaning and order.

In his *Philosophy of Right* Hegel described modern society as a "system of needs" and thus articulated the decisive importance of needs as the glue of modern society.[5] All human beings are inherently insufficient in themselves. It is in struggling to meet their needs that they become aware of themselves, of history, and of nature. Awareness of one's own lack leads to social relationships in which persons engage each other in order to meet each other's needs. The human project is the progressive, mutual meeting of our needs.

NEEDS IN THE MARKET SOCIETY

But it was not long before needs began to lose the sense of Stoic control still maintained by Hume. Bentham and Mill, reflecting the expanding economic dominance of Britain's ruling class, understood progress to be the move from bodily natural needs to higher needs, which are produced artificially by culture. Neither the transcendentalists nor the naturalists reckoned adequately with the potential of the human spirit to create spiritualized, artificial scarcity in the midst of plenty. They did not see clearly the way in which needs would be connected with infinity, insatiability, and necessity, that is, with a new "metaphysics" or religion of need. In previous eras desires and needs of the individual were in perpetual tension with social norms of a stable society, but the modern concept of needs is so unequivocal about the centrality of the needs of the individual that society is reduced to a handmaid of these needs.

In the market society needs must be as expansive and limitless as the desired growth. Neoclassical economic theory employs *need* as the centerpiece, a technical term meant to guarantee the unlimited growth of the economy. It interprets a unique historical phenomenon, the *acquisitive orientation,* as a universal human inclination.[6] In so doing it breaks with earlier capitalist views of needs.[7] If there is no end to the growing abundance of society, the avoidance of enjoyment through ascetic self-control appears irrational. Any sense of salvation connected with repression and thus with economics had to be eliminated as irrational. Need satisfaction becomes simply a dimension of rational economic behavior. The household no longer has to grapple with the question of true and false needs. And it appears of no value to inject God into the question.

But if economic theory was going to depend on the notion of unlimited needs, it had to confront the problem of satiation in nature. The urgency of need declines with increasing satisfaction. People can have too much of a good thing. If they are satiated, it does not make sense to increase the volume of goods and services they can use. They will not desire an ever-increasing standard of living. If each individual could reach a point where more goods and services yielded less satisfaction, economic growth would be desirable neither for individuals nor nations. Orthodox economists depict this fact with the term "declining marginal utility."

How, then, can it be argued that new needs can always be created? By portraying the human being as *naturally* insatiable. This was done by conflating needs in general with "natural" bodily appetites and by arguing that the natural process itself creates continuous tension aimed at pleasurable satisfaction.[8] Thus it could be claimed that unceasing economic growth was rooted in nature. All economic activity could be explained on the level of physiological need satisfaction. "If everything we are producing, selling and consuming today in the advanced complex Western economies could be interpreted as satiating a quasi-physiological drive or need, our economic activity would need no further justification."[9] Reducing needs to their "natural" origin meant just the opposite from what the classical "naturalist" tradition had meant: Needs are not limited and satiable but in principle unlimited and insatiable. The groundwork was laid for the notion of *unlimited growth.*

Needs are also crucial to the theory of distribution in the economy. The market can take care of all distribution if we guarantee the liberty of each individual to determine his or her needs and to choose how to meet those needs within the market mechanism. The market offers a theory of distribution without traditional theories of justice and without the means of coercion required by these theories. No one should be able to tell me what I need. It would be "unnatural" for the state or anyone else to dictate what I need, since my needs arise from the well of my own natural existence. The attraction of this theory of distribution lies largely in its simplicity and its noncoercive regulation of conflict by the rules of the market. The theory would not be so effective, however, were it not for the experience and language of need that pervade our culture.

GOD CONCEPTS
IMPLICIT IN MODERN NEEDS

There are tendencies in the traditional depiction of God that are reflected in modern conceptions of the human needs. An example is the notion of the God who has no needs (aseity). Although our public household views all human beings as "in need," the God without needs reappears as the desired image of fulfilled humanity in whom all needs are met. The individual in whom needs are realized is construed as the epitome of power and freedom. Such an individual would be an independent being without relationships to others.

A second tendency is the traditional identification of God's lordship with God's ability to decide without constraint. The infinity of God's decision reappears in modern economic anthropology as the freedom of pure choice. This means particularly the freedom to choose and meet one's own needs. For many people in our public household, freely choosing and meeting their needs comes close to defining the essence of life. We have made the meaning of needs the meaning of life.

Finally, Christian theology has had the tendency to picture God's will as cosmic necessity. The necessitous will of God is reflected in economic anthropology in terms of the identification of human needs with necessity. And thus the Aristotelian definition of freedom as living according to the necessity of one's life gets interpreted as freedom means realizing the necessity of one's needs. This is the heart of morality in a needs-driven society.

Implicit in these ideologies of need are notions of God in whose captivity the church is unable to recognize and criticize the ways in which "needs" are used to prevent the access of many to livelihood in the public household and also to the household of the church. Let us turn to a critique of these God concepts.

DIVINE ASEITY AND THE LIBERTY OF THE INDEPENDENT HUMAN BEING

The idea that consumers' needs and wants should be satisfied and that the consumer is king is universally accepted in neoclassical economic theory. Orthodox economic theory maintains that giant corporations serve the satisfaction of human wants originating naturally within the psyche of the individual consumer. If one assumes that a free competitive market leads to the maximum possible satisfaction of such needs originating in the individual, the free market is justified because it allegedly assures consumers' sovereignty.

What view of God supports the human compulsion to meet every need? God conceived as one, indivisible divine essence identified with the Father finds a reflection in the individual whose needs emerge in isolation from all others and who lives for the satisfaction of every need. The problem with many traditional doctrines of God was that they did not begin with the social experience of the Spirit. Thinking of God without the experience of Jesus and the Spirit leads to thinking of God as the unrelated self. God as a radical individual essence is the being who has no needs and no external relationships, who cannot go beyond God's self and give self away. This is the being who is free from others through being "apathetic," that is, incapable of suffering with others. God is a private individual meditating for eternity upon his own perfections.

This God is a model for the individual who, according to the logic of the market household, lives privately and narcissistically. Intimate experience of the self's wants is the only measure of the meaning of reality.[10] I know my needs "immediately," but how can I know the needs of others? Evaluating an economy according to how it satisfies the original needs of individual consumers promotes the attitude that private wants are inherently superior to public needs. Our culture is increasingly deprived of belief in the public. But the absence of communal meaning forces the individual into the anxiety of making all life decisions on his or her own.[11] The drive to define one's own needs in isolation from others leads to a society of strangers.

The New Testament narratives, however, do not support a view of God consonant with the individual chooser of needs. They did not have an essence of God in mind as a starting point, but rather the experience of Jesus as the coming redemption of the world. And it is precisely this experience of Jesus that the New Testament writers call *pneuma*, Spirit.[12] All New Testament theologies thematize this communal experience of Jesus in the Holy Spirit. God is not a radical individual; neither is the human being. Needs cannot be defined and satisfied in terms of our individuality. Our needs are a function of our communal being.

DIVINE SOVEREIGNTY
AND NEEDS AS NECESSITY

A paradox in the traditional doctrine of God is reflected in the juxtaposition of freedom and necessity in the economic sphere. God's sovereignty has generally been regarded in terms of God's freedom. God's lordship or divinity consists in being able to make free decisions and eternal decrees. But, on the other hand, God's freedom is thought as the other side of God's lordship. The free choice of God's will is best depicted, claims much of the tradition, in the categories of necessity. God's freedom is also God's necessity. The discourse of needs in our public household utilizes a strange conflation of freedom and necessity which has nevertheless become second nature to us.

Why do sensible people subject themselves to needs? Why are we in love with our needs? Why do we assume that needs are good things without which society could not operate? Why do we disregard the needs of those who have been excluded from the public household? The answer in large part is that we have lost the ability to agree on the character of needs.[13] For some needs it is not necessary to ask, What for? "I am hungry," "I am cold," "I am lonely" seem to express needs of such universality that no one questions them, at least in terms of their own needs. But on many needs there is no consensus as to what they are needed for.

In response to this predicament we give to need the character of necessity. Need brings together by association facts, nature, necessity, and the centrality of the self. Needs serve the function of reconciling self and the objective world. By replacing drive with need, the conflict between the pleasure principle and the reality principle is abolished at a stroke. Determinism and individualism, freedom and necessity can be embraced at the same time. A world reduced to factual needs appears to make life simpler. Our life is governed by a set of facts: need to work, needs of children, need for security.

By diverting attention from goals, values, goods, and ends, needs hide the lack of consensus in a pluralistic society. Dissensus seems to disappear as soon as the discourse of needs takes over. Instead of debating goals and alternatives, we can talk simply about the meeting of needs. Without reference to values and goals, we imagine that the imperative derives from the need, which is believed to be a fact. We imagine that people would not do anything if they did not *need* to.[14] They need to have children. They need to work. They need to shop. The airline attendant says, "I need you to put your luggage under the seat." Needs bring with them the connotation of necessity. I don't have to say that I am ambitious; only that I need to do or have something. Established needs signify a right, a necessary claim to something and thus one can want it without condemnation.

The effect of not considering goals is that the need becomes absolute. It ceases to be a means toward something and becomes an end in itself. We change into necessities work, sex, and family life which were intended to be free responses to God's abundant goodness. The duty of parents to love children is reduced to talk about the needs of children. Needs refer to the objective facts of how things are, facts of the psychology of childhood. Parents are compelled in their decisions by the needs of their children. If a job has ceased to be a means toward a goal of income, creativity, fulfillment, joy, identity, or reducing loneliness, it becomes an end in itself. When work is nothing but a need, it is blind and easily controllable by others. Politicians gain public support by speaking of needs and immediately turn them into imperatives. The need for Strategic Defense Initiative is immediately the necessity of the Strategic Defense Initiative.

The individual is supposed to be in control of his or her destiny, but we cannot stand the loneliness and responsibility this casts upon us. We have proclaimed the right to choose needs a sacred right. But our free choice constantly confounds us. As Augustine said long ago, we can never be certain whether we have chosen rightly. Grace, therefore, claimed Augustine, would be necessary for a humane life. But in a society of absolute free choice, there is no grace. So, we make choices on our own, but then hide behind the rhetoric of need in order to avoid responsibility for the choice. We baptize our choices under the name of need; they become unquestionable as need. Need removes the fear of freedom from us as effectively as did heteronomous authority in medieval times.

Thus we become convinced that without our needs we would not be able to make sense of our lives.[15] Once needs are thought of as giving meaning and order to our lives, they play an important moral function. They are a way of talking about and justifying our actions. Divinely revealed law and autonomous morality are replaced by needs. In the everyday language of need we try to derive moral imperatives from a supposedly factual world of needs. Expressed needs, we think, immediately justify the enormous consumption of wealthy people in the North Atlantic community, while others in the global economy do not have their most basic needs met. And the state of our public discourse is such that need no longer seems even helpful in describing and facing this situation of gross inequality. The language of needs in the market society has made the language of justice highly problematic.

There have been in the modern world numerous critics who have detected the paradox in the market society that upholds the liberty to determine needs and yet defines needs in terms of imperatives. The market ideology argues for the free choice of consumers while ignoring how these supposedly free choices are subtly but grossly manipulated by the corporations and ideology of our society. Rousseau already sounded the alarm that has been heard also from many critics of civilization in our century: We are liable to enslave ourselves by false needs and be exploited by those who define and meet our needs.[16] Needs defined by the individual's freedom and necessity do not lead to an ordered system, but rather to an increasingly exploitative society.

The severest critique of the neoclassical view of needs has come from a neo-Marxism which is itself also grounded in the naturalist tradition.[17] Capitalism was supposed to dissolve because of the internal contradictions of overproduction and underconsumption. A new natural theory of needs seeks to explain how it is that a constantly expanding production continues to find a market for its commodities in consumers who, in their dual roles as workers and consumers, do not seem to resent a double exploitation, having both to produce and consume the commodities capitalism requires.[18]

Neo-Marxism conflates the Marxian notion of "false consciousness" with the Freudian "unconscious." "Capitalism is able to reproduce itself by generating in its subjects a constant and expanding desire for its products, which in turn are geared to the promotion of certain psychic needs which feed off this calculated stimulus."[19] The unconscious is penetrated by the socioeconomic structure itself, so that libidinal instincts—the desire for love, self-esteem, other-esteem, security, sexual gratification, and so on—are placed at its service.[20] Anything in this society can potentially be sold. Selling means identifying an artificial need and then identifying the need with a marketable commodity.[21]

The psychic repression on which Freud thought culture was based is now described as a repressed awareness of the evils of capitalism, a repression willingly exchanged for the greater gratifications of capitalist society. Sublimated needs do not produce civilization; rather they enable a repressive society to keep its members enslaved.[22] In this setting alienation is experienced not as a sense of injustice at the exploitation of labor, but a more generalized psychic malaise in which, although an ever-increasing range of satisfactions is offered, a deep discontent persists.

This theory of repressed and artificial needs has been used to explain exploitation, imperialism, conspicuous consumption, deprivation, and waste. The problem is that it denies the ethical character of these problems. It puts these problems further out of reach by insisting that false needs are embedded in the unconscious, possibly even in the instinctual structure itself and are therefore beyond scrutiny, control, and responsibility of the individual and society.[23] The theory leaves unclear how people could resist ideology at all. It depends on the notion that there must be a social system in which all false needs will be eliminated.[24] But this theory does not offer a way to bring about such a society without forced engineering. It assumes that the false needs of capitalism are so embedded in the psyche of the morally deficient masses that select elites will have to run the revolution until the masses can be educated to understand their own needs. It does not demonstrate a transformative praxis because it is not incarnational.

DIVINE INFINITY
AND HUMAN INSATIABILITY

Another distortion of the Trinity views God as pure spirit. When God is depicted as the Spirit without communion with the Son the church tends to conform to society's growth-orientation based on insatiability. Spiritualist movements characteristically understand the Spirit in nontrinitarian ways. The Spirit is an absolutely distinct third party, an independent second mediator, or even a separate dynamistic or animistic force.[25] Moreover, they see the experience of the Spirit as concentrated in the isolated feelings of the individual. And, finally, they emphasize the affects and effects of the Spirit, the work and subjective power instead of the person of the Spirit. If the Spirit is the "divine" cut loose from the Father and the crucified Son, then in the end it will be a spirit that can be co-opted for any conceivable purpose of the human spirit. In fact, the more the Holy Spirit is separated from God in Jesus Christ, the more the Holy Spirit is viewed as the sheer motivation and blind dynamism on which the prevailing economic ethos lives.

Classical theology depicted the infinity of God as the boundary of human finiteness. The God concept behind the market view of the human being depicts God as pure decision. Infinity means unhindered capacity for choice. This empty infinity in God is the reverse side of the sense of insatiability in the human being. The God who is sheer spirit and the corresponding human being who is sheer spirit support a society that focuses all of its economic problems on the spiraling increase in insatiable wants and the doctrine of growth which has become the secular religion of our society. Market theory eschews direct coercion as a way of expansion, but it replaces it with another element of "necessitous expansion"—the quality of insatiability in the human being, an inherent aspect of the drive to amass wealth. Human insatiability means that the normal reach of power is unbounded in aim. It is "rational" for the human being to be engaged in an endless quest for aggrandizement.[26] The sin of avarice cannot be overcome; therefore it should be used "rationally."[27]

Human need, when connected with money as the depository of value as such, justifies dominative and exploitative relationships as natural. According to Marx, money as the ultimate commodity fetish has a physical-metaphysical character. What money can obtain seems infinite:

> The hoarding drive is boundless in nature. Qualitatively or formally considered, money is independent of all limits, that is, it is the universal representative of material wealth because it is directly convertible into any other commodity. But at the same time every actual sum of money is limited in amount, and therefore has only a limited efficacy as a means of purchase. This contradiction between the quantitative limitation and the qualitative lack of limitation of money keeps driving the hoarder back to his Sisyphean task: accumulation. He is in the same situation as a world

conqueror who discovers a new boundary with each country he annexes.[28]

Because of this "limited infinity" connected with money, the hoarder of money must constantly renounce the material reality of wealth "in order to chase after the eternal treasure [infinitized capital] which can be touched neither by moths nor by rust, and which is wholly celestial and wholly mundane."[29] Avarice, the desire of the infinity associated with money, leads to the manifold practices necessary to the dynamism of commodity relationships. From the perspective of the owners of capital, money infinity is the source of all human creativity; without the creativity of capital, labor would be nothing.[30]

The "spirit of capital" is this giving of the human spirit, human subjectivity, to commodities, money, and capital. Everything from money, to the market, to possessed commodities can be spiritualized, that is, made into idols. Bank commercials would have us relate to our money animistically as they exhort: Make your money work for you. Our economic life is filled with animism, not unlike that of many primitive societies. A sign of the "spirit" is increased needs; a sign of the blessing of the "spirit" is growth in accumulated wealth.

There are no bounds imposed on the size of wealth and few on the means by which wealth is gained. Thus there is a justification for the commodification of life in which society is scanned for all conceivable ways of reducing human activities and instilled wants to profit-making relationships. In so doing, human beings give themselves and their decisions over to "the infinite" which is both symbolized and enfleshed in commodity relationships. Religion, then, is not a superstructure, but a "form of social consciousness that corresponds to a situation in which human beings have delegated the decision-making power over their own life or death to a commodity mechanism for whose results they do not accept responsibility—even though this mechanism is the work of their own hands. This lack of responsibility is then projected onto a God who enjoys an infinitely legitimate arbitrary power, who is the God of private property. . . ."[31]

In North American spiritualist movements this God concept has the effect of strengthening the consumerist ethos of North America. In the high-intensity market setting individuals are led to interpret their needs exclusively as needs for commodities.[32] The sense of satisfaction in our society is more and more becoming the consumption of commodities. Marketing and consumption are substituted for the experience of love, compassion, and hope, of a longing for equity, of trusting and being trusted. Fulfilling private wants through commodities truncates the ways of knowing that yield newness and commitment in life, work, and love. Persons come to be valued by the same criteria by which a commodity is valued: marketability, profitability, and consumability. When the objects of need are reduced to commodities, owners are possessed by wealth instead of possessing it. Marketing and consuming ultimately reveal us to ourselves as things. "We *are* only insofar as we possess. We are what we possess. We are, consequently, possessed by our possessions, produced by our products. Remade in the image and likeness of our own handiwork, we are revealed as commodities."[33]

A TRINITARIAN UNDERSTANDING OF THE HOLY SPIRIT: GOD AND SCARCITY

What both the concept of "God without Spirit" and "Spirit without God" do is separate the Spirit from the Father and the Son by denying the cross. The old-line churches and the spiritualist-fundamentalist churches are equally guilty of this. But according to the witness of the New Testament, the Holy Spirit can be understood only through the cross, which is the center of the Christian proclamation.

Both the Gospels and Paul speak about the relationship between the Father and Son as one in which the Father has delivered over the Son and the Son has delivered over himself to death on the cross.[34] The deepest suffering of the Son is the experience of being Godforsaken, of being infinitely separated from the one with whom he had claimed the greatest intimacy: "My God, my God, why hast thou forsaken me?" (Mark 15:34). The deepest suffering of the Father, on the other hand, is his suffering the death of the Son. This is a deeper suffering, just as our suffering through the death of a loved one is greater than our suffering our own death. The Father gives away the Son, and the Son gives away himself; both go outside themselves and both suffer.

Thus with the cross before us we must criticize every concept of God that defines God as radically individual, self-sufficient, and passionless, just as we must criticize every concept of the divine that depicts the Spirit as sheer dynamism, motivation, or empowerment without suffering. God's economic work in the cross continues in the history of the Holy Spirit, through whose power Jesus has offered himself up to the Father (Heb. 9:14) for us. The Holy Spirit *is* the reality of love between the Father and the Son, their sacrifice "for us," their going beyond themselves, and the self-giving of each for us.

The work of the Holy Spirit is about *access* to God's economy. The Holy Spirit is God working economically so that God's creatures and the whole creation may live and live abundantly. This is the reason that the Holy Spirit is identified with God's righteousness, which appears paradigmatically in God's raising of Jesus from the dead (Rom. 1:4) and is called the "spirit that gives life" (1 Cor. 15:45). God the Holy Spirit makes present God's righteousness, which is God's power for life against death.

Scarcity or Plērōma?

A trinitarian understanding and experience of the Holy Spirit occasions a conflict between the economy of God and the economic ethos of our society: the conflict between scarcity and what the New Testament calls the *plērōma* or the fullness of God's blessings and gifts in the Holy Spirit. The Christian perspective on needs and consumption is that God the Holy Spirit is providing enough of what it takes for all to live and live abundantly. Christianity will therefore be subversive in calling into question the deepest assumption of modern economics, namely, scarcity. Nothing is deeper in the spirit of capitalism, and of socialism as well, than the belief that there is not enough to go around. The church, however, is called to live and organize itself out of the faith that God the Holy Spirit is willing and providing whatever is necessary for all persons and the whole creation to live.

This is not to deny the shortfall of what it takes to be human in the world. People are dying for lack of food and live in misery for lack of decent housing, potable water, adequate sanitation, and health care. Of course there are shortages and limits to plenty in nature. Oil, coal, minerals, arable land, forests, and food are limited (though their limits have always had much to do with the unjust use of nature by human beings). Economic systems are faltering for lack of fuel and natural resources. Human beings are humiliated by the lack of meaningful work and caring human relationships. Lack is not an illusion. Insufficiency is real enough. But insufficiencies, lacks, and shortages are not the same thing as the modern economic definition of scarcity.

The insatiability of human nature is said to be the ground of scarcity. What the market mechanisms actually require is scarcity in the sense of withheld or blocked access to what people need for livelihood and work. Scarcity in this sense is the condition for exclusive private property. But as justification for this, the meaning of scarcity is made to trade on the character of the human being as infinite desirer and infinite acquisitor.

Our society tries to instill artificial scarcity in order to feed the compulsion to growth by spiritualizing work and sexuality. If we really believe that we become free and human through work, the result will be that we cannot work enough. The fullness of *being* human is held to be scarce, unattainable except for those who earn meaning through work. And thus is born our lust after work as an end in itself. But whenever we acknowledge the presence of the Holy Spirit, there is a deep crisis for us and for our society: We cannot justify ourselves through work and thus work is thoroughly demystified. In the presence of the Holy Spirit all we can do is confess the abundance, the richness, the fullness of God's righteousness. To be human and to live abundantly is exclusively the gift of God's grace, of which there is no scarcity, no lack. Demystified work is a response to the abundance of God's grace. It will not be an end in itself, but rather a servant of the abundance of life. That is why the celebration of the resurrection comes on the first day of the week as the precondition of work, not on the last day of the week as recuperation from work.

In order to create a system of debt, on which our economy depends, we have to spiritualize both money and commodities. We have to convince people that if they do not possess certain products, they are not fully human. And thus a deep sense of scarcity is instilled in the minds and hearts of people through the media and their daily experiences. To want more is a sign that we are alive and more deserving than those with fewer needs. The level of satisfaction connected with a product is determined by its ability to satisfy imagined needs. Is it not, quite frankly, impossible to sell any product if it is not more than we need? Shaving cream has to be "great foaming comfort" or it will not satisfy the sense of scarcity for which consumption is the messianic message of salvation. Since none of these deepest human hopes can be fulfilled in any product, the mere consumption of them is never enough. More of the product, or a new, inspired product, is the only relief offered to our human longing. Consumption becomes more important than life itself, for its motivation is the dread of lifelessness.

In our public household advertising is the predominant form of the social creation of wants.[35] It is the task of advertising to add to buying and consuming images of fulfillment and dignity. Buying is valuable in itself. Once buying is seen as a way of dealing with guilt, failure, the loss of self-esteem, and the fear of death, it will be elevated to the status of worship.

Planned obsolescence is the social correlate to the emergence of tension in the physiological field. Changing styles and models and exploiting the desire for conformity force people to develop a need for change much like the need for food, which arises automatically through physiological reasons. The same purpose is accomplished by the continuous development of new products for new kinds of need satisfaction. Once the new product is convincingly connected with a new kind of need, the pressure of conformity actually creates a "need."

The spiritualization of work and money as a way of forcing work and growth constantly breaks down as we move from a society of production to a society of consumption. The more affluent a society becomes, the more difficult it is to create notions of scarcity on the basis of the spiritualization of work and money. Our society has discovered that sexuality can be used as an almost universal means of creating in human beings an artificial sense of scarcity.[36] The object is so to spiritualize sex that it becomes ahistorical and unrealizable. If spiritualized images of sex are presented often enough as objects that must be attained in order to be really alive, people will feel a constant emptiness in their lives, a scarcity, a gnawing void that keeps them unsatisfied and constantly involved in competitive work and consumptive pleasure to fill that void. We buy names and images that are identified with the intimacy and happiness which we lack. When buying automobiles, beverages, tubes of all kinds, the objects we are really trying to purchase are friendship, love, self-esteem, and happiness.

The Crisis of Consumerism in a Consumerist Society

The structuring of the household so that some freely define their needs while the life-maintaining needs of others are not met leads not only to the exploitation of those who are left without livelihood; it also dehumanizes the life of those who are within. The school of thought initiated by Thorstein Veblen has been peculiarly adept at showing how the distortion of human needs ruins not only the economy but also its adherents.[37] Veblen argued that in the modern market economy the meaning of a consumer object has little to do with its use but is embedded in owning and consuming. "Conspicuous consumption," which helps explain the expansiveness of consumption, produces waste and destroys the household relationships necessary to a viable economy.

Recent thinkers in the Veblenian tradition have been more concerned with the problems of satiation which paradoxically lead to an intensifying sense of scarcity and relative deprivation in those who are affluent. They stress the joylessness of a consuming public, the harriedness of today's leisure class, and the inevitability of frustration in positional goods.[38]

Life in the triune community of righteousness destroys false senses of scarcity. Paul wrote to Corinthian Christians who were obsessed with becoming ever richer in spiritualized things and spiritualized human relationships. Paul's message was, "You are already filled. Already you are rich" (1 Cor. 4:8). But this *plērōma*, this fullness has come from "the Spirit who is from God" (2:12), not from the spirit of the accumulation. This fullness and abundance we have from God is nothing other than the power of God's suffering love in the cross. "For you know the grace of our Lord Jesus Christ, that though he was rich, yet for our sake he became poor, so that by his poverty you might become rich" (2 Cor. 8:9). The power of suffering love is the fullness of God by which the Spirit is seeking to build the household of God. To participate in the Spirit is to be filled with the power to suffer with others. A faithful future of the churches of which we are a part depends upon the Holy Spirit making plain to us that the abundance of God's love removes the scarcity we instill with our spiritualized love of things.

Scarcity may not be made the starting point of a system of economic justice. As *starting point,* scarcity is an illusion. In almost all situations of human life scarcity has been caused by human injustice. Sometimes the ideological arguments about scarcity by the economic powers lead to strange solutions of allocation. The shrewdness of faith should prompt us immediately to ask what kind of economics is being constructed on the assumption of such arguments about scarcity. For in general the biblical faith teaches that there is enough *if* the righteousness of God is present and acknowledged as the source of life.

God's Righteousness and Scarcity

In the biblical traditions it becomes clear over and over again that the crucial issue is not how many goods are present, but whether the righteousness of God is present. This is so because the righteousness of God destroys artificial scarcity. The righteousness of God brings manna in the wilderness; there is enough. The pretense of scarcity is not tolerated as the starting point for economics. The righteousness of God creates justice, which enables five thousand people to share five loaves and two fish; there is enough. No, the story ends with marvelous semitic hyperbole, there is more than enough. If the righteousness of God is not present, then poverty is hell and people are subjected to death. In that case, some people are poor because others are rich.

The heart of God's economy is found in God's own self-giving, which produces abundance for life. Thus the church, though it be an incredible scandal to the world, will say with Paul: "He who did not spare his only Son but gave him up for us all, will he not also give us all things with him?" (Rom. 8:32). The early church spoke of the presence of the Holy Spirit in superlatives, in the language of abundance and superabundance: "God is able to provide you with every blessing and abundance, so that you may always have enough of everything and may provide an abundance for every good work" (1 Cor. 9:8; cf. Ps. 78:19). "Those who seek the Lord lack no good thing" (Ps. 34:106).

Jesus serves the building of the household of God out of the power and grace of God's righteousness. Jesus does not put people in need so that they would then become dependent upon him to meet their needs. In fact, one cannot describe Jesus' ministry simply as meeting needs. It is more accurate to say that in the presence of God's righteousness Jesus makes it possible for people to enter into ministry. The point of the gospel is not simply to have one's needs met, but to have one's needs met so that one can meet the needs of others. So the Gerasene demoniac cannot remain in the dependent relationship to Jesus that he desires; he must go home with his new empowerment to engage in his own ministry of meeting needs. When the church represents itself as merely a place where people can have their needs met, it robs them of their right to the joy of their own ministry.

Preoccupation with one's own needs and wants leads to hoarding possessions (Luke 8:14). "Take heed, and beware of all covetousness; for a man's life does not consist in the abundance of his possessions" (Luke 12:15; cf. 1 Corinthians 6). The temptation of amassing wealth for meeting one's own needs diminishes readiness for the approaching righteousness by which God intends a household which meets the needs of all people. Greed and avarice divide the household (Luke 12:13–14). The parable of the rich landowner shatters the seductive hold of life centered in self-definition of wants (Luke 12:13–34). The landowner builds new and bigger barns to store a bumper crop in order to play the futures market or as security for an early retirement and a life of ease. By playing upon scarcity he profits from the needs of others. Not only has the rich man threatened his neighbor with the loss of livelihood, but he has also disabled his own life through hoarding. The ultimate damnation of avarice is that it leads to loneliness: "Woe to you who join house to house, who add field to field, until there is no more room, and you are made to dwell alone in the midst of the land" (Isa. 5:8).

God's verdict is that such acts make one a "fool" (Ps. 14:1). The fool thinks and acts as if there is no accountability to God and community. Faced with death, he realizes that his commodities have deceived him because he has falsely accounted his needs. Fulfilling needs defined as self-enhancement have separated him from God and neighbor. He has falsely assumed that he could regard his life as his own and that it could be measured by possessions. He has falsely assumed that his property was meant to fulfill only his own needs, thereby violating God's lordship and his own role as a responsible steward. The images of the building of storage barns, the business that prevents the acceptance of an invitation, the rich man protecting his hall with a spear are all images of the decision for death before death (Luke 11:21–22).

The deepest scarcity of the human being comes from the scarcity created by our finitude and mortality, the scarcity of time, energy, and life. Each of us is subject to anxiety and regret because there is never enough time, never enough energy, never enough life. This can be translated into the gnawing sense of lack that can be assuaged only by buying, possessing, storing, and consuming. It is the form of life that leads to death, because it precludes the trust of the gospel. A household that trades on these senses of scarcity and anxiety is already a household in love with death. The economy of God rests ultimately on God's destruction of death in Jesus and God's promise of the ultimate destruction of death in the whole creation.

Because of God's intention to meet the needs of all of God's creatures (Luke 12:31), anxiety about "the cares of this life" have no place in the faith devoted to the Economist's *basileia* (Lk. 21:34). The only need human beings have is for the reign of God's righteousness. Everything else human beings need is given with God's righteousness. If Abba so abundantly provides for the needs of nature, "how much more" will Abba's own children be provided. Do not be anxious, seek the *basileia* "and these things shall be yours as well" (Matt. 6:31).

God's destruction of scarcity through God's righteousness creates a new human being, the creature who finds satisfaction in serving God's righteousness and justice. Faith in the God of "enough through justice" does not relieve the human being of all hungers but transposes them into the hunger after righteousness. The purpose of human life is not to consume or accumulate but to do justice. All needs should be defined in relation to that.

JUSTICE AND THE
MEANING OF SOCIAL GOODS

As we have seen, the language of needs serves many functions in the modern market society, but it seldom serves the just distribution of access to life and life abundant in the public household. The language of needs in the market society is distorted, and, as a result, so is the language of rights. In this situation Michael Walzer has proposed that we complement our focus on needs and rights by an emphasis on the meaning of social goods that are to be distributed.

We do not know how to produce or distribute or consume if we do not know the shared meanings of social goods.[39] We do not know what is due to a member of the community until we know how the members relate to each other through the things they make and distribute. The conception and creation of goods precedes and controls their distribution. A community or society may be said to be just if its life and arrangements are faithful to the shared understandings of its members. We cannot expect a radical redesign of the economy without radically changed shared meanings of its members.

What are the shared meanings of social goods because of the character of God the Economist? What does the character of God suggest about the relationships and rules for distribution? It is characteristic of the biblical narratives that in rendering God they at the same time provide the communal shared meanings of social goods. For example, the history of God's relationship to bread communicates a shared meaning of bread and how bread is to be distributed and to whom and under what household relationships. This history does not simply establish an abstract right to bread or a subjective need for bread, but rather provides a social meaning of bread by narrating historical relationships.

The history of bread begins with Joseph, whom we referred to in chapter 4 as the first great economist in our memory. Something exceedingly important had happened to the shared social meaning of bread in the time between Joseph's economic miracle and the people's crying out from starvation in the new famine in Egypt. It was placed in the storehouse economy of Pharaoh and Joseph. Bread had become a commodity, and now that it was a commodity it had to be exchanged. It had to be a market item. As a commodity bread can be used as a political instrument or as a bargaining chip in international relationships. This shared communal understanding meant that bread could become a means of dominating those who had nothing to exchange.

But when the people leave the economy of Pharaoh and begin living in God's household, bread must have a new meaning. The people should cry not for Pharaoh's bread but for God's bread. A new shared communal meaning of the social good bread is given: The "staff of life" is an expression of God's righteousness. Unleavened bread reminds us of the difference between the bread of grace and the bread of slavery (Exod. 12:15–20), the bread of joy and the "bread of tears and affliction" (Ps. 80:5; cf. Ps. 127:2).

Who is God? God is the giver of bread. God gives a strange kind of bread, a bread that is not a commodity, a bread that cannot be put into exchange relationships. The manna cannot be stored (except for the sabbath); if you store it, it will rot. In God's economy food cannot be used as a way of gaining political power and domination over other people.

Who is God? God is the doer of righteousness who gives bread for life in just distribution. How shall God's bread be distributed? According to the logic of gifting, according to what each could eat, no more, no less. "And the people of Israel did so; they gathered, some more, some less. But when they measured it with an omer, he that gathered much had nothing left over, and he that gathered little had no lack; each gathered according to what he could eat" (Exod. 16:17–18).

It is the bread we have looked for ever since:

> Ho, everyone who thirsts, come to the waters; he who has
> no money, come, buy and eat! Come, buy wine and milk
> without price. Why do you spend your money for that which
> is not bread, and your labor for that which does not satisfy?
> Harken diligently to me, and eat what is good, and delight
> yourselves in fatness.
>
> (Isa. 55:1–2)

Because a gift is something that is consumed, used up, devoted to the future, or eaten, food has been the most common image for the gift. Needs are not met, hunger appears, and death threatens when the gift ceases. The peculiar reality of gifting is that when the gift is used, it is not used up. A commodity is truly consumed when it is sold because nothing about the exchange assures its return. The gift that is passed along remains abundant. In fact, a gift multiplies. Gifts that remain gifts can support an affluence of satisfaction, even without numerical abundance. Those who share are satisfied. Hoarding means that you are fed only while you eat; the meal finishes in hunger.

> The desire to consume is a kind of lust. We long to have the world flow through us like air or food. We are thirsty and hungry for something that can only be carried inside bodies. But consumer goods merely bait this lust, they do not satisfy it. The consumer of commodities is invited to a meal without passion, a consumption that leads to neither satiation nor fire. He is a stranger seduced into feeding on the drippings of someone else's capital without benefit of inner nourishment, and he is hungry at the end of the meal, depressed and weary as we all feel when lust has dragged us from the house and led us to nothing.[40]

At the Eucharist we can learn the meaning of the social goods in the community.[41] The Supper begins with bread but encompasses ultimately all social goods. When Jesus takes, blesses, breaks, and gives bread, he is explaining the shared communal meaning of the social good, bread. The extremely complex history of God and bread culminates in Jesus' own utterance of the shared communal meaning of bread, "This is my body which is broken for you and for many (all)."

Centering on bread, the Eucharist uncovers the fundamental shared meaning of all social goods. All are invited freely to this meal, the only proviso being one's awareness of all those others who are also invited to share the meaning of all social goods through Christ's body, namely, the poor, the oppressed, the sinners, and the dying. This meal blocks all use and exchange of things for the purpose of domination. The meaning of this good requires its distribution in ways additional to exchange. It teaches us that certain goods appropriate to the life and dignity of people are not exhaustively commodities, namely, those social goods necessary for life and life abundant and which, if put exhaustively into the market, will be withheld from some.

The celebration of the Lord's Supper is under orders from God the Economist and is a concrete instance of God's providential *oikonomia* with implications for all eating and drinking everywhere. For this reason the disciples of Jesus should pray boldly for daily bread (Luke 11:3). They should keep the command to eat and drink, recognizing that it includes the command that they should share daily bread with all of God's people.

The household of God is meant to be a peculiar sphere of distribution because it has a special meaning of social goods derived from the life, death, and resurrection of Jesus Christ. Its household rules of distribution are meant to conform to God's own distribution of righteousness. This distribution does not do away with every need, but it sees every need in relation to God's justice. This distribution does not do away with every hunger, but it transfigures every hunger and thirst into the hunger and thirst for God's righteousness.

Aubrey R. Johnson's reading of Psalm 23 depicts the work of God's economy overcoming scarcity in God's household:

> With Yahweh as my shepherd there is nothing that I lack;
>   he seeth that I lie down where there is grass for pasture.
> He leadeth me where restful water may be found,
>   satisfying my need to the full.
> He guideth me along the right tracks,
>   thus answering to his name.
> Even if my way lieth through a valley deep in shadow,
>   I dread no evil;
>   for thou art with me,
>   my fears allayed by thy club and thy staff.
> Thou dost show mine enemies
>   that I am welcome at thy table,
>   pouring oil on my head,
>   my cup filled to overflowing.
> Yea, I shall be pursued in unfailing kindness
>   every day of my life,
>   finding a home in the Household of Yahweh
> for many a long year.[42]

Conclusion

In juxtaposing God and economy we have discovered new perspectives on both. We have attempted to understand God as the community of righteousness united in self-giving love, and we have argued that Economist is a proper and necessary metaphor for the triune God. The Trinity serves as criticism of the old authority attributes of God, which have been taken over by the human being as defined by the modern market theory. We have have become aware that the church's worship, structure, and life can uncritically sanctify unaccountable power and mask privilege in economy. Even if economic theory assumes the absence of God in the market, focusing on the doctrine of the Trinity as a way of critically retrieving traditional views of God's economy has led us to criticize God concepts that justify assumptions abetting domination in the economic sphere. These assumptions behind the market mechanisms endorse conditions under which many people are led into an economic dependency that is just as antagonistic to personal rights as is political dependency. Under such conditions, communities are corroded and people cannot realize their capacities. The conditions of economic dependency for the many in our society also destroy the full human development of the few who are powerful in their wealth. Democratic culture cannot thrive under such conditions, and, without democratic culture, democratic institutions soon wither.

Perceiving God as Economist has reminded us that the partitioning and narrowing of economy in the modern world have occurred at great cost to the human being. Despite its sensational successes in the modern world, modern economistic theory has forgotten that economy must be fundamentally concerned with livelihood. A more humane public household will depend on our learning that human dignity in community is prior in value to economic organization. Economic action is not an end in itself; it is a means toward communal human praxis determined democratically. Economy should serve democratic community, which in turn serves the creation of conditions of human beings finding their calling. The great success of the market economy and its tendency to draw everything into commodity exchange relationships has conditioned us to treat ever more dimensions of life as private, that is, unaccountable. The future of our society and its possible constructive contribution to the global household depend on our learning to restore many aspects of economy to community accountability.

If we rightfully appreciate the market's logic of the exchange of commodities as a tremendous instrument of economy, we nevertheless have to be aware that there are many social goods whose shared communal understanding should require different logics of property, work, and distribution. This means that the market should be blocked in some spheres of society. This, of course, cannot happen without democratic politics, which, in turn, are impossible without communities of shared values.

Seeking to live the economy of God, the congregation can contribute to a more just public household. The church's economy and ultimately its mission to the public economy should take shape in the peculiar "economic instruments" of the Holy Spirit: the Word as Gospel, baptism, the eucharist, hospitable *koinōnia*, and *diakonia*. Together they point to alternative ways of producing and distributing what is necessary for an inclusive household of life. And thus will the church claim in its life that God's economy is the foundation of livelihood for all of God's creatures and in so doing will be a living hope for a just society.

The parable of the prodigal son (Luke 15) is a story about economy *par excellence*. In it we have a picture of the Host who yearns for a new household that can be hospitable to the poor, the forsaken, the lost, the dying, for economy is the question of giving access to life to the Host's own child. In what kind of household can this take place?

It is a resurrection household that God is struggling to build. The decisive fact is that the resurrection changes the household rules. So it is when the prodigal son returns from the heroin nightmare of his extreme liberal bout with unaccountable freedom, expecting to find a new lease in the conservative legalism of the old household rules. Redemption happens on the road, beyond all best thoughts of liberalism and conservatism, when the father breaks every rule of what appears to be proper household management. The father rushes to embrace the foul-smelling, dirt-caked child, whereas all power-shrewd people know that he should have stayed in his wing-backed chair surrounded by all of the symbols of his paternal authority. He forgives the son even before the confession is completed, whereas after considerable parental experience, one is convinced that one should let the children spill all the beans for future evidence. The father orders clothes, not work clothes or casual wear, but the three-piece suit, which should have been saved for the highest event of the year. The father calls for a ring, not his fraternity ring, but his father's own ring, which should have been saved for the older son. The father asks for meat, not the rump roast, but filet mignon, which should have been saved for holiest feast of the year. The father announces a party, not a regular Saturday-night soiree, but the most joyous occasion in the household's memory, which should have been saved for the celebration of the older son's patrimony. Why all this? "For this my son was dead, and he is alive."

The story does not end happily because the older son does not go into the celebration of the resurrection economy. And those of us who are older daughters and sons know why: It is simply not fair that the household rules be changed. But who of us, after all, is not an older daughter and son? We stand between the economies. On the one hand is the old household in which each of us knows what we will inherit and are so intent upon it that we do not even question the old household rules. And on the other hand is the new household that God is building. The church in the developed world is standing in the position of the older son. The household rules are changing. Whether we shall work for the household of life and experience its joy is our question.

The invitation to dance is being given freely in the new household. The medieval pictures of the risen Lord dancing, with his cloak extended to include everyone in the dance, catch the spirit of this resurrection household. Would that we let the Holy Spirit catch us up into this dance. Would that we devote our work and our property to this new household, with its strange, frightening but utterly joyful dance. In a world that seeks everything but home, the only unity and consensus worth searching for is that found in the crucified One who nevertheless dances because of an economy that gives to all access to life and life abundant.

Notes

INTRODUCTION

1. Recent publications include: J. Philip Wogaman, *The Great Economic Debate: An Ethical Analysis* (Philadelphia: Westminster Press, 1977); idem, *Economics and Ethics: A Christian Inquiry* (Philadelphia: Fortress Press, 1986); Larry L. Rasmussen, *Economic Anxiety and Christian Faith* (Minneapolis: Augsburg Publishing House, 1981); Bruce C. Birch and Larry L. Rasmussen, *The Predicament of the Prosperous* (Philadelphia: Westminster Press, 1978); Robert Lee, *Faith and the Prospects of Economic Collapse* (Atlanta: John Knox Press, 1981); Albert T. Rasmussen, *Christian Responsibility in Economic Life* (Philadelphia: Westminster Press, 1965); Robert Benne, *The Ethic of Democratic Capitalism: A Moral Reassessment* (Philadelphia: Fortress Press, 1981); *The Annual of the Society of Christian Ethics*, ed. Larry L. Rasmussen, et al. (Waterloo, Ontario: Council on the Study of Religion, Wilfrid Laurier University, 1982); Richard K. Taylor, *Economics and the Gospel* (Philadelphia: United Church Press, 1973); Prentiss L. Pemberton and Daniel Rush Finn, *Toward a Christian Economic Ethic* (Minneapolis: Winston Press, 1985); Robert Stivers, *The Sustainable Society and Economic Growth* (Philadelphia: Westminster Press, 1976); Jon P. Gunnemann, "Capitalism and Commutative Justice," in *Annual of the Society of Christian Ethics* (1985), 101–22; David M. Beckman, *Where Faith and Economics Meet* (Minneapolis: Augsburg Press, 1981); John F. Sleeman, *Economic Crisis: A Christian Perspective* (London: SCM Press, 1976); Dietmar Mieth and Jacques Pohier, eds., *Christian Ethics and Economics: The North-South Conflict* (New York: Seabury Press, 1980); Stephen Mott, *Biblical Ethics and Social Change* (New York: Oxford University Press, 1982); Max L. Stackhouse, *Public Theology and Political Economy: Christian Stewardship in Modern Society* (Grand Rapids: Wm. B. Eerdmans, 1987); Walter L. Owensby, *Economics for Prophets: A Primer on Concepts, Realities, and Values in Our Economic System* (Grand Rapids: Wm. B. Eerdmans, 1988); Oliver F. Williams and John W. Houck, eds., *The Judeo-Christian Vision and the Modern Corporation* (Notre Dame: University of Notre Dame Press, 1982), Warren R. Copeland, *Economic Justice: The Social Ethics of U.S. Economic Policy* (Nashville: Abingdon Press, 1988).

2. Nor shall we be debating the technical merits or demerits of capitalism or socialism, since the existing forms of both basically share many of the same distorted God concepts that undergird common beliefs in scarcity, progress, growth through technology, managerialism,

and the machination of fiscal systems and military might to protect markets.

3. For earlier attempts to correlate God and basic questions of economy see Robert Lowry Calhoun, *God and the Common Life* (New York: Charles Scribner's Sons, 1935); H.N. Wieman, *The Source of the Human Good* (Chicago: University of Chicago Press, 1947); and William Temple, *Christianity and the Social Order* (London: SPCK, 1976).

4. See John Reumann, "The Use of Oikonomia and Related Terms in Greek Sources to about A.D. 100, as a Background for Patristic Applications" (Ph.D. diss., University of Pennsylvania, 1957; Ann Arbor, Mich.: University Microfilms, 1957); idem, "'Stewards of God'—Pre-Christian Religious Application of *Oikonomos* in Greek," *Journal of Biblical Literature* 77 (1958), 339–49; idem, "*Oikonomia* as 'Ethical Accommodation' in the Fathers, and Its Pagan Backgrounds," *Studia Patristica* III (Berlin: Akademie-Verlag, 1961), 370–79. See also Thomas F. Torrance, "The Implications of *Oikonomia* for Knowledge and Speech of God in Early Christian Theology," in *Oikonomia: Heilsgeschichte als Thema der Theologie* ed. Felix Christ (Hamburg-Bergstedt: Herbert Reich Verlag, 1967), 223–38.

5. Daniel Bell, *The Cultural Contradictions of Capitalism* (New York: Basic Books, 1976).

6. On the ambiguity of the liberal tradition in the United States, see John Patrick Diggins, *The Lost Soul of American Politics: Virtue, Self-Interest, and the Foundations of Liberalism* (New York: Basic Books, 1984).

7. Ellen Meikeins Wood, "The Separation of the Economic and the Political in Capitalism," *New Left Review* (May–June 1981), 69–95.

8. The early Christian theologians, such as Clement of Alexandria, Basil, Chrysostom, Ambrose, and Augustine never tired of making this point. Many of the pertinent texts are collected in Charles Avila, *Ownership: Early Christian Teaching* (Maryknoll, N.Y.: Orbis Books, 1983).

9. "Goods with their meanings—because of their meanings—are the crucial medium of social relations; they come into people's minds before they come into their hands; distributions are patterned in accordance with the shared conceptions of what the goods are and what they are for." Michael Walzer, *Spheres of Justice*, 7.

10. Ibid.

11. Ibid., 17–19.

12. C.B. Macpherson, *The Political Theory of Possessive Individualism* (New York: Oxford University Press, 1962).

13. Jürgen Moltmann, "The Social Understanding of the Trinity," in *Humanity in God* (New York: Pilgrim Press, 1983), 90–106.

14. See, e.g., Heinz Kohler, *Economics: The Science of Scarcity* (Hinsdale, Ill.: The Dryden Press, 1976).

15. M. Douglas Meeks, "Gott und die Ökonomie des Heiligen Geistes," *Evangelische Theologie* 40(1979): 51–58.

1. GOD'S ECONOMY
AND THE CHURCH

1. For studies of present economic quandaries, see Daniel Bell and Irving Kristol, eds., *The Crisis in Economic Theory* (New York: Basic Books, 1981); Robert L. Heilbroner, *An Inquiry into the Human Prospect* (New York: W. W. Norton, 1974); Robert Lekachman, *Economists at Bay* (New York: McGraw-Hill, 1976); Charles K. Wilbur and Kenneth P. Jameson, *An Inquiry into the Poverty of Economics* (Notre Dame: University of Notre Dame Press, 1983).

2. Lyuba Zarsky, et al., eds., *The Economic Report of the People* (Boston: South End Press, 1986); Barry Bluestone and Bennett Harrison, *The Deindustrialization of America: Plant Closings, Community Abandonment, and the Dismantling of Industry* (New York: Basic Books, 1982); Thomas Byrne Edsall, *The New Politics of Inequality* (New York: W. W. Norton, 1984), esp. 202–42; Robert Lekachman, *Greed is Not Enough: Reaganomics* (New York: Pantheon Books, 1982).

3. David T. Ellwood, *Poor Support: Poverty in the American Family* (New York: Basic Books, 1988); Michael Harrington, *The New American Poverty* (New York: Holt, Rinehart and Winston, 1984).

4. See *Statistical Abstract of the United States*, 107th edition (Washington: U.S. Department of Commerce, 1987).

5. William Julius Wilson, *The Truly Disadvantaged: The Inner City, the Underclass, and Public Policy* (Chicago: The University of Chicago Press, 1987).

6. Susan George, *How the Other Half Dies: The Real Reasons for World Hunger* (Montclair, N.J.: Allanheld, Osman, 1977).

7. Paul Harrison, *Inside the Third World: The Anatomy of Poverty* (New York: Penguin Books, 1983); Penny Lernoux, *The Cry of the People* (New York: Penguin Books, 1982).

8. Andrew Carnegie, "Wealth," *North American Review*, 1889. See James Sellers, *Warming Fires: The Quest for Community in America* (New York: Seabury Press, 1975), 94–97. See also Andrew Carnegie, *The Gospel of Wealth and Other Timely Essays* (Cambridge: Harvard University Press, 1962).

9. See M. Douglas Meeks, "The Holy Spirit and Human Needs: Toward a Trinitarian View of Economics," *Christianity and Crisis* 40 (November 10, 1980), 307–16.

10. See Jürgen Moltmann and M. Douglas Meeks, "The Liberation of Oppressors," *Christianity and Crisis* 38 (December 25, 1978): 310–17.

11. For a historical survey of economic ethics in the American context, see Max L. Stackhouse, "Jesus and Economics: A Century of Reflection," in *The Bible in American Law, Politics, and Political Rhetoric*, ed. James Turner Johnson (Philadelphia: Fortress Press, 1985), 107–151.

12. *Economic Justice for All: Catholic Social Teaching and the U.S. Economy* (Washington, D.C.: National Conference of Catholic Bishops, 1986). The full text, together with responses from a wide range of perspectives, can be found in *The Catholic Challenge to the American Economy*, ed. Thomas

M. Gannon (New York: Macmillan, 1987). See also Charles P. Lutz, ed., *God, Goods, and the Common Good: Eleven Perspectives on Economic Justice in Dialogue with the Roman Catholic Bishops' Pastoral Letter* (Minneapolis: Augsburg Publishing Co., 1987); David M. Byers, *Justice in the Marketplace: Collected Statements of the Vatican and the United States Catholic Bishops on Economic Policy, 1891-1984* (Washington, D.C.: United States Catholic Conference, 1985); Donald Dorr, *Option for the Poor: A Hundred Years of Vatican Social Teaching* (Maryknoll, N.Y.: Orbis Books, 1983); David J. O'Brien and Thomas A. Shannon, *Renewing the Earth: Catholic Documents on Peace, Justice and Liberation* (Garden City, N.Y: Doubleday, 1979); David Hollenbach, *Claims in Conflict* (New York: Paulist Press, 1982).

13. See, e.g., Audrey Chapman Smock, ed., *Christian Faith and Economic Life* (New York: United Church Board for World Ministries, 1987); "Christian Faith and Economic Justice," a paper prepared for the General Assembly of the Presbyterian Church in the United States by the Council on Theology and Culture, 1983.

14. "Once Western culture became Christian (A.D. 325), the concept of God became the symbolic center for every aspect of life and for the understanding of nature, society, and human existence generally. Consequently, it became not only the object of endless philosophical and theological speculation but also the foundation of every special discipline of thought, every representative mode of action, and all important social institutions. Thus, inevitably, this notion and the modes of thinking that expressed it made union with the sciences, with ethical, legal, and political theories, and above all, with the philosophy of each epoch," Langdon Gilkey, "God," in *Christian Theology*, ed. Peter C. Hodgson and Robert H. King (Philadelphia: Fortress Press, 1982), 66. The God concept has also always "made union with" the economics of a time. This fact is thoroughly masked in the modern market society. Required therefore is what Ernst Bloch calls "detective work" or what Michael Foucault calls cultural "archaeology" to see God concepts at work in and behind economic modes of thought.

2. RECONCEPTUALIZING
GOD AND ECONOMY

1. Arthur C. McGill, *Suffering: A Test of Theological Method* (Philadelphia: Westminster Press, 1982), 65.

2. Bob Goudzwaard, *Capitalism and Progress: A Diagnosis of Western Society*, trans. Josina Van Nuis Zylstra (Grand Rapids: Wm. B. Eerdmans, 1979), xxii.

3. Quoted by Leonard Silk, *The New York Times*, September 30, 1983, 32.

4. Hence, the so-called new economics is increasingly interested in the "noneconomic factors" of economic behavior, including religious faith. See, e.g., Victor R. Fuchs, *How We Live* (Cambridge, Mass.: Harvard University Press, 1983).

5. See Robert L. Ayres, *Banking on the Poor: The World Bank and World Poverty* (Cambridge, Mass.: MIT Press, 1984); Jaques Loup, *Can the Third World Survive?* (Baltimore: Johns Hopkins University Press, 1984); Penny Lernoux, *In Banks We Trust* (Garden City, N.Y.: Doubleday, 1984); John H. Makin, *The Global Debt Crisis* (New York: Basic Books, 1984); G. Arrighi, A. Frank, and Immanuel Wallerstein, *Dynamics of the Global Crisis* (New York: Monthly Review Press, 1984); Brandt Commission, *Common Crisis North-South: Cooperation for World Recovery* (Cambridge, Mass.: MIT Press, 1983); Harold Lever and Christopher Huhne, *Debt and Danger: The World Financial Crisis* (Boston: The Atlantic Monthly Press, 1986).

6. Harold Lever, "The Debt Won't Be Paid," *New York Review of Books* 31 (June 28, 1984): 3–5.

7. See Lawrence Malkin, *The National Debt* (New York: Henry Holt & Co., 1987).

8. M. Douglas Meeks, "Gott und die Ökonomie des Heiligen Geistes," *Evangelische Theologie* 40 (1979): 40–48; idem, "The Holy Spirit and Human Needs: Toward a Trinitarian View of Economics," *Christianity and Crisis* 40 (November 10, 1980), 307–16.

9. Wayne A. Meeks, *The First Urban Christians: The Social World of the Apostle Paul* (New Haven, Conn.: Yale University Press, 1983); John H. Elliott, *A Home for the Homeless: A Sociological Exegesis of 1 Peter, Its Situation and Strategy* (Philadelphia: Fortress Press, 1981); Elisabeth Schüssler Fiorenza, *In Memory of Her: A Feminist Theological Reconstruction of Christian Origins* (New York: Crossroad, 1983). See also David C. Verner, *The Household of God: The Social World of the Pastoral Epistles* (Chico, Calif.: Scholars Press, 1983); Abraham J. Malherbe, *Social Aspects of Early Christianity*, 2nd ed. (Philadelphia: Fortress Press, 1983), 60–112; David L. Balch, *Let Wives Be Submissive: The Domestic Code in 1 Peter* (Chico, Calif.: Scholars Press, 1981); Gerd Theissen, *The Social Setting of Pauline Christianity* (Philadelphia: Fortress Press, 1982); Fernando Belo, *A Materialist Reading of the Gospel of Mark*, trans. Matthew J. O'Connell (Maryknoll, N.Y.: Orbis Books, 1981); J. G. Gager, *Kingdom and Community: The Social World of Early Christianity* (Englewood Cliffs, N.J.: Prentice-Hall, 1975); Howard Clark Kee, *Christian Origins in Sociological Perspective* (Philadelphia: Westminster Press, 1980); Douglas E. Oakman, *Jesus and the Economic Questions of His Day* (Lewiston, N.Y.: Edwin Mellen Press, 1987); Michael H. Crosby, *House of Disciples: Church, Economics, and Justice in Matthew* (Maryknoll, N.Y.: Orbis Books, 1988).

10. Elliott, *A Home for the Homeless*, 213.

11. Ibid, 192.

12. *Oikos* is used over 1600 times in the Septuagint, often conveying the communal identity and socioreligious solidarity of Israel. Elliott, *Home for the Homeless*, 182–86.

13. Apostasy results in the dissolution of the household (Deut. 13:6–18). Oikos is particularly a reference for coming exile: "I have forsaken my house, I have abandoned my heritage" (Jer. 12:7; cf. 22:5; Ezek. 12:11; 17:12), and for God's postexilic rebuilding of the house (Jer. 1:10; 31:38;

24:5,6; 33:7; cf. 3:18–19). Those who once suffered homelessness (*apoikia*) will experience the time of new building (*oikodomein*) in the reunited *oikos* of God (Jer. 3:18; 16:14–15; 31:27–28, 38–40; 32:36–44).

14. For the interrelatedness of ecological questions, see Charles Birch and John B. Cobb, Jr., *The Liberation of Life: From Cell to Community* (Cambridge: Cambridge University Press, 1982); Hazel Henderson, *The Politics of the Solar Age: Alternatives to Economics* (Garden City, N.Y.: Doubleday, 1981); Wendell Berry, *Home Economics* (San Francisco: North Point Press, 1987).

15. See Robert Bellah, et al., *Habits of the Heart: Individualism and Commitment in American Life* (Berkeley: University of California Press, 1985), 284f.: "How do living things, including human beings, exist in relation to each other in their common habitat? Habitat for economy is also habitat of all other living things on the planet. Every ecological fact has ethical significance. Every economic fact has ethical significance."

16. Robert Frost, *The Complete Poems of Robert Frost* (New York: Holt, Rinehart and Winston, 1961), 53.

17. In fact, in these narratives human beings and animals share the same table. See Bernhard W. Anderson, "Creation and Ecology," in *Creation in the Old Testament*, ed. Bernhard W. Anderson (Philadelphia: Fortress Press, 1984), 158ff.

18. See esp. Karl Polanyi, *The Great Transformation* (Boston: Beacon Press, 1957 [1944]); *The Livelihood of Man*, ed. Harry W. Pearson (New York: Academic Press, 1977).

19. M. Douglas Meeks, "The Church and the Poor in Supply-Side Economics," *Cities*, Fall 1983, 6–9.

20. The "surplus value" gained through exchanges can meet the internal standards of justice of a community. But "it will also be crucially important whether this surplus value is convertible, whether it purchases special privileges in the law courts, or in the educational system, or in the spheres of office and politics. Since capitalism develops along with and actually sponsors a considerable differentiation of social goods, no account of buying and selling, no description of free enterprise, can possibly settle the question of justice. We shall need to learn a great deal about other distribution processes and about their relative autonomy from or integration into the market. The dominance of capital outside the market makes capitalism unjust," Michael Walzer, *Spheres of Justice: A Defense of Pluralism and Equality* (New York: Basic Books, 1983), 315.

21. Fred Hirsch, *The Social Limits of Growth* (Cambridge: Harvard University Press, 1976), 87.

22. See Charles E. Rosenberg, *The Care of Strangers: The Rise of America's Hospital System* (New York: Basic Books, 1987).

23. Some parallels may be found in David Tracy's illuminating analysis of possibilities for a "systematic analogical imagination" in *The Analogical Imagination: Christian Theology and the Culture of Pluralism* (New York: Crossroad, 1981), esp. 405–38.

24. Max Weber, *The Protestant Ethic and the Spirit of Capitalism*, trans. Talcott Parsons (New York: Chas. Scribner's Sons, 1958); idem, *The*

Theory of Social and Economic Organization, ed. Talcott Parsons (New York: The Free Press, 1947). See also Talcott Parsons, "Religious and Economic Symbolism in the Western World," in *Religious Change and Continuity,* ed. Harry M. Johnson (San Francisco: Jossey-Boss, 1970), 1–48. and R.H. Tawney, *Religion and the Rise of Capitalism* (New York: Harcourt, Brace and Co., 1926).

25. One of the most creative uses of a materialist critical method is found in Norman K. Gottwald, *The Tribes of Yahweh: A Sociology of the Religion of Liberated Israel 1250–1050 B.C.E.* (Maryknoll, N.Y.: Orbis Books, 1979). Cf. Norman K. Gottwald, "The Theological Task after *The Tribes of Yahweh,*" in *The Bible and Liberation: Political and Social Hermeneutics,* ed. Norman K. Gottwald (Maryknoll, N.Y.: Orbis Books, 1983). Far from being merely a Marxian method, the critical approach can also find expression in the Reformed tradition's concern with idolatry and appears focally in the recent "political theology" of Jürgen Moltmann and Johannes Metz. See, e.g., Jürgen Moltmann, *On Human Dignity: Political Theology and Ethics,* trans. with an Introduction by M. Douglas Meeks (Philadelphia: Fortress Press, 1984); Johannes Metz, *Faith in History and Society,* trans. David Smith (New York: Seabury Press, 1980). See also Hans-Joachim Kraus, *Theologische Religionskritik* (Neukirchen-Vluyn: Neukirchener Verlag, 1982).

26. Cf. Matthew L. Lamb, *Solidarity with Victims: Toward a Theology of Social Transformation* (New York: Crossroad, 1982), 65–88.

27. Also suggestive for a methodology juxtaposing God and economy and focusing on the mission of the church are the arguments of Francis Schüssler Fiorenza, *Foundational Theology: Jesus and the Church* (New York: Crossroad, 1984).

3. GOD AND THE MARKET LOGIC

1. Useful studies on the development of modern economic theory include Fernand Braudel, *Capitalism and Civilization,* 3 vols. (New York: Harper & Row, 1981, 1982, 1984); Alexander Gray, *The Development of Economic Doctrine: An Introductory Survey,* 2nd ed. (London: Longman, 1980); Robert L. Heibroner, *The Worldly Philosophers,* 5th ed. (New York: Simon and Schuster, 1980); idem, *The Making of Economic Society* (Englewood Cliffs, N.J.: Prentice-Hall, 1962); Charles Gide, *Principles of Political Economy,* trans. E.F. Row (Westport, Conn.: Greenwood Press, 1970 [1929]); Douglass C. North, *The Rise of the Western World: A New Economic History* (Cambridge: Cambridge University Press, 1973); Richard Rosecrance, *The Rise of the Trading State: Commerce and Conquest in the Modern World* (New York: Basic Books, 1987).

2. This process of separating God and the market was prepared by a long and complicated history beginning perhaps as early as Nicolas of Cusa's attempt in the fifteenth century to explicate God on the mathematical model. Cusa sought to strengthen the theory of God by orienting it to the clear and certain concepts and theories of mathematics. God would then be thought in terms of the "absolute maximum," the *coincidentia oppositorum,* and the "incomprehensible,"

terms similar to the "dark knowing" of the mystics, but also evoking fascination with the mathematical way of dealing with infinity. Cusa typifies the Renaissance insights into the doctrine of God. The rediscovery of the wide variety of classical philosophical methods suggested the possibility of many alternative conceptions of God. Furthermore, there was discovered a correlation between the meaning of God and the meaning of the human being. New conceptions of the human being led to new conceptions of God, and vice versa. The attitude grew that if society were to be reformed, there would be required a reform in the doctrine of God. To foster the social unification of society, Cusa viewed God as the reconciling unity of all human aspirations and ideals.

On the one hand, the God-human relationship is more and more thought of in terms of philosophical naturalism. A God caught up in determining the laws of nature does not function to liberate human beings in history. God's reality is assimilated to the workings of an impersonal cosmic order that lacks the presence of a caring God. The eschatological elements of God's economy with the world are steadily eliminated. God is reduced to something like a "divine geometer" of the universe (Galileo and Leibniz). Bruno identifies God with the sole substantial reality of the universe. God is the absolute identity of matter and form. With Francis Bacon the study of God is no longer held together with the study of nature. Any elaborate treatment of God and of the spiritual character of the human being is left to the piety of religion. Only if a scientist happens to be pious, will he or she find any religious significance in nature.

On the other hand, the God-human relationship is increasingly linked to Stoic values, which are now considered the best human ethics for a world responsible to the human being. Human dignity is no longer based on the human being's place in the universe but rather on what the human being can freely become and make out of himself or herself. God serves as a measure of human value.

In both cases God is a function of the human project. God is an agent of cosmology or of the attempt to create a peaceful society. It will not be long before many human projects can be pursued without any reference whatsoever to God's agency.

The seventeenth century prepared the transition to the practical atheism of public life that began to triumph in the eighteenth century. Skepticism was one of the great cultural forces that led to the market conception of reality. The goal of skepticism was to disintegrate all human certitude. Two intellectual movements attempted to answer skepticism: rationalism and deism. The great seventeenth century rationalist philosophers fought against skepticism by making God a necessity in their philosophical systems. But the price paid for this protection against skepticism was that the meaning of God became completely functional. "God" performs crucial tasks within the system; God is instrumental to the total plausibility or meaning of an outlook on reality. For Descartes God functioned to guarantee the veracity of our memory and the reliability of our belief in the external world. As a guarantor of the *cogito*, God is an implicate of human certitude. For Spinoza God is the originative truth. God is charged with systematic responsibilities. Necessary as the producer of the universe, God cannot be a free and personal creator, since this would introduce an insoluble problem of divine transcendence and freedom. In Leibniz's thought, God functions as a universal enforcer of those intelligible laws that underlie the reality reference of all ideas and reasons.

The eighteenth century saw the last attempt to establish a cosmological and teleological theism. It was an effort to prove and describe God as the basis of modern science's unlocking of the secrets of nature. Theology, it was claimed, could be done hand in hand with the newest discoveries of science. For all the excitement that this way of thinking God provided (and still stimulates occasionally today), it actually further reduced the meaning of God to the cosmology that scientists thought they had to presuppose.

The eighteenth century, especially in England and France, took in the end a decidedly different tack. Many of its great thinkers were no longer committed to restoring God as the centerpiece of all human thought and effort or as a necessary function of philosophical systems. In fact, it was thought that God should be "pared back," that there should be a minimal reference to God.

The wars of religion had so damaged the European conscience that many felt compelled to find ways of removing differences over doctrines of God that had been used as the source of social and political conflict. A skepticism that would deconstruct or disintegrate God concepts was now thought a useful tool of social harmony. The ideal of tolerance became a standard assuring social concord. Deism arose as a way of living with a minimum of belief and a way of solving theoretical and practical issues without reference to God.

The two most significant figures in the transition to public atheism were Thomas Hobbes and John Locke. Hobbes not only called into question any attempt to rest the doctrine of God on a causal principle by which God could be inferred from nature; he also questioned any appeal to the spiritual attributes of God. Adumbrating Feuerbach in some senses, Hobbes claimed that the divine names refer merely to their sources in human suffering. Religion is basically a devotion to what human beings fear. Hobbes's chief concern was how the institutions of religion get expressed in civil religion. Belief in God is important so long as it gets expressed politically. So the question of God is ultimately a question of the disposition of power within society, not a question of truth. But if the meaning of God purports no claim to truth, it soon becomes uninteresting for politics. A thoroughgoing politicization of God reduces the interest of politics in God.

Locke carries forward the tendency of reducing the functional necessity of God for thought and public life. Locke does not assume that there is an immanent, pregiven truth of God. In his *Essay Concerning Human Understanding* (1690), Locke presupposes that God will become meaningful in the same way that other objects gain meaning, that is, out of a scrutiny of human experience. God is demonstrable, Locke claims, but the view of God's power and infinity construed out of observation of human experience yields a God with a much reduced function. God is hardly needed any more, even on epistemological grounds. Locke was a leader in "shifting Western political economy from its roots in the biblical tradition of economic obligation into the soil of sensate pleasure and possessive individualism." Prentiss L. Pemberton and Daniel Rush Finn, *Toward a Christian Economic Ethic* (Minneapolis: Winston Press, 1985), 67. See also C. B. Macpherson, *The Political Theory of Possessive Individualism* (New York: Oxford University Press, 1962). Locke's improvisation of a moral doctrine of a deistic God featured (1) a flawed but not totally depraved sinful human nature and (2) an idealistic natural law in which the privileged, middle, and upper classes were to govern.

3. James Collins, "Idea of God, 1400–800," in *Dictionary of the History of Ideas*, (New York: Chas. Scribner's Sons, 1973), 2:351; idem, *God in Modern Philosophy* (Chicago: Henry Regnery, 1959).

4. This does not mean that Smith wanted to eliminate God from the total picture of society. The hope of discovering a mechanics of society was still only a dream whose realization was not to be attempted until the nineteenth century.

5. Georg Wilhelm Friedrich Hegel, *Introduction to the Philosophy of Right*, trans. T.M. Knox (Oxford: Clarendon Press, 1952), 126–45.

6. This state of affairs was accompanied by the general demise of "political economy." As the uneasy medieval symbiosis of the great control systems of church authority and state authority was replaced by the modern constellation of state control and market control, politics was increasingly eclipsed from the human pursuit of economy. Liberal democracy maintained certain roles for the state. But the authority of the state was clearly restricted to the resolution of conflicts of volition outside the market. Communist theory was even more extreme in its view of political authority. It claimed that scientific analysis and planning would eventually be capable of replacing the state altogether. Of course, in order to realize the objectives of the capitalist and communist models of control, the state has in fact become stronger everywhere in the developed world.

In actual practice political-authority and market systems are intimately related, but both market and communist theory have indoctrinated us to perceive them as in decisive ways separated. The principal activities of government are heavily economic (taxation, education, ecological protection and energy conservation, national defense, transportation and communication, social security, health care delivery, promotion of economic growth and stability). On the other hand, the workings of the economy (despite the theories of neoclassical economics) are thoroughly political. The government is not primarily a conflict resolver, as much of political science has viewed it since Hobbes's *Leviathan*. Rather, government is a conflict over who will control government and what the terms of cooperation will be. Conflict emerges over economic interests: How power and authority should be organized to serve certain economic interests. Strategically theology should realize that economic interests want to eliminate political authority but yet invariably use political authority.

7. Karl Polanyi, *The Livelihood of Man* (New York: Academic Press, 1977), 9.

8. Robert Nozick, *Anarchy, State, and Utopia* (New York: Basic Books, 1974).

9. For the following, see Charles E. Lindblom, *Politics and Markets* (New York: Basic Books, 1977), 10; and Polanyi, *Livelihood of Man*, 19–34.

10. Market theory is utopian and at the same time ideological. The utopian character of the market is the postulation of an "original nature" or "original state" against which everything is measured. It is claimed that rational human beings are originally created in a state of freedom and equality. Economic theorists invent the "perfect market," which has never existed and cannot. To imagine one such a perfect market, however, permits economists to say that markets fail for all the reasons that deny the postulated perfections. Thus their conventional list of defects includes both impossibilities and difficulties. Lindblom, *Politics and Markets*, 78. This utopian force has been extremely effective in the revolutionary impact of the market. Yet once the market is in place, market theory itself resists change. It wants little or no change in what is viewed as necessary to the historical revolution of the market, e.g., property, claims about scarcity, and the definition of the human being as infinite desirer. For if these assumptions changed, the market as a tool of social organization would have to be significantly reconceived.

11. Karl Polanyi, *The Great Transformation* (Boston: Beacon Press, 1957 [1944]).

12. Lindblom, *Politics and Markets*, 10.

13. See Polanyi, *Livelihood of Man*, 19–34.

14. Schlomo Maital, *Minds, Markets, and Money: Psychological Foundations of Economic Behavior* (New York: Basic Books, 1982), 10.

15. An economy which put all relations exhaustively into market relationships would be intolerable, since it would strip the individual of all but one claim on other members of society, namely, the claim I have on another because I have something to offer in exchange. We would not be able to ask for help in distress as in traditional premarket societies. Marx's complaint was that the market had resolved personal worth into exchange value. The only bond left then was naked self-interest, callous "cash payment." Other methods of organization have been intertwined in varying degrees with the market system to soften its severity.

16. Lionel Robbins, *An Essay on the Nature and Significance of Economic Science* (London: Macmillan, 1952 [1935]), 16.

17. Polanyi, *Livelihood of Man*, 19–21.

18. Ibid., 5–6.

19. Cf. also Karl Polanyi, *Primitive, Archaic, and Modern Economies: Essays of Karl Polanyi*, ed. George Dalton (Boston: Beacon Press, 1968). Polanyi argues that what we call market economy did not exist until the nineteenth century. Primitive, archaic, ancient, medieval, in fact, all economies up until the nineteenth century were not organized institutionally by long-distance markets and economizing. Two recent articles have attempted, with different arguments, to answer the challenge Polanyi makes to the neoclassical economistic theory of resource allocation with his theory of nonmarket economies. Douglass C. North, "Markets and Other Allocation Systems in History: The Challenge of Karl Polanyi," *The Journal of European History* 6 (Winter 1977): 703–16; Morris Silver, "Karl Polanyi and Markets in the Ancient

Near East: The Challenge of the Evidence," *The Journal of Economic History* 43 (December 1983): 795–829. See also Douglass C. North, *Structure and Change in Economic History* (New York: W. W. Norton, 1981), 180–86.

20. See Polanyi, *Great Transformation*, 68–76.

21. Whereas Adam Smith refused to follow the Physiocrats's lead in founding wealth and thus political economy on nature, another clergyman, William Townsend, made patent the fatal assumptions that were to capture the mind of market society. Based on his famous theorem about the contest between goats landed on an island by privateers to provide food in case of future visits and dogs landed on the same island by the Spanish to eliminate the food supply of those who were molesting their trade, Townsend developed his notion of the regulation of the human species through hunger. "Hunger will tame the fiercest animals, it will teach decency and civility, obedience and subjection, to the most perverse. In general it is only hunger which can spur and goad them [the poor] on to labor; yet our laws have said they shall never hunger. The laws it must be confessed, have likewise said, they shall be compelled to work. But then legal constraint is attended with much trouble, violence and noise; creates ill will, and never can be productive of good and acceptable service: whereas hunger is not only peaceable, silent, unremitting pressure, but, as the most natural motive to industry and labor, it calls forth the most powerful exertions; and, when satisfied by the free bounty of another, lays lasting and sure foundations for good will and gratitude. The slave must be compelled to work but the free man should be left to his own judgment, and discretion; should be protected in the full enjoyment of his own, be it much or little; and punished when he invades his neighbor's property." *Dissertation on the Poor Laws*, quoted by Polanyi, *Great Transformation*, 113–14. Polanyi comments, "Here was a new starting point for political science. By approaching human community from the animal side, Townsend by-passed the supposedly unavoidable question as to the foundations of government; and in doing so introduced a new concept of law into human affairs, that of the laws of Nature," 114.

22. Polanyi, *Great Transformation*, 86–102 and passim.

23. Jürgen Moltmann, *On Human Dignity: Political Theology and Ethics*, trans. M. Douglas Meeks (Philadelphia: Fortress Press, 1985), 97–122; idem, "Political Theology," in *The Experiment Hope*, trans. M. Douglas Meeks (Philadelphia: Fortress Press, 1975), 101–18; idem, "Toward a Political Hermeneutic of the Gospel," *Religion, Revolution and the Future*, trans. M. Douglas Meeks (New York: Chas. Scribner's Sons, 1969), 83–107; Johann Baptist Metz, *Theology of the World*, trans. William Glen-Doepel (New York: Seabury Press, 1969); idem, *Faith in History and Society*, trans. David Smith (New York: Seabury Press, 1980); idem, *The Emergent Church: The Future of Christianity in a Postbourgeois World*, trans. Peter Mann (New York: Crossroad, 1981); Francis Fiorenza, "Political Theology as Foundational Theology," *Catholic Theological Society of America Proceedings* 32 (1977): 142–77; Helmut Peukert, ed., *Diskussion zur "Politischen Theologien"* (Mainz: Matthias Grünewald, 1969); John B. Cobb, Jr., *Process Theology as Political Theology*

(Philadelphia: Westminster Press, 1982); José Míguez Bonino, *Toward a Christian Political Ethics* (Philadelphia: Fortress Press, 1983), Leroy S. Rouner, ed., *Civil Religion and Political Theology* (Notre Dame: University of Notre Dame Press, 1986).

24. Gustavo Gutiérrez, *The Power of the Poor in History*, trans. Robert S. Barr (Maryknoll, N.Y.: Orbis Books, 1983); Juan Luis Segundo, *Faith and Ideologies*, trans. John Drury (Maryknoll, N.Y.: Orbis Books, 1984); Rebecca S. Chopp, *The Praxis of Suffering: An Interpretation of Liberation and Political Theologies* (Maryknoll, N.Y.: Orbis Books, 1986); Frederick Herzog, *God-Walk: Liberation Shaping Dogmatics* (Maryknoll, N.Y.: Orbis Books, 1988). See also Cornel West, *Prophesy Deliverance: An Afro-American Revolutionary Christianity* (Philadelphia: Westminster Press, 1982); and James H. Cone, *God of the Oppressed* (New York: Seabury Press, 1975).

25. Michael Walzer, *Spheres of Justice: A Defense of Pluralism and Equality* (New York: Basic Books, 1983).

26. In precapitalist societies wealth had no purpose beyond its existing. Great surpluses became wealth in the form of citadels and military force, religious shrines, or monumental works or luxury objects which aggrandized rulers. Great wealth expressed the grandeur and power of rulership itself. Wealth had "use value." See Aristotle, *Politics*, Book II.

27. Robert L. Heilbroner, *The Nature and Logic of Capitalism* (New York: W. W. Norton, 1985), 52.

28. Ibid., 35.

29. Ibid., 36.

30. See Polanyi, *Livelihood of Man*, 24–34.

31. "Wherever there is great prosperity, there is great inequality. For one rich man there must be at least five hundred poor, and the affluence of the rich supposes the indigence of the many." Adam Smith, *The Wealth of Nations* (Oxford: Clarendon Press, 1976), 709–10.

32. Heilbroner, *Nature and Logic of Capitalism*, 38.

33. For interesting studies of the perception of justice in the American economy, see Jennifer L. Hochschild, *What's Fair: American Beliefs about Distributive Justice* (Cambridge, Mass.: Harvard University Press, 1981); and Herbert McClosky and John Zaller, *The American Ethos: Public Attitudes toward Capitalism and Democracy* (Cambridge, Mass.: Harvard University Press, 1987).

34. Lindblom, *Politics and Markets*, 46.

35. The orthodox liberal argument is inadequate unless it justifies exclusive private property as itself consistent with freedom, a point on which it is silent. It does not discuss the possible coerciveness of private property. In liberal thought a world of exchange is without conflict; everyone does what he or she wishes. When all social coordination is thoroughly voluntary exchange, no one imposes his or her will on anyone else. But this is possible only because the conflicts over who gets what have already been settled through a distribution of property rights in society. Distribution is not conflict free. The present distribution of wealth is the result of centuries of conflict.

36. For examples of how this gets played out in politics, see Thomas Byrne Edsall, *The New Politics of Inequality* (New York: W. W. Norton, 1984).

37. Heilbroner, *Nature and Logic of Capitalism*, 66. It is argued that market liberties, together with the fragmentation of property and decision-making that are characteristics of market systems, are necessary to political freedom and democracy. According to the classical liberal case for market systems, liberty exists through and on the basis of market relations. The classic arguments are Friedrich A. Hayek, *The Road to Serfdom* (Chicago: University of Chicago Press, 1944); and Milton Friedman, *Capitalism and Freedom* (Chicago: University of Chicago Press, 1962). Michael Novak has attempted to make these arguments on moral grounds: *The Spirit of Democratic Capitalism* (New York: Simon & Schuster, 1982). For counter-arguments see J. M. Buchanan, *The Limits of Liberty: Between Anarchy and Leviathan* (Chicago: University of Chicago Press, 1975); Michael J. Sandel, *Liberalism and the Limits of Justice* (Cambridge: Cambridge University Press, 1982); Allen F. Buchanan, *Marx and Justice: The Radical Critique of Liberalism* (Totowa, N.J.: Rowan & Littlefield, 1982); William A. Galston, *Justice and the Human Good* (Chicago: University of Chicago Press, 1980); Samuel Bowles, et al., *Beyond the Waste Land: A Democratic Alternative Economic Doctrine* (Garden City, N.Y.: Doubleday Anchor Books, 1983); Herbert Gintis, "Social Contradictions and the Liberal Theory of Justice," in *New Directions in Social Justice*, ed. Roger Skurski (Notre Dame, Ind.: University of Notre Dame Press, 1983), 90–112; Samuel Bowles and Herbert Gintis, *Democracy and Capitalism: Property, Community, and the Contradictions of Modern Social Thought* (New York: Basic Books, 1986); Andrew Devine, *Liberal Democracy: A Critique of Its Theory* (New York: Columbia University Press, 1981).

38. Heilbroner, *Nature and Logic of Capitalism*, 66.

39. Bowles and Gintis, *Democracy and Capitalism*, 127–30.

40. Most people remunerated in market systems spend their working time in an authority system, that is, in an organized business enterprise in which the rational authority of bureaucracy reigns. Freedom is constantly threatened in an organization in which a few people command thousands of others in the standardized patterns of bureaucracy. Lindblom, *Politics and Markets*, 47. Libertarians reply that employees accepting managerial authority are still free because they voluntarily accept that authority and are free to terminate it. Here again liberal theory refuses to accept livelihood as the chief character of economy and utterly represses human suffering.

People who work within exchange systems often suffer, against their volition, for the sake of the production of new exchange relations of which they are not a part. One way in which existing economic organization can be changed is by the termination of existing exchange relations, such as the termination of jobs by a corporation. This method is coercive. People must move, leave their homes, change their occupation—none of which is their choosing. The injury inflicted through termination of an exchange relationship is an exception that the law does not cover (so that the market system can persist). Liberal market theory is blind to this suffering.

Furthermore, the mere threat of termination can be coercive, as menacing as any governmental command.

41. Ibid., 49.

42. Ibid.

43. Ibid., 48.

44. Milton L. Myers, *The Soul of Modern Economic Man: Ideas of Self-Interest from Thomas Hobbes to Adam Smith* (Chicago: University of Chicago Press, 1983); Norman Fischer, *Economy and Self: Philosophy and Economics from the Mercantilists to Marx* (Westport, Conn.: Greenwood Press, 1979), 42–60.

45. See Robert Kuttner, *The Economic Illusion: False Choices between Prosperity and Social Justice* (Boston: Houghton Mifflin, 1984).

46. Lyuba Zarsky, et al., eds., *Economic Report of the People* (Boston: South End Press, 1986), 23–40. See also Frank Ackerman, *Harzardous to Our Health* (Boston: South End Press, 1984); idem, *Reaganomics: Rhetoric vs. Reality* (Boston: South End Press, 1982); John Weeks, *Capital and Exploitation* (Princeton: Princeton University Press, 1981).

47. For Adam Smith this force was still the Deity, whose will, though incomprehensible to human reason, was working for the comprehensive benefit of society. For Marx the force was the relations of capital and labor, the "laws of motion," which remained hidden because of the fetishism that blinds people to their real social situation. For neoclassical economics the ordering impulse is the universal drive of individuals to gain material wealth in face of the constraint of competition with all others.

48. Most of the victims of the disaster at the Union Carbide plant in Bhopal, India on December 3, 1984 were not in exchange relationships with the company, yet had enormous, unchosen costs imposed on them. A series of explosive, water-induced chemical reactions sent lethal methyl isocyanate vapors into the city, causing 2,000 deaths directly and massive, long-lasting physical and psychological disabling among the 400,000 people exposed to the lung-burning gas. See, Joydeep Gupta, *World Press Review* (February 1986), 56.

49. Bowles and Gintis, *Democracy and Capitalism*, 199–203.

50. Except, of course, the transactions of those who possessed the divine right of ownership. There were, however, defined rights and freedoms within distinct social spheres of feudal and tributary societies, many of which have been lost under the regime of capital.

51. The formation of this personality can be seen in Myers, *The Soul of Modern Economic Man*; Martin Hollis and Edward J. Nell, *Rational Economic Man: A Philosophical Critique of Neo-Classical Economics* (Cambridge: Cambridge University Press, 1975); Maital, *Minds, Markets, and Money*; Walter A. Weisskoff, *Alienation and Economics*; Gary Becker, *The Economic Approach to Human Behavior* (Chicago: University of Chicago Press, 1957); Polanyi, *Livelihood of Man*.

52. Franz J. Hinkelammert, "The Politics of the Total Market, Its Theology and Our Response," *North-South Dialogue* 1 (Fall 1985): 7.

53. Cf. Eberhard Jüngel, *God as the Mystery of the World,* trans. Darrell L. Guder (Grand Rapids: Wm. B. Eerdmans, 1983), 281–98.

54. J.W. Hill, *The Three-Personed God: The Trinity as a Mystery of Salvation* (Washington, D.C.: Catholic University Press of America, 1982), 172. "The precedence of the doctrine of *de Deo uno* over the doctrine of the Trinity and its substantiation by natural theology had disastrous effects for the whole Western doctrine of God, because it gave grounds for the development of atheism and has itself pre-Christian features" (Jürgen Moltmann, *The Church in the Power of the Spirit: A Contribution to Messianic Ecclesiology,* trans. Margaret Kohl [San Francisco: Harper & Row, 1977], 370).

55. Robert Jensen, *The Triune Identity* (Philadelphia: Fortress Press, 1982), ix.

56. See Jürgen Moltmann, *The Trinity and the Kingdom,* trans. Margaret Kohl (New York: Harper & Row, 1981); *The Crucified God: The Cross of Christ as the Foundation and Criticism of Christian Theology,* trans. R.A. Wilson and John Bowden (New York: Harper & Row, 1974). See also Arthur C. McGill, *Suffering: A Test of Theological Method* (Philadelphia: Westminster Press, 1982).

4. GOD THE ECONOMIST

1. For complementary ways of modeling God, see Sallie McFague, *Models of God: Theology for an Ecological, Nuclear Age* (Philadelphia: Fortress Press, 1987).

2. Gerhard von Rad, *Old Testament Theology,* Vol. I (New York: Harper & Row, 1962, 1965), 370, cf. 373. For righteousness as the power/activity of God's salvation cf. Is. 46:13; 51:5, 6, 8; 56:1). I follow John Reumann's ground-breaking work but, instead of differentiating *oikonomia* and *sdq/diakaiosyne,* I see them as much more closely connected. Righteousness is the work of God's economy. See Reumann, "The 'Righteousness of God' and the 'Economy of God': Two Great Doctrinal Themes Historically Compared." in *AKSUM THYATEIRA: A Festschrift for Archbishop Methodios of Thyateira and Great Britain,* ed. George Dion. Dragas (London: Thyateira House, 1985), 615–37.

3. Robert Alter, *The Art of Biblical Narrative,* (New York: Basic Books, 1981), 12.

4. For the use of Yahweh's "home," "house," and "household," see Aubrey R. Johnson, *The Cultic Prophet and Israel's Psalmody* (Cardiff: University of Wales Press, 1979), 20ff. and passim.

5. Paul van Buren, *A Christian Theology of the People of Israel* (New York: Seabury Press, 1983), 76.

6. Michael Welker, "Security of Expectations: Reformulating the Theology of Law and Gospel," *Journal of Religion* 66 (1986), 237–60.

7. Robert Gnuse, *You Shall Not Steal: Community and Property in the Biblical Tradition* (Maryknoll, N.Y.: Orbis Books, 1985), 17.

8. Sharon H. Ringe, *Jesus, Liberation, and the Biblical Jubilee* (Philadelphia: Fortress Press, 1985).

9. Von Rad, *Old Testament Theology,* 1:136ff.

10. Ibid., 1:150ff.

11. There is not space here to deal with the Davidic trajectory. Here the notion that God is the royal owner of the land and of the whole creation is more fully developed. In these traditions the economic role of God can often be designated with the metaphor "benefactor." See Frederick Danker, *Benefactor: Epigraphic Study of a Greco-Roman and New Testament Semantic Field* (St. Louis: Clayton Publishing House, 1982). But if the Davidic emphases get worked out in the New Testament in terms of God as the "Chief Benefactor," whose beneficence will ultimately create the "New City," the city no longer subject to death, sin, and evil, then this trajectory nevertheless comes close to the notion of God as the Economist/Steward in the claim that *Jesus' own donation is his life.* In Jesus, God gives God's life away as the benefaction that leads to life for the public household and the creation.

12. M. Douglas Meeks, "God as Economist and the Problem of Property," *Occasional Paper,* Institute for Ecumenical and Cultural Research, Winter 1984.

13. John H. Elliott, *A Home for the Homeless: A Sociological Exegesis of 1 Peter, Its Situation and Strategy* (Philadelphia: Fortress Press, 1981), 221.

14. Ibid., 197. Cf. the treatment of divine *oikonomia* in Letty M. Russell, *The Future of Partnership* (Philadelphia: Westminster Press, 1979), 26–43; and *Household of Freedom: Authority in Feminist Theology* (Philadelphia: Westminster Press, 1987), 29–41 and passim. See also John Koenig, *New Testament Hospitality* (Philadelphia: Fortress Press, 1985); Thomas W. Ogletree, *Hospitality to the Stranger: Dimensions of a Moral Understanding* (Philadelphia: Fortress Press, 1985).

15. According to Aristotle's "science of the master," "the rule of the household is a monarchy, for every house is under one head: whereas constitutional rule is a government of freemen and equals." *Politics, The Basic Works of Aristotle,* trans. Richard McKeon (New York: Random House, 1941), 1255, p. 1135. Householders, "those who are in a position which places them above toil," use their possessions, slaves, and other members of the household not only as instruments "for maintaining life" but also instruments "of action." A slave by definition is a "part of property"; a free man a possessor of property. "For that some should rule and others be ruled is a thing not only necessary, but expedient; from the hour of their birth, some are marked out for subjection, others for rule." 1253, p. 1132. According to Aristotle, as paraphrased by M.I. Finley, "A man who possessed claims, privileges and powers in all matters against the whole world would be a god, not a man." *Economy and Society in Ancient Greece* (New York: Pengiun Books, 1983), 77. Such a one who did indeed possess such claims against the whole world was what antiquity termed deity.

16. Elisabeth Schüssler Fiorenza, *In Memory of Her: Feminist Theological Reconstruction of Christian Origins* (New York: Crossroad, 1983), 105–54.

17. Ibid., 120. See also George V. Pixley, *God's Kingdom,* trans. Donald A. Walsh (Maryknoll, N.Y.: Orbis Books, 1981); and *On Exodus: A Liberation Perspective* (Maryknoll, N.Y.: Orbis Books, 1987). For Pixley the Jesus movement explicitly worked out a strategy for "structural change" in economy. See also Luise Schottroff and Wolfgang Stegemann, *Jesus and the Hope of the Poor,* trans. Matthew J. O'Connell (Maryknoll, N.Y.: Orbis

Books, 1986); Willy Schottroff and Wolfgang Stegemann, eds., *God of the Lowly: Socio-historical Interpretations of the Bible,* trans. Matthew J. O'Connell (Maryknoll, N.Y.: Orbis Books, 1984).

18. Fiorenza, *In Memory of Her,* 122–30.

19. Ibid., 148. Schüssler Fiorenza claims that the later New Testament literature, including the Catholic epistles and the pseudo-Pauline epistles, takes over the Greco-Roman household codes and thus perpetuates the domination of the *pater familias.*

20. Elliott, *Home for the Homeless,* 232.

21. Ibid., 68.

22. Ibid., 226.

5. GOD AND PROPERTY

1. Through the seventeenth century people were said to have a property not only in lands and goods and claims on revenues from rents, mortgages, and patents, etc., but also a property in their lives and liberty. In an early draft, the American Declaration of Independence read "the right to life, liberty and property."

2. Douglass C. North, *Structure and Change in Economic History* (New York: W.W. Norton, 1981), 21. In one sense, politics is about the power conflict over who gets to decide property rights. In Federalist Paper No. 10, James Madison argued that the United States should not have direct rule by the people, a democracy, but rather representatives of the people, a republic. Madison makes it clear that the representatives should be the enlightened and virtuous property owners. With a complicated form of government designed to prevent a facile changing of property rights, property-owning representatives should be able to prevent rule by factions. And what is the worst thing about factions? If property owners rule, Madison explains, "A rage for paper money, for an abolition of debts, for an equal division of property, or for any other improper or wicked project, will be less apt to pervade the whole body of the Union. . . ." *The Federalist Papers* (New York: New American Library, 1961), 84. Madison here maintains a prevalent viewpoint that government exists primarily to protect property. Creel Froman, *The Two American Political Systems: Society, Economics, and Politics* (Englewood Cliffs, N.J.: Prentice-Hall, 1984), 14: "The source of American ideology concerning the ownership, control, disposition, and protection of property come from those who, like Madison, Jefferson, Adams, Hamilton, and others, were major controllers of property. And it is this ideology, based on property, that is transmitted, via the schools and families, to new members of society, the most important of these being children." Again, 27: "When we speak of 'society,' then, we must be careful to distinguish between its general functions of organization and protection on the one hand, and the ways in which it is organized so that some people have more property and some have less. This distinction will make us more sensitive to how certain groups within the larger society control the *content* of the whole society's ideology, determine its legal rules and procedures for settling conflict, and receive

an unequal share of its benefits." See also Marcus Cunliffe, *The Right to Property: A Theme in American History* (Atlantic Highlands, N.J.: Humanities Press, 1974).

3. An archaeology of property will show that the concept of property has changed between archaic, ancient, medieval, and modern market societies. There are radical differences in property among hunting, gathering, cultivating, and irrigating societies. The common property of Germanic tribes and the private property of Roman society are as different as are the ancient Russian rural institution of the *Mir* and the Chinese village. Various property rights have been developed to justify claims of slave owners, feudal lords, popes, mercantilists, entrepreneurs, and corporation managers. New definitions of property have usually sprung up during periods of conflict, when epochal changes were taking place within the social and economic relations of society.

4. Karl Polanyi, *Primitive, Archaic and Modern Economies: Essays of Karl Polanyi,* ed. George Dalton (New York: Anchor Books, 1968); Karl Polanyi, Conrad M. Arensberg, and Henry W. Pearson, eds., *Trade and Market in the Early Empires* (New York: Free Press, 1957).

5. Wolfgang J. Friedmann, "Property," *Dictionary of the History of Ideas* (New York: Charles Scribner's Sons, 1973), 650.

6. For the following, see C.B. Macpherson, "The Meaning of Property" and "Liberal Democracy and Property," in *Property: Mainstrean and Critical Positions,* ed. C.B. Macpherson (Toronto: University of Toronto Press, 1978), 1–13, 199–207.

7. Hannah Arendt, *The Human Condition* (Garden City, N.Y.: Doubleday Anchor Books, 1959), 23–69.

8. Macpherson, *Property,* 10.

9. For the following, see Macpherson, *Property,* 1–13, 199–207; Anthony Parel and Thomas Flanagan, eds., *Theories of Property: Aristotle to the Present,* (Waterloo, Ont.: Wilfred Laurier University Press, 1979); Richard Schlatter, *Private Property: The History of an Idea* (New York: Russell & Russell, 1973 [1951]), 77ff.; C.B. Macpherson, *The Theory of Possessive Individualism* (New York: Oxford University Press, 1962).

10. Schlatter, *Private Property,* 156: "Before 1690 no one understood that a man had a natural right to property created by his own labor; after 1690 the idea came to be an axiom of social science. That date might be taken to mark the year when the middle class rose to power; the year in which their experience, dressed up in philosophical language by John Locke, was presented to the world as the eternal truth of things." Once Locke had articulated the standard middle-class doctrine against feudal privilege and royal absolutism, "life, liberty, and property" became the slogan under which the liberal political economy could be slowly constructed over the next one hundred years.

11. Friedmann, "Property," 652. Whereas *quiritarian* property was transferred only with great legal difficulty, a second kind of property, *bonitarian* property, was easily transferred to meet the needed mobility and flexibility of a commercial society. This difference in property reflected the history of conflict between patricians and plebians over

the control of land and other forms of property, a conflict in the
background for the contrast between public and private property.

12. M. I. Finley, *The Ancient Economy* (Berkeley: University of California
Press, 1971); Alan Watson, *The Law of Property in the Later Roman
Republic* (Oxford: Clarendon Press, 1968).

13. It is true that the emperor in Greece and Rome was different from
the absolute despot of the East, insofar as he did not have exhaustive
control of property. But the emperor remained the symbolic model of
absolute control over property.

14. Cicero and Seneca developed these theories before they were
expressed in Roman Law, through whose influence medieval and
modern views of property were largely shaped. The early church
theologians' criticism of private property, even if they did not propose
abolishing private property except in ascetic settings, was more
profound than modern interpreters such as Ernst Troeltsch have
suggested; see his *Social Teaching of the Christian Churches*, trans. Olive
Wyon (New York: Harper Torch Books, 1960), 115–16. Troeltsch implies
that the Fathers spiritualized their view of property, but the case is
actually just the opposite. See also Martin Hengel, *Property and Riches
in the Early Church: Aspects of a Social History of Early Christianity*
(Philadelphia: Fortress Press, 1974); Redmond Mullin, *The Wealth of
Christians* (Maryknoll, N.Y.: Orbis Books, 1984); and L. William
Countryman, *The Rich Christian in the Church of the Early Empire:
Contradictions and Accommodations* (New York: Edwin Mellen Press,
1980).

15. Ambrose, *S. Ambrosii De Nabuthe Jezraelita: A Commentary with an
Introduction and Translation,* trans. Martin R. P. Mcquire (Washington,
D.C.: Catholic University of America Press, 1927), 2–3.

16. *De Nabuthe,* quoted by Charles Avila, *Ownership: Early Christian
Teaching* (Maryknoll, N.Y.: Orbis Books, 1983), 66.

17. Justifying property by "first occupancy" usually masked the violence
by which the property was seized. Chrysostom queries, "From whom did
you receive [that large estate], and from whom he who transmitted it to
you? . . . But can you, ascending through many generations, show the
acquisition just? It cannot be. The root and origin of it must have been
injustice. Why? Because God in the beginning did not make one man rich
and another poor. . . . He left the earth free to all alike. Why, then, if it
is common, have you so many acres of land, while your neighbor has not a
portion of it? . . . Is this not an evil, that you alone should enjoy what is
common?" In *Epistolam I ad Timotheum,* 12, 4, quoted by Avila, *Ownership:
Early Christian Teaching,* 94.

18. John Locke, *Two Treatises of Civil Government* (New York: E.P.
Dutton, 1970 [1690]), 129.

19. Locke, *Civil Government,* 130. "That labour puts a distinction
between them [acorns or apples] and common. That added something
to them more than Nature, the common mother of all, has done, and so
they become his private right. . . . We see in commons, which remain
so by compact, that it is the taking any part of what is common, and
removing it out of the state Nature leaves it in, which begins the

property, without which the common is no use. And the taking of this or that part does not depend on the express consent of all of the commoners. Thus, the grass my horse has bit, the turfs my servant has cut, and the one I have digged in any place, where I have a right to them in common with others, become my property without the assignation or consent of anybody. The labour that was mine, removing them out of that common state they were in, both fixed my property in them."

20. Schlatter, *Private Property*, 157–61. Locke returned to the old theory that property was the conventional creation of human beings.

21. Schlatter, *Private Property*, 160.

22. The state is established to protect unequal property, which is held to be prior to government. In antiquity, military, legal, and religious power led to wealth; in modernity, wealth leads to power. Now the assumption was no longer that rulers needed property to perform the duties proper to their dignity but that people of property should be the rulers. The power to rule no longer gives one the right to property but rather property gives one the right to rule in order to protect one's property. C. B. Macpherson, "Human Rights as Property Rights," *Dissent* 24 (Winter 1977): 73. The equality of property in the sense of access of all to what they need to fulfill their lives became unthinkable because it would take from the rich the possibility of being rich. See Schlatter, *Private Property*, 98–99.

23. Lawrence C. Becker, "The Moral Basis of Property Rights," in *Property*, ed. J. Roland Pennock and John W. Chapman (New York: New York University Press, 1980), 193f.

24. According to Locke's theory of property, before the invention of money there were definite limits to private property. Property acquired by labor included only those things which a single person could extract from nature; it was limited to the amount the person could use, and the appropriator from nature had to leave enough for the needs of others. Nature gives property and also sets limits to property. "As much as anyone can make use of to any advantage of life before it spoils, so much he may by his labor fix a property in. Whatever is beyond this is more than his share, and belongs to others." *Civil Government*, 131.

25. Macpherson, *Property*, 204–5.

26. When labor is reduced to a commodity, it, too, shows the characteristics of "commodity fetishism," which Karl Marx likened to idolatry. A commodity, claimed Marx, can be viewed as a "social hieroglyphic" because it embodies social relationships which have gone into its production but which have been mystified or hidden. Robert L. Heilbroner, *Marxism: For and Against* (New York: Norton, 1980), 102. The commodity of human labor in the market society divulges all the distorted relationships of the whole society.

Marx's program of demystifying society depended on showing that the exchange ratios of economy did not ultimately rest in "nature," as classical economics had claimed, but that they are determined by social relationships. The "profit" drive in our system, according to Marx, causes the capitalist constantly to arrange human labor so that surplus value can be created (e.g., the division, simplification, routinization, mechanization of labor). The exclusive right or property of the capitalist in the produced commodity alienates the laborer from the fruits of his or her labor. Once the laborers have sold their property, their labor, they lose the right to that with which they have mixed their labor. Furthermore the capitalist owns the raw materials and machines with which the laborer works. The laborer is thus separated from nature and his or her means of livelihood.

A commodity has a *use value* (it embodies usefulness or pleasure for human beings) and an *exchange value* (it is able to command other objects or money in everyday transactions); see Heilbroner, *Marxism*, 96. The amount of labor that goes into producing a commodity determines the exchange value. A commodity has a fetish character insofar as it hides the fact that there is always a quantum of unpaid labor in the commodity owned by the capitalist. This is Marx's theory of "surplus value." The notion of surplus value depends upon the difference between labor and labor power. Labor power is the *capacity for work* that an employer buys when he or she hires a worker for a day or a week. Labor, on the other hand, is the *actual expenditure of human energy and intelligence* that becomes embodied in the commodities that laborers create. Marx's theory of surplus value asserts that there must be a systematic difference between the two—that one must always be able to buy the capacity for work for less than the value that will be created when that capacity is put to use and commodities are produced. Indeed, it is only because this difference exists that capital itself can be brought into being; see Heilbroner, 107.

27. C. B. Macpherson, "Human Rights as Property Rights," 73ff.

28. For what Lawrence C. Becker considers an exhaustive list of the elements of modern ownership, see his article "The Moral Basis of Property Rights," 190–91. See also Lawrence C. Becker, *Property Rights: Philosophical Foundations* (Boston: Routledge & Kegan Paul, 1977); Virginia Held, comp., *Property, Profits and Economic Justice* (Belmont, Calif.: Wadsworth Publishing Co., 1980); Lawrence Becker and Kenneth Kipnis, *Property: Cases, Concepts, Critiques* (Englewood Cliffs, N.J.: Prentice-Hall, 1984).

29. M. Douglas Meeks, "The Holy Spirit and Human Needs: Toward a Trinitarian View of Economics," *Christianity & Crisis* 40 (November 10, 1980): 307–16.

30. Macpherson, *The Political Theory of Possessive Individualism.*

31. John R. Wikse, *About Possession: The Self as Private Property* (University Park, Penn.: Pennsylvania State University Press, 1977). See also Russel Scott, *The Body as Property* (New York: Viking, 1981).

32. Perhaps more than any other philosopher, Hegel argued for the necessity of property because it both allows and requires human beings to shape themselves and the objective world. Putting one's will in external things and manifesting one's "right of appropriation" are necessary to becoming an actual will. But that Hegel does not carefully enough reflect on the danger of idolatry is shown in Marx's critique of Hegel. See Peter G. Stillman, "Property, Freedom, and Individuality in Hegel's and Marx's Political Thought," in *Property*, ed. Pennock and Chapman, 130–67.

33. Cf. for this, Jürgen Moltmann, *The Trinity and the Kingdom*, trans. Margaret Kohl (New York: Harper & Row, 1974), 191–200.

34. According to the New Testament *koinōnia* means mutual coinherence of the believers and Jesus Christ. From this follows the mutual coinherence of the believer and the community (1 Cor. 1:9, 12:12–13; Hebrews 2:14; 1 Peter 1:4). Having a share in Jesus Christ means "giving a share" in the household of life (Philem. 17; Phil. 4:15; Gal. 6:6; 1 Cor. 9:11).

35. The modes of sharing in the New Testament texts can probably be divided up according to the institutionalized relationships of *reciprocity* (mutual gift-giving, mutual sharing of interests, e.g., Phil. 2) and *redistribution* (sharing out of a community of goods, e.g., Acts 3). Cf. Polanyi, *The Livelihood of Man* (New York: Academic Press, 1977), 35–43.

36. They lived from a common purse, which provided their daily needs and their means to pay the Temple tax and alms (Matt. 17:27; John 13:29). A group of Galilean women provided for the livelihood of this band of "hard-core unemployed" (Lk. 8:1–3). As his constant companions, these women ministered to Jesus, stayed with him through his public humiliation and execution, were the first evangelists to proclaim his resurrection, and were the nucleus of followers from which the early church originated (Luke 23:49, 55–56; 24:1–11; Acts 1:14; 2:1).

37. As Michael Harrington has put it in *Socialism* (New York: Saturday Review Press, 1972), 4: "One need not any longer ask whether the future is going to be collective—if we do not blow ourselves to smithereens, that issue has already been settled by a technology of such complex interdependence that it demands conscious regulation and control." Factories, unions, corporations, banks, medical centers, universities, insurance companies, and government bureaucracies are factually putting the lie to any notion that freedom can be conceived in terms of the isolated, self-interested individual.

38. For a discussion of the theological difference between "making" and "creating," see Jürgen Moltmann, *God in Creation: A New Theology of Creation and the Spirit of God*, trans. Margaret Kohl (San Francisco: Harper & Row, 1981), 72–79.

39. Terence E. Fretheim, *The Suffering of God: An Old Testament Perspective* (Philadelphia: Fortress Press, 1984).

40. Of course, gifting as "benefacting" can have its hidden means of dominating or controlling. See the strange arguments about "gifting" in George Gilder, *Wealth and Poverty* (New York: Bantam Books, 1982). "Gifting" is not normally thought of as a dimension, much less, the foundation of our economy. But there is a growing scholarly interest in the *gift* or *grant* economy. Kenneth E. Boulding, *The Economy of Love and Fear: A Preface to Grant Economics* (Belmont, Calif.: Wadsworth Publishing Co., 1973); David Collard, *Altruism and Economics: A Study in Non-Selfish Economics* (Oxford: Oxford University Press, 1978).

41. Paraphrase of Basil, see Avila, *Ownership*, 53.

42. According to Clement, "It is God himself who has brought our race to a *koinōnia*, by sharing Himself, first of all by sending His Word (*Logos*) to all alike, and by making all things for all." *Paidagogos*, book 2, chapter 12, quoted by Avila, *Ownership*, 37.

43. See Luise Schottroff and Wolfgang Stegemann, *Jesus and the Hope of the Poor*, trans. Matthew J. O'Connell (Maryknoll, N.Y.: Orbis Books, 1986), 67–120; George V. Pixley, *God's Kingdom*, trans. Donald D. Walsh (Maryknoll, N.Y: Orbis Books, 1981), 63–87.

44. Avila, *Ownership*, 132. Jacob Viner, *Religious Thought and Economic Society*, ed. Jacques Melitz and Donald Winch (Durham, N.C.: Duke University Press, 1978), 15ff.

45. "The Educator," 2, 3, in S.P. Wood, *Clement of Alexandria*, (New York: Fathers of the Church, 1954), 193.

46. Jewish law, which is a summation of obligations to God, understands property essentially as a means of fulfilling these obligations. See the article "Eigentum," in *Theologische Realenzyklopedie*, (Berlin: Walter de Gruyter, 1982): 9:404–60.

47. Jesus' saying about the needle's eye (Lk. 18:24–30; cf. Mk. 10:23–31; Matt. 19:23–30) epitomizes his teaching about possessions. Ingeniously interpreted throughout the tradition to avoid its harshness, this typical semitic exaggerated metaphor shows the basic incompatibility between the abundance of riches and faithful discipleship. There is no optimism about rich persons relinquishing possessions and becoming disciples. Only the righteousness of God will give the strength to abandon their trust in their possessions and do whatever is necessary to live a life freed from their bondage and free for the economy of God's household. The story of Zacchaeus (Luke 19:1–10) attests that it can happen.

48. For the following, see Walter E. Pilgrim, *Good News to the Poor: Wealth and Poverty in Luke-Acts* (Minneapolis: Augsburg Publishing House, 1981), 87ff.

49. See Walter Wink, *Unmasking the Powers: The Invisible Forces That Determine Human Existence* (Philadelphia: Fortress Press, 1986).

50. Lewis Hyde, *The Gift: Imagination and the Erotic Life of Property* (New York: Vintage Books, 1983), 3ff.

51. See George Dalton, ed., *Tribal and Peasant Economies: Readings in Economic Anthropology* (Garden City, N.Y.: Natural History Press, 1967); Richard Titmuss, *The Gift Relationship: From Human Blood to Social Policy* (New York: Pantheon, 1971); Marcel Mauss, *The Gift: Forms and Functions of Exchange in Archaic Societies*, trans. Ian Cunnison (New York: W. W. Norton, 1967).

52. See Jürgen Moltmann and M. Douglas Meeks, "The Liberation of Oppressors," *Christianity & Crisis* 38(1978): 310–17.

53. Moltmann, *Trinity and the Kingdom*, 54–55.

54. Luke does not make total abandonment of possessions a once-for-all mark of Christian discipleship. Luke 22:35–38 seems to legitimate a new form of discipleship after Jesus' departure: a bag, and purse, and sword may be needed.

55. According to Clement, "Goods were made to be possessed. Goods are called goods because they do good, and they have been provided by God for the good of humanity. . . . You can use [wealth] rightly; it ministers to righteousness. But if one uses it wrongly it is found to be a minister of wrong, for its nature is to minister, not to rule." "The Rich Man's Salvation," 12–13, *PG* 9:616–17, in *Clement of Alexandria: The*

Exhortation to the Greeks; The Rich Man's Salvation; To the Newly Baptized,
trans. G. W. Butterworth (London: Heinemann, 1953), 267. According to
Philo, every possession is a loan from God which can at any time be
demanded back. Property is a kind of endowment for a purpose. One
should not destroy one's property without good reason. One can tear
one's garment, but one should not overdo it. The body, health, and
property stand in God's service and may not be destroyed or harmed.

56. The way property is held should be determined by the character of
property as created and intended by God. Here we have to make a
distinction in the Christian tradition between the Augustinian and the
Thomist approach. The traditional Christian appropriation of Stoicism
claimed that by God's creation all property is common and made for
common use of all. There was, however, provisional, private use as long
as it was used for the well-being of the community. Thus it was said that
property should be owned in common and used privately.

The Augustinian theory was combined with the primitive Germanic
law to give birth to the feudal conception of property. Richard McKeon,
"The Development of the Concept of Property," *Ethics* 48 (April 1938),
297–367. According to Augustine, God is lord and owner of the world.
God grants the right to use God's property to the righteous, providing
they render fealty to God. In feudal theory, property and political
authority were both denoted by dominion. The conventions of
government and property are not natural but are necessitated by sin.
Thus did both pope and king have the justification for claiming feudal
lordship over the world insofar as they represented God's ownership of
the world for the sake of order. The property right of each vassal was
respected as long as the vassal rendered fealty and homage.

Aquinas, synthesizing the traditional Christian thought and
Aristotle, gave reasons for rejecting the traditional Christian/Stoic
conception of property. In some ways he strengthened feudalism, while
in other ways he contributed to overcoming it. Instead of "own in
common, use privately for the common good," Aquinas urged, "own
privately, use in common." Aquinas held that property and the political
authority that protected it had always existed and were natural. That
property should be determined by right reason in accordance with
natural law meant for Aquinas that it should be distributed according
to the elaborate hierarchy of classes, the most perfect form of social
organization. This was a defense of wealth by both popes and kings
against each other's claims and by the rising middle class against both.
But it has also been used to justify the intervention of the state to
provide for the necessities of life for all. Aquinas's view of justice led to
approximately the same understanding of the use of property as found
in the older Christian tradition: hold all things in such a way that they
may be common for all.

57. It is true that the early theologians also often speak of property as
the means of *autarkeia*, self-sufficiency. The Stoic notion of *autarkeia*
connotes contentedness, satisfaction, and self-determination that would
keep the individual from being a burden to others. But the Fathers did
not understand self-sufficiency in the modern sense as a way of making
oneself independent of the community. The early theologians used this
term to affirm that God has supplied us with what we need, the

necessities (*ta anangkaia*). Certain things are easy to acquire because they are necessary. They need no more justification than God's patent desire that God's creatures live. But even more crucial for the early theologians, self-sufficiency of property is the means of providing others in the household with whatever will prevent their becoming dependent. *Autarkeia* can also be a way of trying to express the Pauline sense of eschatological distancing from property in which Paul's advice was to "Let those who buy [live] as though they had no goods, and those who deal with the world as though they had no dealings with it. For the form of this world is passing away" (1 Cor. 7:30–31).

58. *Summa Theologiae*, II–II, q. 66, aa. 2 and 7.

59. *Enarratio in Psalmum*, 12; quoted by Avila, *Ownership*, 113. According to Ambrose, "When we minister the necessities of life to those who are in want, we are returning to them their own, not being bountiful with what is ours; we pay a debt of justice rather than fulfill works of mercy."

60. Calvin reaffirmed the old idea that "ownership entailed obligations and was contingent on the right use of property." See *Institutes*, III, vii and x. This protected the good owner since it maintained that his or her property was bestowed by God, not the state, but it also encouraged people to use their property for the poor beyond the injunctions of the law.

61. Gregory of Nyssa says, "If one should seek to be absolute possessor of all, refusing even a third or a fifth [of his possessions] to his brothers, then he is a cruel tyrant, a savage with whom there can be no dealing, an insensate beast gloatingly shutting its jaws over the meal it will not share." Quoted by William Walsh and P. Langan, "Patristic Social Consciousness: The Church and the Poor," in *The Faith That Does Justice*, ed. John C. Haughey (New York: Paulist Press, 1977), 127.

62. The *Didache* exhorts, "Share your possessions with your brother, and do not claim anything is your own. If you and he are joint participators in things immortal, how much more in things mortal." *Didache*, 1.4.8, in *Early Christian Writings*, trans. M. Stariforth (London: Penguin Books, 1972), 229.

63. Aquinas, *Summa Theologiae*, II–II, q. 66, art. 7: "It is not theft, properly speaking, to take secretly and use another's property in case of extreme need: because that which he takes for the support of his life becomes his own property by reason of that need."

64. Robert Gnuse, *You Shall Not Steal: Community and Property in the Biblical Tradition* (Maryknoll, N.Y.: Orbis Books, 1985).

65. John T. Noonan, *The Scholastic Analysis of Usury* (Cambridge, Mass.: Harvard University Press, 1957); Benjamin N. Nelson, *The Idea of Usury: From Tribal Brotherhood to Universal Otherhood* (Princeton: Princeton University Press, 1949); Luther, "Trade and Usury," in *Luther's Works*, vol. 45, ed. Walther I. Brandt (Philadelphia: Fortress Press, 1962), 245–310.

66. Luke T. Johnson, *Sharing Possessions: Mandate and Symbol of Faith* (Philadelphia: Fortress Press, 1981).

67. Macpherson, *Property*, 74.

68. For a discussion of the difficulty of such a community of being, doing, and gifting in the context of our social policies, see Stanley Hauerwas, *A Community of Character: Toward a Constructive Christian Social Ethic* (Notre Dame, Ind.: University of Notre Dame Press, 1981), 72–86.

69. "For if the conception of a good has to be expounded in terms of such actions as those of practice, of the narrative unity of a human life and of a moral tradition, then goods, and with them the only grounds for the authority of laws and virtues, can only be discovered by entering into those relationships which constitute communities whose central bond is a shared vision of and understanding of goods." Alasdair MacIntyre, *After Virtue: A Study in Moral Theory* (Notre Dame, Ind.: University of Notre Dame Press, 1981), 240.

6. GOD AND WORK

1. One of the best studies of this phenomenon is E.P. Thompson, *The Making of the English Working Class* (New York: Vintage Books, 1966).

2. Quoted in Max Weber, *The Protestant Ethic and the Spirit of Capitalism*, trans. Talcott Parsons (New York: Charles Scribner's Sons, 1958), 281.

3. Peter D. Anthony, *The Ideology of Work* (London: Tavistock Publications, 1981), 43.

4. Studs Terkel, *Working* (New York: Pantheon Books, 1974), xi.

5. Several studies give firsthand accounts of work and its effects on family relations, health, emotions, income, longevity, living conditions, loyalty, etc. In addition to Terkel, *Working*, see Ronald Frazer, ed., *Work*, 2 vols. (Harmondsworth, Eng.: Penguin Books, 1969); Barbara Garson, *All the Livelong Day* (New York: Doubleday, 1975); Richard Sennet and Jonathan Cobb, *The Hidden Injuries of Class* (New York: Alfred A. Knopf, 1972); Harry Braverman, *Labor and Monopoly Capital: The Degradation of Work in the Twentieth Century* (New York: Monthly Review Press, 1975); Richard Balzer, *Clockwork* (New York: Doubleday, 1976); U.S. Department of Health, Education and Welfare, *Work in America* (Cambridge: MIT Press, 1973). See also James B. Gilbert. *Work without Salvation: America's Intellectual and Industrial Alienation* (Baltimore: Johns Hopkins University Press, 1977); David M. Gordon, et al., *Segmented Work, Divided Workers: The Historical Transformation of Work in the United States* (Cambridge: Cambridge University Press, 1982).

6. David Bleakley, *Work: The Shadow and the Substance: A Reappraisal of Life and Labour* (London: SCM Press, 1983).

7. Adriano Tilgher, *Homo Faber: Work through the Ages*, trans. Dorothy Canfield Fisher (Chicago: Henry Regnery, 1965), 149–63.

8. See Robert M. Pfeffer, *Working for Capitalism* (New York: Columbia University Press, 1979). Barry Bluestone and Bennet Harrison estimate that 32 to 38 million jobs were lost during the 1970s because of private disinvestment of American businesses. *The Deindustialization of America* (New York: Basic Books, 1982). Lester C. Thurow, *Generating Inequality: Mechanisms of Distribution in the U.S. Economy* (New York: Basic Books, 1975).

9. But it is clear that this view of work has not always been held. In fact it is not sufficient to explain the behavior of everyone in our time. Neither the "free-rider" phenomenon nor altruistic behavior can be explained by the strict market logic. "Neoclassical economic theory can explain how people acting in their own self-interest behave; it can explain why people do not bother to vote; it can explain why, as a result of the free rider problem, people will not participate in group actions where the individual gains are negligible. It cannot, however, explain effectively the reverse side of the coin, that is, behavior in which calculated self-interest is not the motivating factor. How do we account for altruistic behavior (the anonymous free donation of blood, for example); for the willingness of people to engage in immense sacrifice with no evident possible gain (the endless parade of individuals and groups in history who have incurred prison or death for abstract causes)? How do we explain the large numbers of people who do vote, or the enormous amount of effort individuals devote to participating in voluntary organizations where the individual returns are small or negligible?" Douglass C. North, *Structure and Change in Economic History*, (New York: W.W. Norton, 1981), 11.

10. Weber, *Protestant Ethic*, 62.

11. Smith was not arguing for an unrestrained economic motivation. His thought was often morally humane; he did not want radically to separate economy from the rest of social life. But Smith's defense of his arguments nevertheless marked the beginning of economic measurement as the criterion of work.

12. The Trinity prevents us from emphasizing only one aspect of God's life, e.g., work or rest, to the exclusion of others. The memory of the diverse perspectives on work in the biblical traditions themselves will support the relativization of work ideologies. The varieties of biblical traditions reflect different economic situations and thus different patterns of work. Work looks different in the nomadic life of the confederacy, the complex economy of the monarchy, and the periods of subjugation to imperial powers. Work is obviously affected by the introduction of new technologies and development in farming. The biblical writers face different ideologies of work in each of these situations. The Mosaic traditions speak of Torah-conformed work as the shape of the joy of obedience which brings freedom under the conditions of oppression. The prophets cry out against the dehumanization of the poor through the manipulation of work and its products (Isa. 31:3). Many of the Psalms are interested in how the household of God can exist under the conditions of exilic work. The wisdom traditions extol work as the best way of securing identity as God's people (Prov. 6:6–11; 12:24).

13. Because the tradition had difficulty conceiving both the work and person of the Third Person of the Trinity, there has been a characteristic deficit in the doctrine of the Holy Spirit. Recent eschatological theologies of the Holy Spirit have begun to correct this. From the perspective of God's ultimate redemption, it can be said that the Holy Spirit takes the initiative and acts upon the Son and together with the Son acts upon the Father who, from this perspective, is passive. The peculiar work of the

Holy Spirit is ingathering, unifying, and glorifying. The Holy Spirit has the active part to play in the building of the community of God and the community of human beings.

14. Jürgen Moltmann, *The Trinity and the Kingdom,* trans. Margaret Kohl (New York: Harper & Row, 1974), 178–90.

15. Of course, slavery ultimately requires its ideology, too. But no specific ideology of work is necessary as long as slavery, forced labor, can be maintained. In fact, a sophisticated ideology of labor was needed only after the medieval conceptions of society were no longer in force and the early stages of industrialization required a large labor force who would "voluntarily" sell their labor. The glorification of work appears in the ancient world only before and at the decline of slavery. C. Mosse, *The Ancient World at Work,* trans. J. Lloyd (New York: W.W. Norton, 1969), 29. Early Greek thinkers, such as Hesiod and Xenophon, prior to the slavery of the Hellenistic world, praised agricultural work as a religious experience and as a disciplining that would prepare one for war. *Works and Days,* Oeconmicus, 4.3 (Loeb Classical Library 390.) "The land, which is a god, teaches justice and humility," Mosse, 25.

16. Plato, *Republic.* Thus education is limited to producing a guardian class exclusively responsible for the examination of the good, the ideal, the beautiful. Aristotle systematized and exaggerated the ordinary Athenian view of work. For him work is inferior, debased, and debasing. "The citizens must not lead the life of mechanics or tradesmen, for such a life is ignoble, and inimicable to virtue. Labor robs persons of the leisure to participate in political and military activities as well as moral and intellectual pursuits, all of which are appropriate only to free citizens. Neither must they be husbandmen, since leisure is necessary both for the development of virtue and the performance of political duties." *Politics,* in *The Basic Works of Aristotle,* trans. Richard McKeon (New York: Random House, 1941), 1328b, pp. 1288–89.

17. Hannah Arendt, *The Human Condition* (Garden City, N.Y.: Doubleday Anchor Books, 1959) 174.

18. Aristotle, *Politics,* 1253b, p. 1131.

19. L.A. Tilly and H.W. Scott, *Women, Work, and Family* (New York: 1978).

20. For example Schleiermacher, Bushnell, Rahner, Pieper, and Huizinga. See Francis F. Fiorenza, "Religious Beliefs and Praxis: Reflections on Catholic Theological Views of Work," in *Work and Religion,* ed. Gregory Baum (New York: Seabury Press, 1980), 92–102; idem, "Work and Critical Theology," in *A Matter of Dignity,* ed. W. J. Heisler and J. W. Houck (Notre Dame: University of Notre Dame Press, 1977), 23–43.

21. According to Horace Bushnell, the progenitor of American liberal theology, the two basic forms of human activity can be divided into work as a conscious effort and play as a spontaneous activity. The desire for play underlies all culture. One works to have the opportunity to play. Religion has developed from being legalistically obedient to being spontaneous. Society under Christianity will become a life of play. See Horace Bushnell, *Work and Play* (New York: Charles Scribner, 1881).

22. Friedrich Schleiermacher hoped that technological mechanization would humanize both technology and nature so that the human spirit could express its religious and artistic nature and could more fully penetrate both nature and society; *Die christliche Sitte,* 2nd ed. (Berlin: G. Rimer, 1884). Schleiermacher is aware that industrial development, with division of labor, often impedes the formation of human personality and personal talents, thus labor should be divided according to the talents of each. Work that dehumanizes human beings by reducing them to machines should be rejected. Christianity should encourage a lessening of mechanical work and an elevation of industrialized work to the realm of art according to the criterion of esthetic and religious freedom.

23. For studies of work in the biblical and church traditions, see Goran Agrell, *Work, Toil and Sustenance,* trans. Stephen Westerholm (Stockholm: Verbum, Hakan Ohlssons, 1976); Walther Bienert, *Die Arbeit nach der Lehre der Bibel* (Stuttgart: Evangelisches Verlagswerk, 1954); Robert L. Calhoun, *God and the Day's Work* (New York: Association Press, 1943); Alan Richardson, *The Biblical Doctrine of Work* (London: SCM Press, 1952).

24. Even though God's creative and redemptive modes of work are distinct, they are not radically different. When the biblical traditions speak of God's creating, they use the language of liberation; when speaking of the liberating work of God, they return to the language of creation, the "new creation." The word *barah* is used exclusively of God's work and thus sets the work of God apart from all human work (Ps. 148:5; 8:3; 2 Cor. 4:6–7). *Barah* had already been used in Israel's theological traditions to refer to God's work of liberating Israel from "the household of bondage." *Barah,* "God creates," means, basically, "God liberates."

For this reason the early church gave a christological interpretation of God's work of creation. The same redemptive work expressed in Jesus Christ is the work by which all things have been called into being, purposed, and held together. For in the Son, Jesus Christ, "all things were created, in heaven and on earth. . . . He is before all things, and in him all things hold together" (Col. 1:16a, 17; cf. Eph. 1:9–10). In all of God's work, God is working for the life and future of God's household, the creation.

25. Claus Westermann, 299–308.

26. Jürgen Moltmann, *God in Creation: A New Theology of Creation and the Spirit of God,* trans. Margaret Kohl (San Francisco: Harper & Row, 1981), 72–78.

27. See, for this, Gregory Baum, *The Priority of Labor: A Commentary on "Laborem Exercens," Encyclical Letter of Pope John Paul II* (New York: Paulist Press, 1982).

28. Jürgen Moltmann, *On Human Dignity: Political Theology and Ethics,* trans. M. Douglas Meeks (Philadelphia: Fortress Press, 1984), 40ff.

29. Walter Harrelson, *The Ten Commandments and Human Rights* (Philadelphia: Fortress Press, 1980), 88.

30. Christian teaching contributed to the gradual process of the revaluation of work in the West. It took over the egalitarian Stoic claim

that slavery was no longer acceptable according to the natural law, even if it was tolerated in the legal code of the state. By the third century A.D., the Stoic notion of the egalitarian state of nature had penetrated Christian doctrine. Augustine argued that human beings were not meant to be set above other human beings. But the Augustinian notion of the fall followed the Stoic assumption that under historical conditions the hierarchies in civic legal codes had to be accepted.

The monastic tradition, following the dictum, *ora et labora,* overcame in principle the classical assignment of virtue and work to different classes of people. From the universally binding natural law every human being receives the two ideals of duty to community and self-sufficiency, which became the primary foci of work up to the modern world. Jean de Meun's *Roman de la Rose* (ca. 1270) mediated to the medieval world the notion that there were in the golden age conditions in which all human beings were equal. There was no private property and no exploitation by work. Covetousness, envy, deceit, and pride brought about the situation in which human beings divide the soil through property and themselves through work. Rousseau indelibly blazoned these ideas in the modern consciousness and argued that the golden age could be again created on earth. He thus had much to do with breaking up the higher medieval synthesis of natural and civil law so carefully woven by Thomas Aquinas.

According to this synthesis human beings cooperate in bringing God's plan to consummation. See Thomas Aquinas, *Summa contra Gentiles,* 3.77, see also 3.69f, 133; *Compendium Theologiae,* 1.148. God preordains a correspondence between an individual's inclination for a particular job and the specific needs of the whole community. See *Summa Theologiae,* II–II, 183.2; *Summa contra Gentiles,* 3.134. Persons fulfill themselves in meeting the needs of the community. Thus vocational fulfillment flows from God's will. Work is therefore a task, an office, and an obligatory service that individuals perform for each other in the community. Each one, including especially the ruler, is justified in his or her work only insofar as he or she contributes to the common good of the family, state, and creational household.

Medieval civilization was founded on an agricultural economy of small, local, self-sufficient communities. The interlocking and interdependent parts found a stable equilibrium within a closed system, which tended to resist change. Service was obligated to a lord in return for protection. A network of rights and protections ran throughout the whole society. Work was necessary for the survival of the family and for paying what was required to the lord. There was no point in working harder, since there would be nothing to do with a surplus. For the most part the rhythms of nature ruled work. The primitive management system of bailiff and reeve (representing roughly the interests of lord and servant) supervised the farming of vassals and tenants. Authority and subordination were justified by a view of society as a system of mutual exchange of services devoted to the good life of the commonweal. The first signs of the breakdown of this system came in the twelfth and thirteenth centuries, when annual cash payments were exacted instead of services. Work was beginning to be connected with wage labor. By the 1380s it was very difficult to support the manorial system.

The ethic taught that work was a social duty through which social order is created. The Jansenist mentality encompassed fidelity to obligations, dedication to hard work, and an earnest and self-sufficient attitude toward life. (These virtues eventually became distinctive of the middle class.) Individuals were educated to perform their specific offices in life. The motive for work was not desire for pleasure. Rather, in the context of the divine plan, work serves as penance for sin. Work is monotonous, necessary, strenuous, not meaningful in itself as an end. It is meaningful only insofar as it demands an orderly life, an ascetic self-discipline, and a methodical control of the details of life. Work means the subjection of life to order, rules, and self-abstinence. But work is not yet meant as a means to profit or advancement. In addition to keeping one free from adultery, work orders time and concentrates human effort. Work brings riches, success, respect, and accomplishment.

The Lutheran theology of work offers an even more extensive theory of the integration of society through work by bringing call and vocation together and by overcoming the splitting of the church into priests and laity. God calls people through faith in the gospel and indirectly through work in one's occupation. This led to a consecration of the vocational-occupational structure of society as divinely ordained. Every honest vocation is service to God. All meanings, characteristics, and hope of the divine call to community with Christ fall on the work appropriate to one's position. One's everyday work gives one a good conscience and even a transcendent sense of belonging to the divine order of things.

31. Weber, *Protestant Ethic*; Jacob Viner, *Religious Thought and Economic Society*, ed. Jaques Melitz and Donald Winch (Durham, N.C.: Duke University Press, 1978), 151–89.

32. The emphasis in the Weberian approach to the Protestant work ethic has been on the anthropological question of salvation. But this is too narrow and does not arrive at the most significant theological issues of work. There is a very definite God concept that correlates with what Weber claimed to see in Puritan pastors. The doctrine of God in the so-called Protestant work ethic has not been sufficiently analyzed and criticized, and thus there has been no starting point for criticizing the anthropology that developed, according to Weber, out of Protestantism, and hence, also, no starting point for criticizing the implicit doctrine of God and anthropology in the secularized form of the Protestant work ethic. See below, ch. 7, n. 7.

33. John Rawls comments: "The striking feature of the utilitarian view of justice is that it does not matter, except indirectly, how the sum of satisfactions is distributed among individuals any more than it matters, except indirectly, how one man distributes his satisfactions over time. . . . There is no reason in principle why the greater gain of some should not compensate for the lesser losses of others, or more importantly, why the violation of the liberty of a few might not be made right by the greater good shared by many." *A Theory of Justice* (Cambridge: Harvard University Press, 1971), 26.

34. Anthony, *Ideology of Work*, 70–71.

35. Eugene D. Genovese, *Roll, Jordan, Roll: The World the Slaves Made* (New York: Pantheon Books, 1974), 6.

36. This dissenting view of work begins at least as early as the Diggers of seventeenth-century England.

37. See Rudolf Siebert, "Work and Religion in Hegel's Thought," in *Work and Religion*, ed. Baum, 117–28. Karl Marx comments on Hegel's view of human self-production: "The great thing in Hegel's *Phenomenology* and its end result—the dialectic of negativity as the moving and productive principle—is simply that Hegel grasps the self-production of man as a process, and objectification as a supercession of this alienation; that he thus grasps the nature of *work* and comprehends objective man. . . . The real active relationship of man to himself as a species-essence, as a real i.e. human essence is only possible as far as he actually brings forth all his *species-powers*—which in turn is only possible through the collective operation of mankind, only as the result of history—and treats them as objects, something which immediately again is possible only in the form of estrangement." *Economic and Philosophical Manuscripts*, quoted by Alisdair Clayre, *Work and Play: Ideas and Experience of Work and Leisure* (New York: Harper & Row, 1974), 45.

38. But there are growing signs of the failure also of managerialism to foster work. The overall relationship of work and management is changing in our time. Automation is replacing workers not only by machines or computers but also by managers, scientists, and technologists. Although the ideal of managers is not to engage in work, they are more and more thought of as doing the work of the corporation. Now ideological appeals are directed to managers. But there is little evidence that managers are being treated in the advanced and sophisticated manner with which they have been trained to relate to subordinates. The management of managers requires that they subordinate all other activities to their company-assigned ends. They, too, can be unwittingly victimized by reorganization, transferral, dismissal at the behest of organizational plans drawn up by distant consultants. One hears increasingly of the alienation of managers.

39. A second sense of passion in God's work can be seen in the Hassidic concept of God's drawing back in order to make room for the creation, or God's drawing into God's self, making a womb, as it were, in which creation can have space to be. See Moltmann, *God in Creation*, 86ff. God suffers self-diminishment in order to give place to creation. God's creating work thus is not sheer activity and dominating control over the object, the other. Rather God's action is preceded by God's suffering. For a treatment of God's suffering in relation to non-being, see Paul S. Fiddes, *The Creative Suffering of God* (Oxford: Clarendon Press, 1988), 207–67.

40. For the following, cf. Moltmann, *On Human Dignity*, 42–45.

41. Moltmann, *God in Creation*, 276–96; Abraham Joshua Heschel, *The Sabbath: Its Meaning for Modern Man* (New York: Farrar, Straus and Giroux, 1951).

42. See E. F. Schumacher, *Good Work* (London: Abacus, 1980), 112–23.

43. Idleness is dangerous because it refuses the mercy of God and means that one is refusing one's basic covenantal obligation. "If anyone

would not work, let that person not eat." (2 Thess. 3:7–12). Idleness means that one becomes a burden to others in the community. The worklife of patience, suffering, and sharing the burdens of others is the way in which Christians carry the cross for others in day-to-day toil.

44. See the articles by Iring Fetscher and Dietmar Mieth in *Unemployment and the Right to Work*, ed. Jacques Pohier and Dietmar Mieth (New York: Seabury Press, 1982), 53–71; Jürgen Moltmann, ed., *Recht auf Arbeit, Sinn der Arbeit*, (Munich: Chr. Kaiser, 1979).

45. Paul Ricoeur, "The Logic of Jesus, the Logic of God," *Christianity and Crisis* 39 (December 24, 1979), 324–27.

46. Cf. Dorothee Soelle with Shirley A. Cloyes, *To Work and to Love: A Theology of Creation* (Philadelphia: Fortress Press, 1984), 93–101.

47. One reason that Japanese businesses, conceived as a large family, show higher rates of productivity than many American plants is that Japanese managers do not make as many short-term decisions to show a profit in a quarterly report. Instead, they seem to make decisions regarding the communal rhythm of work extending to the generations.

48. W. J. Heisler and John W. Houck, eds., *A Matter of Dignity: Inquiries into the Humanization of Work* (Notre Dame: University of Notre Dame Press, 1977).

49. Paul Bernstein, *Workplace Democracy: Its Internal Dynamics* (New Brunswick, N.J.: Transaction Books, 1980).

7. God and Needs

1. No crude hedonist, Epicurus adumbrated Maslow by ranking needs in this order: the first natural and necessary, the second natural and unneccesary, and the third neither natural nor necessary.

2. While a primitivist tendency is noticeable, the Stoics and Epicureans (and later Rousseau) did not have in mind a golden age of natural needs that could be empirically observed. Rather, they thought of a social arrangement advanced cognitively and technologically enough to satisfy human needs without a culture stimulating proliferated needs.

3. Albert O. Hirschman, *The Passions and the Interests: Political Arguments for Capitalism before Its Triumph* (Princeton: Princeton University Press, 1977).

4. Michael Ignatieff, *The Needs of Strangers: An Essay on Privacy, Solidarity and the Politics of Being Human* (New York: Viking Penguin, 1985).

5. Georg Wilhelm Friedrich Hegel, *Introduction to the Philosophy of Right* (Oxford: Clarendon Press, 1952), 126ff.

6. But nowhere did the theory provide any convincing account of what it means to be a person. See Richard Warner, *Freedom, Enjoyment, and Happiness: An Essay on Moral Psychology* (Ithaca, N.Y.: Cornell University Press, 1987).

7. The *ethos* of early capitalism was not directed at acquisition as such. Not yet structured by profit-loss and capital accounting, it did not show its subsequent predatory and speculative penchant. Early

capitalism required self-restraint and thus was pervaded by an anticonsumption ethic. It imposed a moral obligation to postpone and sacrifice satisfaction of needs except as necessary for staying alive and fit. There was a clear renunciation of idleness, enjoyment of the senses, and even a hostility to relaxation and close human relations. Max Weber argued that the "spirit of capitalism" involved an intensive impulse-control unknown in previous noncapitalist economies. One reason that the repression provided by Protestantism stood out so emphatically for Weber was that he wrote about it in the same period in which neoclassical price theory was gaining ascendancy. Weber saw in the "worldly asceticism" of the capitalist spirit a pattern of enormous repression, a repression connected with religious belief. The repression necessitated by unrelenting work and production sought its justification in the religious repository of Puritan pastoral care. Satisfaction of needs should be postponed because economic success was a sign of salvation.

As capitalism produced abundance, this repression was more and more called into question. The self-controlled, inner-directed God of worldly asceticism began to appear under the new religious belief system of social Darwinism as acquisitive and achievement-oriented. For the individual now committed to both self-control and enjoyment through consumption, such a God of action and success could provide a good conscience. The enjoyment of economic success became virtuous in itself.

It was enough if people held merely to a rational self-control ethic in pursuit of production and profit. Repression could be justified simply by the goal of acquisition and of economic success according to economic means-ends rationality. Economic success could now prove the individual's worth in comparison with those who fail in economic competition.

8. Alfred Marshall in *Principles of Economics,* 9th ed. (New York: Macmillan, 1961), 323–80, developed the notion of equilibrium, modeled according to physiological needs and their satisfaction. The physiological interpretation of need satisfaction presupposes an appetite caused by an actual bodily lack, which in turn causes a drive aimed at a state of saturation or temporary equilibrium. The pain of tension is relieved by the pleasure of satisfaction. So far we have the basis for the ancient understanding of needs within the household. Needs emerge within biological necessity. Economic activity then would consist of a never-ending metabolic cycle of production, consumption, digestion, which would be constantly repeated at the same level without any increase and without any economic growth. Walter A. Weisskopf, *Alienation and Economics* (New York: Dell, 1971), 156.

9. Weisskopf, *Alienation and Economics,* 158.

10. Christopher Lasch, *The Culture of Narcissism: American Life in an Age of Diminishing Expectations* (New York: W. W. Norton, 1978).

11. Peter L. Berger, *Homeless Mind,* (New York: Random House, 1973), 191: "More and more time is spent in private life. This shift in the 'time budget' of most people has put additional strain upon the private sphere and its solutions to the problems of modern discontents. The search for

satisfactory meanings for individual and collective existence has become, in consequence, more frantic."

12. Heribert Mühlen, *Der Heilige Geist als Person in der Trinität, bei der Inkarnation und in Gnadenbund: Ich-du-wir.* (Munster: Aschendorf, 1969).

13. For the following, see Tony Walter, *Need: The New Religion* (Downers Grove, Ill.: Inter Varsity Press, 1986).

14. The popular reception of Freud has concluded that the gratification of our needs is what motivates all human behavior. It is bad to repress any need. This is a shallow understanding of Freud's complex theory of the struggle between needs and conscience. But it coincides with the predominant psychological trend, to find an objective starting point in physiological needs that can be understood mechanistically and thus unambiguously.

15. Walter, *Need*, 113–25.

16. A contemporary exponent is Ivan Illich, *Toward a History of Needs* (New York: Pantheon, 1978); idem, *Tools for Conviviality* (New York: Harper & Row, 1973). Far from trusting needs to bring about social order, Rousseau believed that the need for self-esteem and esteem from others created false needs and ended up as the means of exploitation by others. After their basic needs are met, people start acquiring all kinds of conveniences that quickly become needs.

17. Marx's labor theory of value was a strictly economic theory, accounting for the generation of wealth by the extraction of surplus value through the exploitation of labor. But it cannot explain how this exploitative system is tolerated when all objective conditions for its destruction are already present. Workers seem increasingly tied to the system that holds them captive. Why do they continually become middle-class?

18. Patricia Stringborg, *The Problem of Human Needs and the Critique of Civilization* (London: George Allen & Unwin, 1981).

19. Ibid., 250.

20. Wilhelm Reich, *The Mass Psychology of Fascism* (Harmondsworth, Eng.: Penguin Books, 1975); Erich Fromm, *The Sane Society* (New York: Holt, Rinehart & Winston, 1955); idem, *The Anatomy of Human Destructiveness* (New York: Holt, Rinehart & Winston, 1973); Herbert Marcuse, *One-Dimensional Man: Studies in the Ideology of Advanced Industrial Society* (Boston: Beacon Press, 1964).

21. Thus, as Marx claimed, "Production creates not only an object for the subject but also a subject for the object," *Grundrisse* (Berlin: Dietz Verlag, 1953), 141. John Kenneth Galbraith argues that "one cannot defend production as satisfying wants if that production creates its own wants." *The Affluent Society* (Boston: Houghton Mifflin, 1958), 153.

22. Stringborg, *Problem of Human Needs*, 250.

23. Ibid., 251.

24. The critics of need actually establish further needs, e.g., needs that are defined by growth psychology and the human potential movement. Human beings, born empty, with mere potential, live under the sign of progress, striving to become complete, to become self-actualized. The

human potential movement also speaks the language of growth, increase, and development. It, too, believes that the discovery of ever higher needs is progress. It disagrees only on what the higher needs are.

25. Like all spiritualist movements since Montanus, present-day spiritualist and charismatic renewal movements are reacting against a static God concept that views the Holy Spirit as an afterthought and against the resulting spiritless reality of church and world. These movements refuse to worship a God who is a self-sufficient individual, since a God so conceived is an instrument of external control by hierarchical, imperialistic, or totalitarian conceptions of authority. Thus spiritualist and pietist movements are usually in the beginning liberation movements. They fight against domination by moving from the God concept of the self-centered, all-powerful being to the experience of the Spirit as the starting point for everything. There is much in these present movements from which old-line churches need to learn. But a large number of contemporary charismatics reject the criticism of society in the older Pentecostalism and are becoming accommodated to the spirit and values of the prevailing economic system. One could point to many leaders on the spiritualist circuit who are flagrantly avowing the worst aspects of our economic life: commodity fetishism, profiteering, consumerism. Some spiritualist conservatives who keep a strict private morality when to comes to sexuality, family, and personal relationships, nevertheless let themselves be caught up in an utter animism when it comes to economics. Over and over, their definitions of the gifts of the Spirit turn out to be the idols of action, growth, and progress. The ecstasy of many spiritualists is not much more than euphoria at being able to believe again religiously in the old-time values of American capitalism.

26. This megalomania, according to Adam Smith, might be an irrational deception of the deity, but it is nevertheless the motivation of all human industry. Adam Smith, *Theory of Moral Sentiments* (Oxford: Clarendon Press, 1976), 182–83.

27. But, as we have seen in chapter 3, the "rational" use of avarice does not mean that the market can control sin, since some people are in a better position to control the market's control mechanisms.

28. Karl Marx, *Capital,* trans. Ben Fowkes (New York: Vintage Books, 1977), 1:230–31.

29. Ibid., 1:128, 129.

30. This assumption is what leads in the writings of George Gilder to the fanciful flights depicting capital as the source of creativity and the "gifting" of capitalists as the mainspring of society. See Gilder, *Wealth and Poverty* (New York: Bantam Books, 1982); and idem, *The Spirit of Enterprise* (New York: Simon & Schuster, 1984).

31. Franz J. Hinkelammert, *The Ideological Weapons of Death: A Theological Critique of Capitalism* (Maryknoll, N.Y.: Orbis Books, 1986), 15.

32. William Leiss, *Limits to Satisfaction: An Essay on the Problem of Needs and Commodities* (Toronto: University of Toronto Press, 1976).

33. John Francis Kavanaugh, *Following Christ in a Consumerist Society: The Spirituality of Cultural Resistance* (Maryknoll, N.Y.: Orbis Books, 1982), 26.

34. See Jürgen Moltmann, *The Crucified God: The Cross of Christ as the Foundation and Criticism of Christian Theology,* trans. R.A. Wilson and John Bowden (New York: Harper & Row, 1974).

35. Weisskopf, *Alienation and Economics,* 162; John Kenneth Galbraith, *The New Industrial State* (Harmondsworth, Eng.: Penguin Books, 1967), 209–12.

36. Philip Slater, *The Pursuit of Loneliness: American Culture at the Breaking Point* (Boston: Beacon Press, 1970), 81–95.

37. Thorstein Veblen was interested in the social, noneconomic components of consumer behavior. He thought the materialistic goals and objects of consumption were as decisive for economy as production. In his study of consumer behavior he raised fundamental doubts about the nature of the American character. Veblen is radical because he calls into question the starting point for modern economics: the meaningfulness of the human desire to consume. Implicit in this starting point is the idea that there is an infinite supply of resources and consumer goods or products and thus that there is no limit to consumption. The interaction that interested Veblen was one in which predatory, socially ambitious grand acquisitors sought to gain vulgar acquisition of status symbols. False need reigned supreme in the leisure society. By isolating people from each other, conspicuous consumption ruined the cooperative relationships within technological and engineering structures on which industry depended. The Veblen concern partly hides and partly reveals the deeper fissures in the social structures. See Thorstein Veblen, *The Theory of the Leisure Class: An Economic Study of Institutions* (New York: B. W. Huebsch, 1899).

38. Tibor Scitovsky speaks of a "joyless economy," in which the intensified pursuit of comfort has the effect of eclipsing pleasure. Tibor Scitovsky, *The Joyless Economy: An Inquiry in Human Satisfaction and Consumer Dissatisfaction* (New York: Oxford University Press, 1976). Satiety and comfort create their own kind of scarcity, namely, the inability to find stimulus for genuine novelty in life. Constant satiation makes pleasure in life impossible. The lifestyle of consuming comfort and fashion defeats enjoyment. A consumer economy requires massive medication for diseases of overconsumption and inactivity. Overconsumption itself is a narcotic for a lack of meaning in consumption.

The frantic attempt to fulfill needs through consuming products causes a scarcity of time. See Staffan B. Linder, *The Harried Leisure Class* (New York: Columbia University Press, 1970). With the increase in leisure goods comes a decrease in leisure time. The economic commitment to buy and maintain everything from the automobile to the washing machine is the "shadow price of high consumption" and results in a time famine. All time becomes an economic calculus for dealing with multiplied things that are supposed to meet our wants. Part of leisure time is converted back into work to generate the income required to buy the maintenance time required for many consumer goods. We are left wanting time.

Fred Hirsch has identified another sense of growing scarcity in his important book *The Social Limits to Growth* (Cambridge: Harvard University Press, 1976). He asserts that the more the basic material needs of the majority of our population are met, the more intense becomes the competitive acquisition of what he calls "positional goods." Market goods are purchased without regard to the effect that universal ownership might have on satisfaction; the enjoyment of a refrigerator is not impaired by the universal ownership of refrigerators. "Positional goods," on the other hand, are those goods whose utility and satisfaction derive from their restricted distribution, such as top jobs, mobility, recreation, education, services, leisure, and the control of other people's time. Positional goods represent status, exclusivity, and the presumed gratification of activity that can be carried on without crowding, intrusion, and interruption.

The value of positional goods is the value placed on others's not possessing them. Instead of expanding their consumption of market goods, those who become richer demand increases in those goods that are ultimately unattainable for everyone. But enjoyment of my vacation house is threatened by the overcrowding that results from many people being able to afford a vacation house. The irony is that, as more and more people gain access to these things, the less and less satisfying they are. People react by trying to make them more scarce by making them more expensive and more exclusive. This raises year by year the destructive competition of positional goods and lowers the ability of human beings to live together in community, in genuine presence to each other. Society becomes less and less a public household and more and more an arena of frantic competition filled with painful frustration.

39. Michael Walzer, *Spheres of Justice: A Defense of Pluralism and Equality* (New York: Basic Books, 1983), 7.

40. Lewis Hyde, *The Gift: Imagination and the Erotic Life of Property* (New York: Vintage Books, 1983), 10.

41. "The eucharist, properly celebrated, is a sign of that generous justice by which God invites the hungry and the thirsty to his table (Isaiah 55:1; Luke 6:21). As the creative prefiguration of the feast which God is preparing for all peoples beyond the conquest of death (Isaiah 25:6-9), the Lord's meal should prompt Christians, who have themselves welcomed equally to the sacrament, towards a fair distribution of the divine bounties at present made tangible in the earth's resources." Geoffrey Wainwright, *Doxology: The Praise of God in Worship, Doctrine and Life* (New York: Oxford University Press, 1980), 427. See also, Joseph A. Grass, *Broken Bread and Broken Bodies: The Lord's Supper and World Hunger* (Maryknoll, N.Y.: Orbis Books, 1985), Monica Hellwig, *The Eucharist and the Hunger of the World* (New York: Paulist Press, 1976); Frederick Herzog, *God-Walk: Liberation Shaping Dogmatics* (Maryknoll, N.Y.: Orbis Books, 1988), 130–41 and passim.

42. Aubrey R. Johnson, "Psalm 23 and the Household of Faith," in *Proclamation and Presence,* ed. John I. Durham and J.R. Porter (Richmond: John Knox Press, 1983), 271.

Bibliography

I
THEOLOGY, ETHICS, BIBLICAL STUDIES, AND ECONOMICS

Alter, Robert. *The Art of Biblical Narrative.* New York: Basic Books, 1981.

Barth, Karl. *Church Dogmatics.* Vol. III/4: *The Doctrine of Creation.* Trans. A. T. Mackay, et al. Edinburgh: T. & T. Clark, 1961.

Baum, Gregory. *Religion and Alienation.* New York: Paulist Press, 1975.

Baum, Gregory, and Duncan Cameron. *Ethics and Economics: Canada's Catholic Bishops and the Economic Crisis.* Toronto: James Lorimer, 1984.

Beckmann, David M. *Where Faith and Economics Meet.* Minneapolis: Augsburg, 1981.

Benne, Robert. *The Ethic of Democratic Capitalism: A Moral Reassessment.* Philadelphia: Fortress Press, 1981.

Birch, Bruce C., and Larry L. Rasmussen. *The Predicament of the Prosperous.* Philadelphia: Westminster Press, 1978.

Birch, Charles, and John B. Cobb, Jr. *The Liberation of Life: From Cell to the Community.* Cambridge: Cambridge University Press, 1981.

Bonhoeffer, Dietrich. *Ethics.* Ed. Eberhard Bethge. New York: Macmillan, 1965.

Brueggemann, Walter. *Genesis.* Atlanta: John Knox Press, 1982.

Byers, David M., ed. *Justice in the Marketplace: Collected Statements of the Vatican and the United States Catholic Bishops on Economic Policy, 1891–1984.* Washington, D.C.: United States Catholic Conference, 1985.

Calhoun, Robert Lowry. *God and the Common Life.* New York: Charles Scribner's Sons, 1935.

Chopp, Rebecca S. *The Praxis of Suffering: An Interpretation of Liberation and Political Theologies.* Maryknoll, N.Y.: Orbis Books, 1986.

Cobb, John B., Jr. *Process Theology as Political Theology.* Philadelphia: Westminster Press, 1982.

Collins, James. *God in Modern Philosophy.* Chicago: Henry Regnery, 1959.

Cone, James H. *God of the Oppressed.* New York: Seabury Press, 1975.

Countryman, L. William. *The Rich Christian in the Church of the Early Empire: Contradictions and Accommodations.* New York: The Edwin Mellen Press, 1980.

Cramp, A. B. *Notes towards a Christian Critique of Secular Economic Theory.* Provisional Paper. Toronto: Institute for Christian Studies, 1975.

Crosby, Michael H. *House of Disciples: Church, Economics, and Justice in Matthew.* Maryknoll, N.Y.: Orbis Books, 1988.

Danker, Frederick W. *Benefactor: Epigraphic Study of a Greco-Roman and New Testament Semantic Field.* St. Louis: Clayton Publishing House, 1982.

Dorr, Donald. *Option for the Poor: A Hundred Years of Vatican Social Teaching.* Maryknoll, N.Y.: Orbis Books, 1983.

Elliott, John H. *A Home for the Homeless: A Sociological Exegesis of 1 Peter, Its Situation and Strategy.* Philadelphia: Fortress Press, 1981.

Fiddes, Paul S. *The Creative Suffering of God.* Oxford: Clarendon Press, 1988.

Fiorenza, Elisabeth Schüssler. *In Memory of Her: Feminist Theological Reconstruction of Christian Origins.* New York: Crossroad, 1983.

Fiorenza, Francis Schüssler. *Foundational Theology: Jesus and the Church.* New York: Crossroad, 1984.

Fretheim, Terence E. *The Suffering of God.* Philadelphia: Fortress Press, 1984.

Gannon, Thomas M., ed. *The Catholic Challenge to the American Economy.* New York: Macmillan, 1987.

Gilkey, Langdon. "God." In *Christian Theology: An Introduction to Its Traditions and Tasks.* Rev. ed., ed. Peter C. Hodgson and Robert H. King, 88–112. Philadelphia: Fortress Press, 1985.

Gottwald, Norman K. *The Tribes of Yahweh: A Sociology of the Religion of Liberated Israel, 1250–1050 B.C.E..* Maryknoll, N.Y.: Orbis Books, 1979.

Gottwald, Norman K., ed. *The Bible and Liberation: Political and Social Hermeneutics.* Rev. ed. Maryknoll, N.Y.: Orbis Books, 1983.

Gunnemann, Jon. "Justice with Strangers: The Ethics of Exchange." *Prism* 2 (Fall 1987): 74–88.

_____. "Capitalism and Commutative Justice." *Annual of the Society of the Christian Ethics* (1985): 101–122.

Gutiérrez, Gustavo. *The Power of the Poor in History.* Tr. Robert R. Barr. Maryknoll, NY: Orbis Books, 1983.

Hall, Douglas John. *The Steward: A Biblical Symbol Come of Age.* New York: Friendship Press, 1982.

Hanson, Paul D. *The People Called: The Growth of Community in the Bible.* San Francisco: Harper & Row, 1986.

Harrelson, Walter. *The Ten Commandments and Human Rights.* Philadelphia: Fortress Press, 1980.

Hauerwas, Stanley. *A Community of Character: Toward a Constructive Social Ethic.* Notre Dame: University of Notre Dame Press, 1981.

Herzog, Frederick. *Justice Church: The New Function of the Church in North American Christianity.* Maryknoll, N.Y.: Orbis Books, 1980.

_____. *God-walk: Liberation Shaping Dogmatics.* Maryknoll, N.Y.: Orbis Books, 1988.

Hill, W. J. *The Three-Personed God: The Trinity as a Mystery of Salvation* Washington, D.C.: Catholic University Press of America, 1982.

Hinkelammert, Franz J. *The Ideological Weapons of Death.* Trans. Phillip Berryman. Maryknoll, N.Y.: Orbis Books, 1986.

Hollenbach, David. *Claims in Conflict.* New York: Paulist Press, 1979.

Jensen, Robert W. *The Triune Identity.* Philadelphia: Fortress Press, 1982.

Johnson, Aubrey R. "Psalm 23 and the Household of Faith." In *Proclamation and Presence,* ed. John I. Durham and J. R. Porter, 255–271. Atlanta: John Knox Press, 1970.

_____. *The Cultic Prophet and Israel's Psalmody.* Cardiff: University of Wales Press, 1979.

Jüngel, Eberhard. *God as the Mystery of the World.* Trans. Darrell L. Guder. Grand Rapids: Eerdmans, 1983.

King, Paul G., and David O. Woodyard, *The Journey toward Freedom: Economic Structures and Theological Perspectives.* Rutherford, N.J.: Fairleigh Dickinson, 1982.

King, Paul G., Kent Maynard, and David O. Woodyard. *Risking Liberation: Middle Class Powerlessness and Social Heroism.* Atlanta: John Knox Press, 1988.

Koenig, John. *New Testament Hospitality: Partnership with Strangers as Promise and Mission.* Philadelphia: Fortress Press, 1986.

Lamb, Matthew. *Solidarity with Victims: Toward a Theology of Social Transformation.* New York: Crossroad, 1982.

_____. "The Production Process and Exponential Growth: A Study in Socio-Economics and Theology." In *Lonergan Workshop,* ed. Fred Lawrence 1 (1978), 257–309. Missoula, Mt.: Scholars Press, 1978.

Lebacqz, Karen. *Justice in an Unjust World: Foundations for a Christian Approach to Justice.* Minneapolis: Augsburg, 1987.

Lee, Robert. *Faith and the Prospects of Economic Collapse.* Atlanta: John Knox Press, 1981.

Lutz, Charles P., ed. *God, Goods, and the Common Good: Eleven Perspectives on Economic Justice in Dialogue with the Roman Catholic Bishops' Pastoral Letter.* Minneapolis: Augsburg, 1987.

Maguire, Daniel. *A New American Justice.* New York: Doubleday, 1980.

Malherbe, Abraham J. *Social Aspects of Early Christianity*. 2nd ed. Philadelphia: Fortress Press, 1983.

Manno, Bruno, and M. E. Jegen, eds. *The Earth is the Lord's*. New York: Paulist Press, 1978.

McFague, Sallie. *Models of God: Theology for an Ecological, Nuclear Age*. Philadelphia: Fortress Press, 1987.

McGill, Arthur. *Suffering: A Test of Theological Method*. Philadelphia: Westminster Press, 1982.

Mealand, David L. *Poverty and Expectation in the Gospels*. London: SPCK, 1980.

Meeks, M. Douglas. "Gott und die Ökonomie des Heiligen Geistes." *Evangelische Theologie* 40 (1979): 40–48.

_____. "The Holy Spirit and Human Needs: Toward a Trinitarian View of Economics." *Christianity and Crisis* 40 (November 10, 1980): 307–316.

_____. "Hope and the Ministry of Planning and Management." *Anglican Theological Review* 64 (April 1982): 147–162.

_____. "God as Economist and the Problem of Property." *Occasional Papers*, No. 21. Collegeville, Minn.: Institute for Ecumenical and Cultural Research, 1984.

_____. "Political Theology and Political Economy," in *Gottes Zukunft—Zukunft der Welt*. Ed. Hermann Deuser, et al., 446–456. Munich: Chr. Kaiser Verlag, 1986.

_____. "The Church and the Poor in Supply-Side Economics," *Cities* (Fall 1983), 6–9.

Meeks, Wayne A. *The First Urban Christians: The Social World of the Apostle Paul*. New Haven: Yale University Press, 1983.

Metz, Johannes B. *Theology of the World*. Trans. William Glen-Doepel. New York: Seabury Press, 1969.

_____. *Faith in History and Society*. Trans. David Smith. New York: Seabury Press, 1980.

Mieth, Dietmar, and Jacques Pohier, eds. *Christian Ethics and Economics: The North-South Conflict*. New York: Seabury Press, 1980.

Migliore, Daniel L. *The Power of God*. Philadelphia: Westminster, 1983.

Míguez Bonino, José. *Toward a Christian Political Ethics*. Philadelphia: Fortress Press, 1983.

Moltmann, Jürgen. *On Human Dignity: Political Theology and Ethics*. Trans. M. Douglas Meeks. Philadelphia: Fortress Press, 1984.

_____. *The Trinity and the Kingdom*. Trans. Margaret Kohl. New York: Harper & Row, 1981.

_____. *God in Creation: A New Theology of Creation and the Spirit of God*. Trans. Margaret Kohl. San Francisco: Harper & Row, 1985.

_____. *The Crucified God: The Cross of Christ as the Foundation and Criticism of Christian Theology.* Trans. R. A. Wilson and John Bowden. San Francisco: Harper & Row, 1974.

Moltmann-Wendel, Elisabeth, and Jürgen Moltmann. *Humanity in God.* New York: Pilgrim Press, 1983.

Moxnes, Halvor. *The Economy of the Kingdom: Social Conflict and Economic Relations in Luke's Gospel.* Philadelphia: Fortress Press, 1988.

Muelder, Walter George. *Religion and Economic Responsibility.* New York: Scribners, 1953.

Neal, Marie Augusta. *A Socio-theology of Letting Go.* New York: Paulist Press, 1977.

Niebuhr, Reinhold. *Christian Realism and Political Problems.* New York: August M. Kelly, 1953.

_____. *Reflections on the End of an Era.* New York: Charles Scribner's Sons, 1934.

Novak, Michael. *The Spirit of Democratic Capitalism.* New York : Simon and Schuster, 1982.

Oakman, Douglas E. *Jesus and the Economic Questions of His Day.* Lewiston, N.Y.: Edwin Mellen Press, 1987.

O'Brien, David J. and Thomas A. Shannon. *Renewing the Earth: Catholic Documents on Peace, Justice and Liberation.* Garden City, N. Y.: Doubleday, 1977.

Ogletree, Thomas W. *Hospitality to the Stranger: Dimensions of Moral Understanding.* Philadelphia: Fortress Press, 1985.

Osthathios, Geervarghese Mar. *Theology of a Classless Society.* London: Lutterworth Press, 1979.

Owensby, Walter L. *Economics for Prophets.* Grand Rapids: Eerdmans, 1988.

Patrick, Dale. *The Rendering of God in the Old Testament.* Philadelphia: Fortress Press, 1981

Pemberton, Prentiss L., and Daniel Rush Finn. *Toward a Christian Economic Ethic.* Minneapolis: Winston Press, 1985.

Pilgrim, Walter E. *Good News to the Poor: Wealth and Poverty in Luke-Acts.* Minneapolis: Augsburg, 1981.

Pixley, George V. *God's Kingdom: A Guide for Biblical Study.* Trans. Donald D. Walsh. Maryknoll, N.Y.: Orbis Books, 1981.

_____. *On Exodus: A Liberation Perspective.* Maryknoll, N.Y.: Orbis Books, 1987.

Preston, Ronald H. *Religion and the Persistence of Capitalism.* London: SCM Press, 1979.

Rasmussen, Albert T. *Christian Responsibility in Economic Life.* Philadelphia: Westminster, 1965.

Rasmussen, Larry L. *Economic Anxiety and Christian Faith*. Minneapolis: Augsburg Press, 1981.

Reumann, John. *The Use of Oikonomia and Related Terms in Greek Sources to about A.D. 100 as a Background for Patristic Applications*. Ann Arbor, Mich.: University Microfilms, 1957.

———. "The 'Righteousness of God' and the 'Economy of God': Two Great Doctrinal Themes Historically Compared." In *AKSUM-THYATEIRA: A Festschrift for Archbishop Methodios of Thyateira and Great Britain* (Athens, 1985), 615–637.

Ringe, Sharon H. *Jesus, Liberation, and the Biblical Jubilee*. Philadelphia: Fortress Press, 1985.

Russell, Letty M. *The Future of Partnership*. Philadelphia: Westminster Press, 1979.

———. *The Household of Freedom: Authority in Feminist Theology*. Philadelphia: Westminster Press, 1987.

Ryan, John A. *Distributive Justice: The Right and Wrong of Our Present Distribution of Wealth*. New York: Macmillan, 1942.

Ryan, William. *Equality*. New York: Pantheon, 1981.

Schottroff, Luise, and Wolfgang Stegemann. *Jesus and the Hope of the Poor*. Tr. Matthew J. O'Connell. Maryknoll, N.Y.: Orbis Books, 1986.

Schottroff, Willy, and Wolfgang Stegemann, eds. *God of the Lowly: Socio-Historical Interpretations of the Bible*. Tr. Matthew J. O'Connell. Maryknoll, N.Y.: Orbis Books, 1984.

Shinn, Roger L. *Forced Options: Social Decisions for the 21st Century*. New York: Harper & Row, 1982.

Sider, Ronald J. *Rich Christians in an Age of Hunger*. Downers Grove, Ill.: Inter-Varsity Press, 1980.

Sleeman, John. *Economic Crisis: A Christian Perspective*. London: SCM, 1976.

Sobrino, Jon. *Theology of Christian Solidarity*. Maryknoll, NY: Orbis Books, 1985.

———. *The True Church and the Poor*. Tr. Matthew J. O'Connell. Maryknoll, N.Y.: Orbis Books, 1984.

Stackhouse, Max L. *Public Theology and Political Economy: Christian Stewardship in Modern Society*. Grand Rapids: Eerdmans, 1987.

———. "Jesus and Economics: A Century of Reflection." In *The Bible in American Law, Politics, and Political Rhetoric*, ed. James Turner Johnson, 107–151. Philadelphia: Fortress, 1985.

Stegemann, Wolfgang. *The Gospel and the Poor*. Trans. Dietlinde Elliott. Philadelphia: Fortress Press, 1984.

Stivers, Robert. *The Sustainable Society: Ethics and Economic Growth*. Philadelphia: Westminster Press, 1976.

————. *Hunger, Technology, and Limits to Growth.* Minneapolis: Augsburg, 1984.

Taylor, Richard K. *Economics and the Gospel.* Philadelphia: United Church Press, 1973.

Temple, William. *Christianity and the Social Order.* London: SPCK, 1976.

Torrance, Thomas F. "The Implications of *Oikonomia* for Knowledge and Speech of God in Early Christian Theology." In *Oikonomia: Heilsgeschichte als Thema der Theologie,* ed. Felix Christ, 223–238. Hamburg-Bergstedt: Herbert Reich Verlag, 1967.

Tracy, David. *The Analogical Imagination: Christian Theology and the Culture of Pluralism.* New York: Crossroad, 1981.

Troeltsch, Ernst. *The Social Teachings of the Christian Church.* Trans. Olive Wyon. 2 vols. New York: Harper Torchbooks, 1960.

Verner, David C. *The Household of God: The Social World of the Pastoral Epistles.* Chico, Calif.: Scholars Press, 1983.

Van Buren, Paul. *A Christian Theology of the People of Israel.* New York: Seabury Press, 1983.

Viner, Jacob. *Religious Thought and Economic Society,* ed. Jacques Melitz and Donald Winch. Durham, N.C.: Duke University Press, 1978.

von Rad, Gerhard. *Old Testament Theology.* 2 vols. Trans. D. M. G. Stalkner. New York: Harper & Row, 1962.

Wainwright, Geoffrey. *Doxology: The Praise of God in Worship, Doctrine, and Life.* New York: Oxford University Press, 1980.

Welker, Michael, "Security of Expectations: Reformulating the Theology of Law and Gospel." *Journal of Religion* 66 (1986): 237–260.

West, Cornel. *Prophesy Deliverance: An Afro-American Revolutionary Christianity.* Philadelphia: Westminster Press, 1982.

Wieman, H. N. *The Source of the Human Good.* Chicago: University of Chicago Press, 1947.

Williams, Oliver F., and John W. Houck, eds. *The Judeo-Christian Vision and the Modern Corporation,* Notre Dame: University of Notre Dame Press, 1982.

Wink, Walter. *Unmasking the Powers: The Invisible Forces that Determine Human Existence.* Philadelphia: Fortress Press, 1986.

Winter, Gibson. *Liberating Creation: Foundations of Religious Social Ethics.* New York: Crossroad, 1981.

Wogaman, J. Philip. *The Great Economic Debate: An Ethical Analysis.* Philadelphia: Westminster Press, 1977.

————. *Economics and Ethics: A Christian Inquiry.* Philadelphia: Fortress Press, 1986.

Woltersdorff, Nicholas. *Until Justice and Peace Embrace*. Grand Rapids: Eerdmans, 1983.

Yoder, John Howard. *The Politics of Jesus*. Grand Rapids: Eerdmans, 1972.

_____. *The Priestly Kingdom: Social Ethics as Gospel*. Notre Dame: University of Notre Dame, 1984.

II
ECONOMIC AND POLITICAL THEORY

Ackerman, Frank. *Hazardous to Our Wealth*. Boston: South End Press, 1984.

_____. *Reaganomics: Rhetoric vs. Reality*. Boston: South End Press, 1982.

Aristotle, *Politics*. *The Basic Works of Aristotle*. Trans. Richard McKeon. New York: Random House, 1941.

Arrighi, G., A. Frank, and Immanuel Wallerstein. *Dynamics of the Global Crisis*. New York: Monthly Review Press, 1982.

Ayres, Robert L. *Banking on the Poor: The World Bank and World Poverty*. Cambridge, Mass.: The MIT Press, 1984.

Barnet, Richard J. *The Lean Years: Politics in the Age of Scarcity*. New York: Simon and Schuster, 1980.

_____. *The Alliance: America, Europe, Japan: Makers of the Postwar World*. New York: Simon and Schuster, 1983.

Barrow, Robin. *Injustice, Inequality and Ethics: A Philosophical Introduction to Moral Problems*. New York: Barnes & Noble Books, 1982.

Bay, Christian. *Strategies of Political Emancipation*. Notre Dame: University of Notre Dame Press, 1981.

Becker, Gary. *The Economic Approach to Human Behavior*. Chicago: University of Chicago Press, 1957.

Bell, Daniel. *The Cultural Contradictions of Capitalism*. New York: Basic Books, 1976.

Bell, Daniel and Irving Kristol, eds. *The Crisis in Economic Theory*. New York: Basic Books, 1981.

Bellah, Robert N., Richard Madsen, William A. Sullivan, Ann Swidler, and Steven M. Tipton. *Habits of the Heart*. Berkeley: University of California Press, 1985.

Benditt, Theodore M. *Rights*. Totowa, NJ: Rowman and Littlefield, 1982.

Bentham, Jeremy. *An Introduction to Principles of Morals and Legislation*. New York: Longwood Press, 1970.

Bernstein, R. J. *The Restructuring of Social and Political Theory*. Oxford: Oxford University Press, 1976.

Berry, Wendell. *Home Economics*. San Francisco: North Point Press, 1987.

Bluestone, Barry, and Bennett Harrison. *The Deindustrialization of America*. New York: Basic Books, 1982.

Boulding, Kenneth E. *Beyond Economics: Essays on Society, Religion and Ethics*. Ann Arbor, Mich.: University of Michigan, 1968.

———. *The Economy of Love and Fear: A Preface to Grant Economics*. Belmont, Calif.: Wadsworth, 1973.

Bowie, Norman E. *Towards a New Theory of Distributive Justice*. Amherst: The University of Massachusetts Press, 1971.

Bowles, Samuel, et al. *Beyond the Waste Land: A Democratic Alternative to Economic Decline*. Garden City, N.Y.: Doubleday Anchor, 1983.

Bowles, Samuel and Herbert Gintis. *Democracy and Capitalism: Property, Community, and the Contradictions of Modern Social Thought*. New York: Basic Books, 1986.

Brandt Commission. *Common Crisis North-South: Cooperation for World Recovery*. Cambridge, Mass.: MIT Press, 1983.

Braudel, Fernand. *Capitalism and Civilization*. 3 vols. New York: Harper & Row, 1981, 1982, 1984.

Buchanan, Allen E. *Marx and Justice: The Radical Critique of Liberalism*. Totowa, NJ: Rowman and Allenheld, 1982.

Buchanan, J. M. *The Limits of Liberty: Between Anarchy and Leviathan*. Chicago: University of Chicago Press, 1975.

Calleo, David P. *The Imperious Economy*. Cambridge, Mass.: Harvard University Press, 1982.

Carnegie, Andrew. *The Gospel of Wealth and Other Timely Essays*. Cambridge: Harvard University Press, 1962.

Carney, Thomas. F. *The Economies of Antiquity: Controls, Gifts and Trade*. Lawrence, Kansas: Coronado Press, 1973.

Collard, David. *Altruism and Economics: A Study in Non-Selfish Economics*. New York: Oxford University Press, 1978.

Csikzentmihaly, Mihaly, and Eugene Rochberg-Halton. *The Meaning of Things: Domestic Symbols and the Self*. New York: Cambridge University Press, 1981.

Dahrendorf, Rolf. *Life Chances*. Chicago: University of Chicago Press, 1980.

Dahl, Robert A. and Charles E. Lindblom. *Politics, Economics and Welfare*. New York: Harper & Row, 1953.

Daly, Herman E. *Steady-State Economics:The Economics of Biophysical Equilibrium and Moral Growth*. San Francisco: W. H. Freeman, 1977.

Daly, Herman E., ed. *Toward a Steady-State Economy*. San Francisco: W. H. Freeman, 1973.

Danziger, Sheldon H., and Daniel E. Weinberg. *Fighting Poverty: What Works and What Doesn't.* Cambridge: Harvard University Press, 1987.

Devine, Andrew. *Liberal Democracy: A Critique of its Theory.* New York: Farrar, Straus & Giroux, 1981.

Diggins, John Patrick. *The Lost Soul of American Politics: Virtue, Self-Interest, and the Foundations of Liberalism.* New York: Basic Books, 1984.

Dorrien, Gary J. *The Democratic Socialist Vision.* Totowa: Rowman & Littlefield, 1986.

Douglas, Mary, and Baron Ischerwood. *The World of Goods.* New York: Basic Books, 1979.

Edsall, Thomas Byrne. *The New Politics of Inequality.* New York: W. W. Norton, 1984.

Eisenstadt, S. N., ed. *The Protestant Ethic and Modernization: A Comparative View.* New York: Basic Books, 1968.

Ellwood, David T. *Poor Support: Poverty in the American Family.* New York: Basic Books, 1988.

Fenichel, Otto. "The Drive to Amass Wealth." *Psychoanalytic Quarterly,* (January 1938): 69–95.

Finley, M. I. *The Ancient Economy.* Berkeley: University of California Press, 1971.

_____. *Economy and Society in Ancient Greece.* Ed. B. D. Shaw and R. P. Saller. New York: Penguin Books, 1983.

Fischer, Norman. *Economy and Self: Philosophy and Economics from the Mercantilists to Marx.* Westport, Conn.: Greenwood Press, 1979.

Friedman, Milton. *Capitalism and Freedom.* Chicago: University of Chicago Press, 1962.

Froman, Creel. *The Two American Political Systems: Society, Economics, and Politics.* Englewood Cliffs, N. J.: Prentice-Hall, 1984.

Fuchs, Victor R. *How We Live.* Cambridge, Mass.: Harvard University Press, 1983.

Galbraith, John Kenneth. *The Affluent Society.* Boston: Houghton Mifflin, 1958.

_____. *The New Industrial State.* Boston: Houghton Mifflin, 1967.

George, Susan. *How the Other Half Dies: The Real Reasons for World Hunger.* Montclair, N.J.: Allanheld, Osmun, 1977.

Georgescu-Roegen, Nicholas. *The Entropy Law and the Economic Process.* Cambridge: Harvard University Press, 1971.

Gewirth, Alan. *Human Rights: Essays on Justification and Application.* Chicago: University of Chicago Press, 1982.

Ghelardi, Robert. *Economics, Society and Culture: God, Money and the New Capitalism.* New York: Delacorte Press, 1976.

Gide, Charles. *Principles of Political Economy.* Tr. E. F. Row. Westport, Conn.: Greenwood Press, 1970.

Gilder, George. *Wealth and Poverty.* New York: Bantam Books, 1982.

————. *The Spirit of Enterprise.* New York: Simon and Schuster, 1984.

Goudzwaard, Bob. *Capitalism and Progress: A Diagnosis of Western Society.* Trans. J. van Nuis Zylstra. Grand Rapids, Mich.: Wm. B. Eerdmans, 1979.

Gray, Alexander. *The Development of Economic Doctrine: An Introductory Survey.* 2nd ed. London: Longman, 1980.

Habermas, Jürgen. *Knowledge and Human Interest.* Trans. Jeremy J. Shapiro. Boston: Beacon Press, 1971.

————. *Legitimation Crisis.* Trans. Thomas McCarthy. Boston: Beacon Press, 1975.

Hardin, Garrett. *Promethean Ethics: Living with Death, Competition, and Triage.* Seattle: University of Washington Press, 1980.

Harrington, Michael. *Decade of Decision.* New York: Simon and Schuster, 1980.

————. *The New American Poverty.* New York: Holt, Rinehart and Winston, 1984.

————. *Socialism.* New York: Saturday Review Press, 1972.

Harris, Marvin. *America Now: The Anthropology of a Changing Culture.* New York: Simon and Schuster, 1982.

Harrison, Paul. *Inside the Third World: The Anatomy of Poverty.* New York: Penguin Books, 1982.

Hartman, Robert H. *Poverty and Economic Justice: A Philosophical Approach.* Ramsey, N.J.: Paulist Press, 1984.

Hayek, Friedrich. *The Road to Serfdom.* Chicago: The University of Chicago Press, 1944.

————. *The Constitution of Liberty.* Chicago: University of Chicago Press, 1960.

Hegel, Georg Wilhelm Friedrich. *Introduction to the Philosophy of Right.* Trans. T. M. Knox. Oxford: Clarendon Press, 1952.

Heilbroner, Robert L. *Beyond Boom and Crash.* New York: W. W. Norton, 1978.

————. *An Inquiry into the Human Prospect.* New York: W. W. Norton, 1974.

————. *The Making of Economic Society.* Englewood Cliffs, N.J.: Prentice-Hall, 1962.

————. *The Limits of American Capitalism.* New York: Harper & Row, 1960.

————. *Marxism: For and Against.* New York: W. W. Norton, 1980.

————. *The Worldly Philosophers.* 5th ed. New York: Simon and Schuster, 1980.

————. *The Nature and Logic of Capitalism.* New York: W. W. Norton, 1985.

————. *Behind the Veil of Economics: Essays in Worldly Philosophy*. New York: W. W. Norton, 1988.

Heilbroner, Robert L., and Lester C. Thurow. *Economics Explained*. Englewood Cliffs, N.J.: Prentice-Hall, 1982.

————. *Five Economic Challenges*. Englewood Cliffs, N.J.: Prentice-Hall, 1981.

Heller, Agnes. *Everyday Life*. Boston: Routledge & Kegan Paul, 1984.

Henderson, Hazel. *The Politics of the Solar Age: Alternatives to Economics*. Garden City, N.Y.: Doubleday, 1981.

Hirschman, Albert. *The Passions and the Interests: Political Arguments for Capitalism Before Its Triumph*. Princeton: Princeton University Press, 1977.

Hobbes, Thomas. *Leviathan*. Oxford: Clarendon Press, 1967.

Hochschild, Jennifer L. *What's Fair: American Beliefs about Distributive Justice*. Cambridge: Harvard University Press, 1981.

Hollis, Martin, and Edward J. Nell. *Rational Economic Man: A Philosophical Critique of Neo-Classical Economics*. New York: Cambridge University Press, 1975.

Hunt, E. K., and Jessie G. Schwartz, eds. *A Critique of Economic Theory*. Baltimore: Penguin Books, 1972.

Jonas, Hans. *The Imperative of Responsibility: In Search of an Ethics for the Technological Age*. Chicago: University of Chicago Press, 1984.

Keynes, John Maynard. *The End of Laissez-faire*. New York: Harcourt and Brace Jonaovich, 1965.

————. *The General Theory of Employment, Interest and Money*. London: Macmillan, 1936.

Kohler, Heinz. *Economics: The Science of Scarcity*. Hinsdale, Ill.: The Dryden Press, 1976.

Kuttner, Robert. *The Economic Illusion: False Choices Between Prosperity and Social Justice*. New York: Houghton Mifflin, 1984.

Leiss, William. *The Domination of Nature*. Boston: Beacon Press, 1974.

Lekachman, Robert. *Greed is not Enough: Reaganomics*. New York: Pantheon Books, 1982.

————. *Economists at Bay*. New York: McGraw-Hill, 1976.

Lernoux, Penny. *The Cry of the People*. New York: Penguin Books, 1982.

————. *In Banks We Trust*. Garden City, N.Y.: Doubleday, 1984.

Levine, Andrew. *Liberal Democracy: A Critique of Its Theory*. New York: Columbia University Press, 1981.

Levy, Jean-Philippe. *The Economic Life of the Ancient World.* Trans. John G. Biram. Chicago: University of Chicago Press, 1967.

Lindblom, Charles E. *Politics and Markets: The World's Political-Economic Systems.* New York: Basic Books, 1977.

Longman, Phillip. *Born to Pay: The New Politics of Aging in America.* Boston: Houghton Mifflin, 1987.

Loup, Jacques. *Can the Third World Survive?* Baltimore: The Johns Hopkins University Press, 1984.

Lutz, Mark A., and Kenneth Lux. *The Challenge of Humanistic Economics.* Menlo Park, Calif.: Benjamin/Cummings, 1979.

McCloskey, Donald N. *The Rhetoric of Economics.* Madison: The University of Wisconsin Press, 1985.

McClosky, Herbert, and John Zaller. *The American Ethos: Public Attitudes Toward Capitalism and Democracy.* Cambridge, Mass.: Harvard University Press, 1987.

MacIntyre, Alasdair. *After Virtue: A Study in Moral Theory.* Notre Dame, Ind.: University of Notre Dame Press, 1981.

————. *Whose Justice? Which Rationality?* Notre Dame, Ind.: University of Notre Dame Press, 1988.

Macpherson, C. B. *Democratic Theory: Essays in Retrieval.* Oxford: Clarendon Press, 1973.

————. *The Political Theory of Possessive Individualism: Hobbes to Locke.* New York: Oxford University Press, 1962.

Maital, Shlomo. *Minds, Markets, and Money: Psychological Foundations of Economic Behavior.* New York: Basic Books, 1982.

Maker, William, ed. *Hegel on Economics and Freedom.* Macon, Ga.: Mercer University Press, 1987.

Makin, John H. *The Global Debt Crisis.* New York: Basic Books, 1984.

Malkin, Lawrence. *The National Debt.* New York: Henry Holt and Company, 1987.

Marshall, Alfred. *Principles of Economics.* 9th ed. New York: Macmillan, 1961.

Marx, Karl. *Capital.* New York: Vintage, 1977, 1981.

————. *Economic and Philosophical Manuscripts.* In Erich Fromm, *Marx's Concept of Man,* 90–196. New York: Frederick Ungar, 1961.

Mauss, Marcel. *The Gift: Forms and Functions of Exchange in Archaic Societies.* Trans. Ian Cunnison. New York: W. W. Norton, 1967.

Mill, John Stuart. *Principles of Political Economy.* Toronto: University of Toronto Press, 1965.

Murphy, Elaine M. *The Environment to Come: A Global Summary.* Washington, D.C.: Population Reference Bureau, 1983.

Myers, Milton L. *The Soul of Modern Economic Man: Ideas of Self-Interest, Thomas Hobbes to Adam Smith.* Chicago: University of Chicago Press, 1983.

Nell, Edward and Martin Hollis. *Rational Economic Man: A Philosophical Critique of Neo-Classical Economics.* New York: Cambridge University Press, 1975.

Nelson, William N. *On Justifying Democracy.* Boston: Routledge & Kegan Paul, 1980.

North, Douglass C. "Non-Market Forms of Economic Organization: The Challenge of Karl Polanyi." *Journal of European Economic History* 6 (1977): 703–716.

_____. *The Rise of the Western World: A New Economic History.* Cambridge: Cambridge University Press, 1973.

_____. *Structure and Change in Economic History.* New York: W. W. Norton, 1981.

Nozick, Robert. *Anarchy, State, and Utopia.* New York: Basic Books, 1974.

Parsons, Talcott. "Religious and Economic Symbolism in the Western World." In *Religious Change and Continuity*, ed. Harry M. Johnson, 1–48. San Francisco: Jossey-Bass, 1970.

Pemberton, Prentiss. "Lockean Liberalism: A Radical Shift from the Biblical Economic Ethic," in *In the Great Tradition*, ed. J. Ban, 107–119. Valley Forge, Pa.: Judson Press, 1982.

Plato. *The Republic.* In *The Collected Dialogues of Plato*, ed. Edith Hamilton and Huntington Cairns, 575–844. New York: Pantheon Books, 1961.

Polanyi, Karl. *The Great Transformation.* Boston: Beacon Press, 1957.

_____. *The Livelihood of Man.* Ed. Harry W. Pearson. New York: Academic Press, 1977.

_____. *Primitive, Archaic, and Modern Economies.* Ed. George Dalton. Boston: Beacon, 1971.

Rawls, John. *A Theory of Justice.* Cambridge: Harvard University Press, 1971.

Reich, Robert B. *The Next American Frontier.* New York: Penguin Books, 1983.

_____. *Tales of a New America.* New York: Times Books, 1987.

Rifkin, Jeremy, with Ted Howard. *Entropy: A New World View.* New York: Bantam Books, 1980.

Robbins, Lionel. *An Essay on the the Nature and Significance of Economic Science.* London: Macmillan, 1952 [1935].

Robinson, Joan. *Freedom and Necessity: An Introduction to the Study of Society.* New York: Vintage Books, 1971.

Ropke, Wilhelm. *A Humane Economy: The Social Framework of the Free Market.* Chicago: Regnery, 1960.

Rosecrance, Richard. *The Rise of the Trading State: Commerce and Conquest in the Modern World.* New York: Basic Books, 1987.

Rosenberg, Charles E. *The Care of Strangers: The Rise of America's Hospital System.* New York: Basic Books, 1987.

Rosenberg, Nathan, and L. E. Birdzell. *How the West Grew Rich: The Economic Transformation of the Industrial World.* New York: Basic Books, 1987.

Sahlins, Marshall. *Stone Age Economics.* Harthorne, N.Y.: Aldine, 1972.

Sandel, Michael J. *Liberalism and the Limits of Justice.* New York: Cambridge University Press, 1982.

Schiller, Bradley R. *The Economics of Poverty and Discrimination.* 3rd ed. Englewood Cliffs, N.J.: Prentice-Hall, 1980.

Schroyer, Trent. *The Critique of Domination.* Boston: Beacon Press, 1975.

Schumacher, E. F. *A Guide for the Perplexed.* New York: Harper & Row, 1977.

Schumpeter, Joseph A. *Capitalism, Socialism and Democracy.* London: George Allen & Unwin, 1976.

Sen, Amartya. *Poverty and Famines: An Essay on Entitlement and Deprivation.* Oxford: Clarendon Press, 1981.

————. *On Economic Inequality.* Oxford: Oxford University Press, 1973.

Sennett, Richard. *The Fall of Public Man: On the Social Psychology of Capitalism.* New York: Random House, 1977.

————. *Authority.* New York: Knopf, 1980.

Shell, Marc. *Money, Language and Thought.* Berkeley: University of California Press, 1982.

Silver, Morris. *Affluence, Altruism, and Atrophy: The Decline of the Welfare State.* Stony Brook: New York University Press, 1980.

————. *Prophets and Markets: The Political Economy of Ancient Israel.* Boston: Kluwer-Nijhoff, 1983.

————. "Karl Polanyi and Markets in the Ancient Near East: The Challenge of Evidence." *The Journal of Economic History* 43 (December 1983): 795–829.

Skurski, Roger, ed. *New Directions in Economic Justice.* Notre Dame: University of Notre Dame Press, 1983.

Smith, Adam. *An Inquiry into the Nature and Causes of the Wealth of Nations.* Chicago: University of Chicago Press, 1976.

————. *Theory of Moral Sentiments.* Oxford: Clarendon Press, 1976.

Tawney, R. H. *Religion and the Rise of Capitalism*. New York: Harcourt, Brace and Co., 1926.

———. *The Acquisitive Society*. New York: Harcourt, Brace & Co., 1948.

Thurow, Lester C. *Dangerous Currents: The State of Economics*. New York: Random House, 1983.

———. *Generating Inequality: Mechanisms of Distribution in the U.S. Economy*. New York: Basic Books, 1975.

———. *The Zero-Sum Society: Distribution and the Possibilities for Economic Change*. New York: Basic Books, 1980.

Vaughan, Frederick. *The Tradition of Political Hedonism: From Hobbes to J. S. Mill*. New York: Fordham University Press, 1982.

Veblen, Thorstein. *The Theory of the Leisure Class: An Economic Study of Institutions*. New York: Huebsch, 1918.

———. *The Theory of Business Enterprise*. New York: New American Library, 1958.

Wallerstein, Immanuel. *The Modern World-System*. New York: Academic Press, 1974, 1980.

———. *Historical Capitalism*. London: Verso, 1983.

Walzer, Michael. *Spheres of Justice*. New York: Basic Books, 1983.

Weber, Max. *The Protestant Ethic and the Spirit of Capitalism*, Trans. Talcott Parsons. New York: Charles Scribner's Sons, 1958

———. *The Theory of Social and Economic Organization*. Trans. A. M. Henderson and Talcott Parsons. New York: The Free Press, 1964 [1947].

———. *Economy and Society*. 2 vols. Ed. Guenther Roth and Claus Wittich. Berkeley: University of California Press, 1978.

Weeks, John. *Capital and Exploitation*. Princeton: Princeton University Press, 1981.

Weisskopf, Walter A. *Alienation and Economics*. New York: Dell, 1971.

Wellman, Carl. *Welfare Rights*. Totowa, N.J.: Rowman and Allanheld, 1982.

Wilbur, Charles K., and Kenneth P. Jameson. *An Inquiry into the Poverty of Economics*. Notre Dame: University of Notre Dame Press, 1983.

Wilson, William Julius. *The Truly Disadvantaged: The Inner City, the Underclass, and Public Policy*. Chicago: The University of Chicago Press, 1987.

Wood, Ellen Meikeins, " The Separation of the Economic and the Political in Capitalism." *New Left Review* (May/June 1981), 66–95.

III
PROPERTY

Arthur, John, and William H. Shaw, eds. *Justice and Economic Distribution.* Englewood Cliffs, N.J.: Prentice-Hall, 1978.

Avila, Charles. *Ownership: Early Christian Teaching.* Maryknoll, N.Y.: Orbis Books, 1983.

Becker, Lawrence. *Property Rights: Philosophic Foundations.* Boston: Routledge and Kegan Paul, 1977.

Becker, Lawrence and Kenneth Kipnis. *Property: Cases, Concepts, Critiques.* Englewood Cliffs, N.J.: Prentice-Hall, 1984.

Brueggemann, Walter. *The Land: Place as Gift, Promise, and Challenge in Biblical Faith.* Philadelphia: Fortress Press, 1977.

————. "Reflections on Biblical Understandings of Property." *International Revue of Missions* 64 (October 1975): 354–361.

Carlyle, A. J. "The Theory of Property in Medieval Theology." In R. W. Carlyle and A. J. Carlyle, *A History of Medieval Political Theory in the West.* Vol. 1:132–146. Edinburgh: William Blackwood, 1928–36.

Countryman, L. William. *The Rich Christian in the Church of the Early Empire: Contradictions and Accommodations.* New York: Edwin Mellen Press, 1980.

Cunliffe, Marcus. *The Right to Property: A Theme in American History.* Atlantic Highlands, N. J.: Humanities Press, 1974.

Dearman, John Andrew. *Property Rights in the Eighth-Century Prophets: The Conflict and Its Background.* 1981. Atlanta: Scholars Press, 1988.

Dickenson, H. J. *Liberty and Property: Political Ideology in Eighteenth Century Britain.* New York: Holmes and Meier, 1978.

"Eigentum." In *Theologische Realenzyklopaedie.* Vol. IX:404–460. Berlin: Walter de Gruyter, 1982.

Ethics, 87 (January 1977).

Finley, M. I., ed. *Studies in Roman Property.* Cambridge: Cambridge University Press, 1976.

Finley, M. I. *Ancient Slavery and Modern Ideology.* New York: Penguin Books, 1983.

Fletcher, Joseph F., ed. *Christianity and Property.* Philadelphia: Westminster Press, 1957.

Friedman, Wolfgang J., "Property." In *Dictionary of the History of Ideas.* New York: Charles Scribner's Sons, 1973.

Gnuse, Robert. *You Shall Not Steal: Community and Property in the Biblical Tradition.* Maryknoll, N.Y.: Orbis Books, 1985.

Grace, Frank. *The Concept of Property in Modern Christian Thought.* Urbana: University of Illinois Press, 1953.

Hartman, Robert H., ed. *Poverty and Economic Justice: A Philosophical Approach.* New York: Paulist Press, 1984.

Held, Virginia, comp. *Property, Profits and Economic Justice.* Belmont, Calif.: Wadsworth, 1980.

Hengel, Martin. *Property and Riches in Early Church: Aspects of a Social History of Early Christianity.* Trans. John Bowden. Philadelphia: Fortress Press, 1974.

Hunt, Emery Kay. *Property and Prophets: Evolution of Economic Institutions and Ideologies.* New York: Harper & Row, 1975.

Hyde, Lewis. *The Gift: Imagination and the Erotic Life of Property.* New York: Vintage Books, 1983.

Little, Lester K. *Religious Poverty and Profit Economy in Medieval Europe.* Ithaca, N.Y.: Cornell University Press, 1978.

Locke, John. *Two Treatises of Civil Government.* New York: Dutton, 1970.

Loiselle, André. "The Fathers of the Church and Social Inequities." In *Attentive to the Cry of the Needy,* ed. W. Vogels, et al., 27–40. S.I.: Canadian Religious Conference.

Macpherson, C. B. "A Political Theory of Property." In *Democratic Theory: Essays in Retrieval,* ed. C. B. Macpherson. Oxford: Clarendon Press, 1973.

_____. "Human Rights as Property Rights." *Dissent* (Winter 1977), 72–77.

Macpherson, C. B., ed. *Property: Mainstream and Critical Positions.* Toronto: University of Toronto Press, 1978.

McKeon, Richard. "The Development of the Concept of Property in Political Philosophy." *Ethics* 48 (1938): 297–367.

Mauss, Marcel. *The Gift: Forms and Functions of Exchange in Archaic Societies.* New York: W. W. Norton, 1967.

Mullin, Redmond. *The Wealth of Christians.* Maryknoll, N.Y.: Orbis Books, 1984.

Nelson, Benjamin N. *The Idea of Usury: From Tribal Brotherhood to Universal Otherhood.* Princeton: Princeton University Press, 1949.

Noonan, John T., Jr. *The Scholastic Analysis of Usury.* Cambridge: Harvard University Press, 1957.

Nowak, Leszek. *Property and Power.* Boston: D. Redel, 1983.

Parel, Anthony, and Thomas Flanagan, eds. *Theories of Property: Aristotle to the Present.* Waterloo, Ontario: Wilfred Laurier University Press, 1979.

Pennock, J. Roland, and John W. Chapman. *Property.* New York: New York University Press, 1980.

De Ste Croix, Geoffrey. "Early Christian Attitudes to Property and Slavery." In *Church, Society and Politics*, ed. D. Baker. Oxford: Blackwells, 1975.

Schlatter, Richard Bugler. *Private Property: The History of an Idea.* New Brunswick, N.J.: Rutgers University Press, 1951.

Schochet, Gordon J., ed. *Life, Liberty and Property: Essays on John Locke's Political Ideas.* Belmont, Calif.: Wadsworth, 1971.

Scott, Russell. *The Body as Property.* New York: Viking, 1981.

Scott, William B. *In Pursuit of Happiness: American Conceptions of Property from the Seventeenth to the Twentieth Century.* Bloomington, Ind.: Indiana University Press, 1977.

Sobran, Joseph. "Christians and Private Property." *Center Journal* 2 (Fall 1983): 79–84.

Titmuss, Richard. *The Gift Relationship: From Human Blood to Social Policy.* New York: Pantheon, 1971.

Watson, Alan. *The Law of Property in the Later Roman Republic.* Oxford: Clarendon Press, 1968.

Wikse, John R. *About Possession: The Self as Private Property.* University Park: The Pennsylvania State University Press, 1977.

Wilber, Charles K. "The Role of Property in an Economic System." In *The Earth is the Lord's,* ed. M. E. Jegen. New York: Paulist Press, 1978.

IV
WORK

Agrell, Goran. *Work, Toil and Sustenance.* Trans. Stephen Westerholm. Stockholm: Verbum, Hakan Ohlssons, 1976.

Anthony, Peter D. *The Ideology of Work.* London: Tavistock, 1981.

Applebaum, Herbert, ed. *Work in Market and Industrial Societies.* Albany: State University of New York Press, 1984.

Arendt, Hannah. *The Human Condition.* Chicago: University of Chicago Press, 1958.

Ballard, Paul H. *Towards a Contemporary Theology of Work.* Cardiff: University College, 1982.

Balzar, Richard. *Clockwork.* New York: Doubleday, 1976.

Baum, Gregory. *The Priority of Labor: A Commentary on "Laborem Exercens," Encyclical Letter of Pope John Paul II.* New York: Paulist Press, 1982.

Baum, Gregory, ed. *Work and Religion.* New York: Seabury Press, 1980.

Barth, Karl. *Church Dogmatics.* III/4: 521ff. Trans. A. T. MacKay, et al. Edinburgh: T. & T. Clark, 1961.

Bell, Daniel. *The Coming of Post-Industrial Society.* New York: Basic Books, 1973.

———. *Work and Its Discontents.* Boston: Beacon Press, 1956.

Bendix, R. *Work and Authority in Industry.* New York: John Wiley, 1956.

Berger, P. L., ed. *The Human Shape of Work.* Chicago: Henry Regency, 1964.

Bernstein, Paul. *Workplace Democratization: Its Internal Dynamics.* New Brunswick, N.J.: Transaction Books, 1980.

Best, Fred, comp. *The Future of Work.* Englewood Cliffs, N.J.: Prentice-Hall, 1973.

Bienert, Walther. *Die Arbeit nach der Lehre der Bibel.* Stuttgart: Evangelisches Verlagswerk, 1954.

Blauner, R. *Alienation and Freedom.* Chicago: University of Chicago Press, 1964.

Bleakley, David. *In Place of Work ... The Sufficient Society.* London: SCM Press, 1981.

———. *Work: The Shadow and the Substance: A Reappraisal of Life and Labour.* London: SCM Press, 1983.

Bonhoeffer, Dietrich. *Ethics.* Ed. Eberhard Bethge. New York: Macmillan, 1955.

Braverman, Harry. *Labor and Monopoly Capital: The Degradation of Work in the Twentieth Century.* New York: The Monthly Review Press, 1975.

Bushnell, Horace. *Work and Play.* New York: Charles Scribner, 1981.

Calhoun, Robert L. *God and the Day's Work.* New York: Association Press, 1943.

Chenu, Marie Dominique. *The Theology of Work: An Exploration.* Trans. Lillian Soiron. Chicago: Henry Regnery, 1966.

Clarke, Roger. *Work in Crisis.* Edinburgh: St. Andrew Press, 1982.

Clayre, Alasdair. *Work and Play: Ideas and Experience of Work and Leisure.* New York: Harper & Row, 1974.

Dahl, Gordon. *Work, Play and Worship in a Leisure-Oriented Society.* Minneapolis: Augsburg, 1972.

Dahrendorf, Rolf. *Class and Class Conflicts in Industrial Society.* Stanford, Calif.: Stanford University Press, 1959.

Dickson, Paul. *The Future of the Workplace: The Coming Revolution in Jobs.* New York: Weybright and Talley, 1975.

Durkheim, Emil. *The Division of Labor in Society.* New York: Free Press, 1964.

———. *Socialism and Saint Simon.* London: Routledge & Kegan Paul, 1959.

Edwards, Richard C. *Contested Terrain: The Transformation of the Workplace in the Twentieth Century.* New York: Basic Books, 1979.

Fiorenza, Francis F. "Work and Critical Theology." In *A Matter of Dignity*, ed. W. J. Heisler and J. W. Houck, 23–43. Notre Dame: University of Notre Dame Press, 1977.

———. "Religious Beliefs and Praxis: Reflections on Catholic Theological Views of Work." In *Work and Religion*, ed. Gregory Baum. New York: Seabury Press, 1980.

Fraser, Ronald, ed. *Work*. 2 vols. Harmondsworth: Penguin, 1969.

Friedman, Geirges. *The Anatomy of Work: Labor, Leisure, and the Implications of Automation*. Trans. Wyatt Rawson. New York: Free Press of Glencoe, 1962.

Fullerton, Kemper. "Calvinism and Capitalism." *Harvard Theological Review* 21(1928): 163–191.

Garson, Barbara. *All the Livelong Day*. New York: Doubleday, 1975.

Genovese, Eugene D. *Roll, Jordan, Roll: The World the Slaves Made*. New York: Pantheon Books, 1974.

Gershuny, Jonathan I. *After Industrial Society? The Emerging Self-Service Economy*. London: Macmillan, 1978.

Gilbert, James B. *Work Without Salvation: America's Intellectual and Industrial Alienation*. Baltimore: Johns Hopkins University Press, 1977.

Gillet, Richard W. *The Human Enterprise: A Christian Perspective on Work*. Kansas City: Leaven Press, 1985.

Gordon, David M., et al. *Segmented Work, Divided Workers: The Historical Transformation of Work in the United States*. Cambridge: Cambridge University Press, 1982.

Gorz, Andre. "Work and Consumption." In *Towards Socialism*, ed. P. Anderson and R. Blackburn. London: Collins, 1965.

Green, James R. *The World of the Worker: Labor in Twentieth-Century America*. New York: Hill and Wang, 1980.

Gutman, Herbert G. *Work, Culture, and Society in Industrializing America: Essays in American Working Class and Social History*. New York: Knopf, 1976.

Harwood, Robert. *Brave New Workplace*. New York: Elisabeth Sifton Books/Viking, 1985.

Heisler, W. J., and John W. Houck, eds. *A Matter of Dignity: Inquiries into the Humanization of Work*. Notre Dame: Univeresity of Notre Dame Press, 1977.

Herzberg, Frederick, et al. *The Motivation to Work*. New York: John Wiley and Sons, 1959.

———. *Work and the Nature of Man*. London: Staples Press, 1966.

Hill, J. E. Christopher. *Reformation to Industrial Revolution*. New York: Penguin, 1971.

Howe, Irving, ed. *The World of the Blue-Collar Worker*. New York: Quadrangle, 1972.

Illanes, Jose Luis. *On the Theology of Work.* Trans. Michael Adams. 2nd ed. Chicago: Scepter Books, 1968.

John Paul II, "On Human Work." Washington: United States Catholic Conference, 1981.

Kaiser, Edwin G. *Theology of Work.* Westminster, Md.: The Newman Press, 1966.

Kane, Margaret. *Gospel in Industrial Society.* London: SCM, 1980.

Marcuse, Herbert. *One Dimensional Man.* Boston: Beacon Press, 1964.

Mason, Ronald M. *Participatory and Workplace Democracy: A Theoretical Development in the Critique of Liberalism.* Carbondale, Ill.: Southern Illinois University Press, 1982.

Mill, John Stuart. *Essay on Liberty.* Oxford: Blackwell, 1946.

Moltmann. Jürgen. *Theology of Play.* Trans. Reinhard Ulrich. New York: Harper & Row, 1971.

———. "The Right to Work," in *On Human Dignity: Political Theology and Ethics.* Trans. M. Douglas Meeks. Philadelphia: Fortress Press, 1984.

More, Thomas. *Utopia.* New York: E.P. Dutton, 1910.

Mosse, Claude. *The Ancient World at Work.* Trans. Janet Lloyd. New York: Norton, 1969.

Palm, Göram. *The Flight from Work.* Trans. Patrick Smith. Cambridge: Cambridge University Press, 1977.

Parker, S. R. *The Sociology of Leisure.* London: George Allen & Unwin, 1976.

Pfeffer, Richard M. *Working for Capitalism.* New York: Columbia University Presss, 1979.

Pohier, Jacques, and Dietmar Mieth, eds. *Unemployment and the Right to Work.* New York: Seabury Press, 1982.

Richardson, Alan. *The Biblical Doctrine of Work.* London: SCM Press, 1952.

Sabel, Charles F. *Work and Politics: The Division of Labor in Industry.* New York: Cambridge University Press, 1984.

Schacht, Richard. *Alienation.* London: Allen and Unwin, 1971.

Schaw, Louis C. *The Bonds of Work: Work in Mind, Time and Tradition.* San Francisco: Jossey-Bass, 1968.

Schleiermacher, Friedrich. *Die christliche Sitte.* Ed. L. Jonas. 2nd ed. Berlin: G. Rimer, 1984.

Schumacher, E. F. *Good Work.* London: Abacus, 1980.

Seligman, B. "On Work, Alienation, and Leisure." *American Journal of Economics and Sociology* (1965), 337–360.

Sennett, Richard and Jonathan Cobb. *The Hidden Injuries of Class.* New York: Knopf, 1972.

Shaiken, Harley. *Work Transformed: Automation and Labor in the Computer Age.* New York: Holt Rinehart and Winston, 1984.

Sölle, Dorothee with Shirley A. Cloyes. *To Work and to Love: A Theology of Creation.* Philadelphia: Fortress Press, 1984.

Stringfellow, William. "Justification, the Consumption Ethic and Vocational Poverty." *Christianity and Crisis* 36 (April 12, 1976): 74–79.

Terkel, Studs. *Working: People Talking about What They Do All Day and How They Feel about What They Do.* New York: Pantheon Books, 1974.

Thompson, E. P. *The Making of the English Working Class.* New York: Vintage Books, 1966.

Tilgher, Adriano. *Homo Faber: Work Through the Ages.* Trans. D. C. Fisher. Chicago: Henry Regnery, 1958.

Tilly, L. A., and J. W. Scott. *Women, Work, and Family.* New York: Henry Holt & Co., 1978.

Todd, John Murray, ed. *Work: Christian Thought and Practice.* Baltimore: Helicon Press, 1960.

U.S. Department of Health, Education, and Welfare. *Work in America.* Cambridge: MIT Press, 1973.

Vroom, V. *Work and Motivation.* New York: Wiley, 1964.

Walzer, Michael. *The Revolution of the Saints.* New York: Atheneum, 1968.

V
NEEDS AND CONSUMPTION

Barbour, Ian G., ed. *Finite Resources and the Human Future.* Minneapolis: Augsburg, 1976

Barnet, Richard J. *The Lean Years: Politics in the Age of Scarcity.* New York: Simon and Schuster, 1980.

Bell, Daniel. *The Cultural Contradictions of Capitalism.* New York: Basic Books, 1976.

Bleaney, M. F. *Underconsumption Theories: A History and Critical Analysis.* New York: Beekman, 1976.

Boulding, Kenneth, et al. *From Abundance to Scarcity.* Columbus: Ohio State University Press, 1978.

Brittain, Samuel. *Capitalism and the Permissive Society.* New York: Macmillan, 1973.

Brown, Lester R. *World Without Borders.* New York: Random House, 1972.

Byron, William. *Toward Stewardship: An Interim Ethic of Poverty, Power, and Pollution*. New York: Paulist Press, 1975.

Cesaretti, C. A., and Stephen Commins, eds. *Let the Earth Bless the Lord: A Christian Perspective on Land Use*. Somers, Conn.: The Seabury Press, 1982.

Cesaretti, C. A., ed. *The Prometheus Question: A Moral and Theological Perspective on the Energy Crisis*. Somers, Conn.: The Seabury Press, 1982.

Cohen, Marshall, et al. *Equality and Preferential Treatment*. Princeton: Princeton University Press, 1977.

Crahan, Margaret E. *Human Rights and Basic Needs in the Americas*. Washington, D.C.: Georgetown University Press, 1982.

Crean, David, and Eric and Helen Ebbeson. *Living Simply: An Examination of Christian Lifestyles*. New York: Seabury Press, 1981.

Deer, Thomas S. *Ecology and Human Need*. Philadelphia: Westminster Press, 1975.

Finnin, William M., Jr., and Gerald Alonzo Smith, eds. *The Morality of Scarcity: Limited Resources and Social Policy*. Baton Rouge: Louisiana State University Press, 1979.

Gabor, Dennis and U. Colombo. *Beyond the Age of Waste*. New York: Pergamon, 1978.

Granty, James, and John Sewell. "Basic Human Needs and the New International Order: A Northern View." In *World Faiths and the New World Order*, ed. Joseph Gremillion, 69–108. Washington, D.C.: Interreligious Peace Colloquium, 1980.

Grassi, Joseph A. *Broken Bread and Broken Bodies: The Lord's Supper and World Hunger*. Maryknoll, N.Y.: Orbis Books, 1985.

Hamrin, Robert G. *Managing Growth in the 1980s: Toward a New Economics*. New York: Praeger, 1980.

Heller, Agnes. *The Theory of Need in Marx*. New York: St. Martin's Press, 1976.

Hellwig, Monica. *The Eucharist and the Hunger of the World*. New York: Paulist Press, 1976.

Hirsch, Fred. *Social Limits to Growth*. Cambridge: Harvard University Press, 1976.

Illich, Ivan. *Toward a History of Needs*. New York: Pantheon, 1978.

Jenks, Christopher, et al. *Who Gets Ahead? The Determinants of Economic Success in America*. New York: Basic Books, 1979.

Kavanaugh, John F. *Following Christ in a Consumer Society: The Spirituality of Cultural Resistance*. Maryknoll, N.Y.: Orbis Books, 1981.

Konner, Melvin. *The Tangled Wing: Biological Constraints on the Human Spirit*. New York: Holt Rinehart and Winston, 1982.

Lappé, Frances Moore, and Joseph Collins. *Food First: Beyond the Myth of Scarcity*. New York: Ballantine, 1978.

Lasch, Christopher. *The Culture of Narcissism.* New York: W. W. Norton, 1978.

Leiss, William. *The Limits to Satisfaction: An Essay on the Problems of Needs and Commodities.* Toronto: University of Toronto Press, 1976.

Linder, Staffan Burenstam. *The Harried Leisure Class.* New York: Columbia University Press, 1970.

Markovic, Mihailo. *From Affluence to Praxis: Philosophy and Social Criticism.* Ann Arbor, Mich.: The University of Michigan Press, 1974.

McRobie, Georg. *Small is Possible.* New York: Harper & Row, 1981.

Meadows, Donella H., et al. *The Limits to Growth.* 2nd ed. New York: Universe Books, 1974.

Meyerson, Rolf, "Abundance Reconsidered." In *On the Making of Americans.* Ed. Herbert J. Gans, et al., 87–104. Philadelphia: University of Pennsylvania Press, 1979.

Mieth, Dietmar and Jacques Pohier, eds. *Christian Ethics and Economics: The North-South Conflict.* New York: Seabury Press, 1980.

Mishan, Edward. J. *The Costs of Economic Growth.* Harmondsworth, Eng.: Penguin, 1973.

Munby, Denys. *Economic Growth in World Perspective.* New York: Association Press, 1966.

Nankivell, Owen. *All Good Gifts: A Christian View of the Affluent Society.* London: Epworth, 1978.

Niebuhr, Reinhold. *The Irony of American History.* New York: Charles Scribner's Sons, 1962.

O'Brien, D. J., and T. A. Shannon, eds. *Renewing the Earth.* New York: Doubleday, 1977.

Olson, Mancur, and Hans H. Landsberg. *The No-Growth Society.* New York: W. W. Norton, 1973.

Ophuls, William. *Ecology and the Politics of Scarcity.* San Francisco: W. H. Freeman, 1977.

Parker, Stanley. *The Sociology of Leisure.* London: George Allen & Unwin, 1976.

Peters, Ted. *Fear, Faith and the Future: Affirming Christian Hope in the Face of Doomsday Prophecies.* Minneapolis: Augsburg Publishing House, 1980.

Pohier, Jacques, and Dietmar Mieth, eds. *The Dignity of the Dispised Earth.* New York: Seabury Press, 1979.

Potter, David M. *People of Plenty: Economic Abundance and the American Character.* Chicago: University of Chicago Press, 1954.

Riesman, David. *Abundance for What? And Other Essays.* Garden City, N.Y.: Doubleday, 1964.

Rifkin, Jeremy and Ted Howard. *The Emerging Order: God in the Age of Scarcity.* New York: G. P. Putnam, 1979.

Rubenstein, Richard L. *The Age of Triage: Fear And Hope in an Overcrowded World.* Boston: Beacon Press, 1983.

Samuel, Vinay, and Christopher Sugden, eds. *The Church in Response to Human Need.* Grand Rapids: Wm. B. Eerdmans, 1987.

Santmire, H. Paul. *The Travail of Nature: The Ambiguous Ecological Promise of Christian Theology.* Philadelphia: Fortress Press, 1983.

Schumacher, E. F. *Small Is Beautiful: Economics as if People Mattered.* New York: Harper & Row, 1973.

Scitovsky, Tibor. *The Joyless Economy: An Inquiry into Human Satisfaction and Consumer Dissatisfaction.* New York: Oxford University Press, 1976.

Sennett, Richard. *The Fall of Public Man.* New York: Vintage Books, 1978.

Shi, David E. *The Simple Life: Plain Living and High Thinking in American Culture.* New York: Oxford University Press, 1985.

Sider, Ronald J. *Evangelicals and Development: Toward A Theory of Social Change.* Philadelphia: Westminster Press, 1982.

Sider, Ronald J., ed. *Lifestyle in the Eighties: An Evangelical Commitment to Simple Lifestyle.* Philadelphia: Westminster Press, 1982.

Springborg, Patricia. *The Problem of Human Needs and the Critique of Civilization.* London: G. Allen & Unwin, 1981.

Stiglitz, Joseph E., ed. *Readings in the Modern Theory of Growth.* Cambridge, Mass.: M.I.T. Press, 1969.

Tavis, Lee A., ed. *Multinational Managers and Poverty in the Third World.* Notre Dame: University of Notre Dame Press, 1982.

Taylor, John V. *Enough is Enough.* London: SCM Press, 1975.

Ward, Barbara, and René Dubos. *Only One Earth: The Care and Maintenance of a Small Planet.* New York: W. W. Norton, 1972.

Warner, Richard. *Freedom, Enjoyment, and Happiness: An Essay on Moral Psychology.* Ithaca: Cornell University Press, 1987.

Wilkinson, Loren, ed. *Earth-Keeping: Christian Stewardship of Natural Resources.* Grand Rapids, Mich.: Wm. B. Eerdmans, 1980.

Wogaman, J. Philip, and Paul McCleary. *Quality of Life in a Global Society.* New York: Friendship Press, 1978.

Wriggins, W. Howard, and Gunnar Adler-Karlson. *Reducing Global Inequities.* New York: McGraw-Hill, 1978.

Zolotas, Xenophon. *Economic Growth and Declining Social Welfare.* New York: New York University Press, 1981.

Indexes

SCRIPTURE

SUBJECTS

AUTHORS/NAMES

Kraus, Hans-Joachim, 191
Kuttner, Robert, 199
Lamb, Matthew, 191
Lasch, Christopher, 219
Lee, Robert, 185
Leibniz, Gottfried
    Wilhelm, 192-193
Leiss, William, 221
Lekachman, Robert, 187
Lernoux, Penny, 187, 189
Lever, Harold, 189
Lindblom, Charles E., 195,
    197
Linder, Staffan, 222
Locke, John, 67, 106-108,
    159-160, 193, 203, 204
Loup, Jacques, 189
Luther, Martin, 122, 210
McClosky, Herbert, 197
McFague, Sallie, 200
McGill, Arthur C., 188, 200
MacIntyre, Alasdair, 125,
    211
Macpherson, C.B., 11, 110,
    186, 194, 203, 205,
    206, 210
Madison, James, 202
Maital, Schlomo, 195, 199
Makin, John H., 189
Malherbe, Abraham J., 189
Malkin, Lawrence, 189
Mandeville, Bernard, 50
Marcuse, Herbert, 159, 220
Marshall, Alfred, 2, 219
Marx, Karl, 2, 41, 143-145,
    159, 166-168, 195,
    199, 205, 217, 221
Maslow, Abraham, 218
Mauss, Marcel, 208
Meeks, M. Douglas, 186,
    187, 189, 190, 201,
    206, 208
Meeks, Wayne, 189
Metz, Johannes, 191, 196
Míguez Bonino, José, 197
Mill, J.S., 108, 160
Moltmann, Jürgen, 186,
    187, 191, 196, 200,
    206, 207, 208, 213,
    214, 217, 218, 222
Montanus, 220
Moore, Thomas, 136
Morgan, J.P., 30
Morris, William, 136
Mosse, C., 213
Mott, Stephen, 185
Mühlen, Heribert, 220
Mullin, Redmond, 204
Myers, Milton L., 199
Nell, Edward J., 199

Nelson, Benjamin N., 210
Niebuhr, Reinhold, 26
Nietzsche, Friedrich, 125
Noonan, John T., 210
North, Douglass C., 191,
    195, 196, 202, 212
Novak, Michael, 69, 198
Nozick, Robert, 194
Oakman, Douglas E., 189
O'Brien, David J., 188
Ogletree, Thomas W., 201
Owensby, Walter L., 185
Parsons, Talcott, 191
Pemberton, Prentiss L.,
    185, 194
Pfeffer, Robert M., 211
Philo, 209
Pilgrim, Walter E., 208
Pixley, George V., 201
Plato, 67, 159, 213
Polanyi, Karl, 38, 50,
    53-55, 113, 190, 194,
    195, 196, 197, 199,
    203
Pullman, George M., 141
Rahner, Karl, 213
Rasmussen, Albert T., 185
Rasmussen, Larry L., 185
Rawls, John, 216
Reich, Wilhelm, 220
Reumann, John, 186, 200
Richardson, Alan, 214
Ricoeur, Paul, 218
Ringe, Sharon, 200
Robbins, Lionel, 53, 195
Rosecrance, Richard, 191
Rosenberg, Charles E., 190
Rousseau, Jean-Jacques,
    159, 166, 215, 218,
    220
Ruskin, John, 136
Russell, Letty M., 201
Saint-Simon, Claud-Henri,
    143
Sandel, Michael J., 198
Schlatter, Richard, 203, 204
Schleiermacher, Friedrich,
    213, 214
Schottroff, Luise, 201, 208
Schottroff, Willy, 202
Schumacher, E.F., 217
Scitovsky, Tibor, 222
Scott, H.W., 213
Scott, Russell, 206
Segundo, Juan Luis, 197
Seneca, 204
Sennet, Richard, 211
Shannon, Thomas A., 188
Siebert, Rudolf, 217
Silk, Leonard, 188

Silver, Morris, 195-196
Skurski, Roger, 198
Slater, Peter, 222
Sleeman, John F., 185
Smiles, Samuel, 142
Smith, Adam, 2, 30, 48,
    131-132, 194, 196,
    197, 199, 212, 221
Soelle, Dorothee, 218
Southey, Robert, 136
Spinoza, Baruch, 192
Stackhouse, Max L., 185,
    187
Stegemann, Wolfgang, 201,
    202, 208
Stillman, Peter G., 206
Stringborg, Patricia, 220
Tawney, R.H., 191
Taylor, Richard K., 185
Temple, William, 186
Terkel, Studs, 128, 211
Theissen, Gerd, 189
Thompson, E.P., 211
Thurow, Lester C., 211
Tilgher, Adriano, 211
Tilly, L.A., 213
Titmuss, Richard, 208
Torrance, Thomas F., 186
Townsend, William, 196
Tracy, David, 190
Troeltsch, Ernst, 204
Van Buren, Paul, 200
Veblen, Thorstein, 173-174,
    222
Verner, David C., 189
Viner, Jacob, 216
Von Rad, Gerhard, 200
Wainwright, Geoffrey, 223
Walter, Tony, 220
Walzer, Michael, 11, 58,
    176, 186, 190, 197,
    223
Warner, Richard, 218
Weber, Max, 41, 190, 211,
    212, 216, 219
Weeks, John, 199
Weisskopf, Walter A., 199,
    219, 222
Welker, Michael, 200
West, Cornel, 197
Westermann, Claus, 214
Wieman, H.N., 186
Wikse, John R., 111, 206
Wilbur, Charles K., 187
Wilson, Julius William, 187
Wink, Walter, 208
Wogaman, J. Philip, 185
Wood, Ellen Meikeins, 186
Xenophon, 213
Zaller, John, 197